PSYCHOLOGY
AND
AMERICAN
CATHOLICISM

PSYCHOLOGY
— AND —
AMERICAN
CATHOLICISM

From Confession to Therapy?

C. KEVIN GILLESPIE, S.J.

A Crossroad Book
The Crossroad Publishing Company
New York

Part of chapter 1 was previously published as "'For the Knowledge of the Soul': The Story of American Catholicism and Psychology," in *Ecumenical People, Programs, Papers,* newsletter of the Institute for Ecumenical and Cultural Research, St. John's University, Collegeville, Minnesota, May 2000, 6–11.

The Crossroad Publishing Company
481 Eighth Avenue, New York, NY 10001

Printed in the United States of America

Library of Congress Cataloging-in-Publication Data

Gillespie, C. Kevin.
    Psychology and American Catholicism : from confession to therapy? / C. Kevin Gillespie.
      p. cm.
    Includes bibliographical references and index.
    ISBN 0-8245-1896-9 (hardcover)
    1. Psychology and religion. 2. Psychology, Religious. 3. Catholic Church–United States–History–20th century. I. Title.
    BF51 .G49 2001
    261.5'15'08822–dc21
                                2001000411

1 2 3 4 5 6 7 8 9 10   06 05 04 03 02 01

To Francis J. Gillespie,
the first to tell me stories,
and to
Sara Cullen Gillespie,
the first to listen to my own

Contents

Foreword

In these pages, Kevin Gillespie tells a story that is at once very American and very Catholic. Catholics may read it to understand their family history, as it recounts from a fresh perspective a tale told in many other ways before. All Americans, however, will find a vivid if seldom chronicled aspect of their own narrative here as well.

If we have learned already of the slow but colorful ascendancy of immigrant Catholics in the realms of American politics, finance, and the popular arts, and heard the marching bands providing the background music for Catholic colleges and universities, we know less of the pilgrims' progress of Catholics in psychology, which, despite its European origins, came not only to be dominated by Americans but also to express their practical genius and temper of mind.

Here, then, is a tale to be told *Rashomon* style, through the eyes of all those who have observed the parallel stories of a nation of believers and experimenters, of romantics and pragmatists, strivers for social position who think that everyone should be equal, researchers of high and noble discovery who immediately try to democratize their findings and make them available to the masses. Americans prize individuality and its advertised choices, but they also aspire to be part of the group; they want to be on their own, but they are afraid of being left out. The America against whose spires and plains this story is told is committed to separating church and state but confounds them regularly.

That is because—and this is of no small relevance to Father Gillespie's explorations—Americans have been profoundly influenced by their belief in both hard science and in hellfire religion. The citizens of this country, as psychologist/philosopher William James once observed, believe in belief. "They believe anything they can," he noted, "and would believe everything if only they could." If the Founding Fathers wisely worked against the intermingling of theology and political science in order to avoid, for example, a state religion, they set wide boundaries for a country in which the influence of fundamentalist religion would predominate for generations. Not only did this religious undercurrent establish the first great universities and their academic tradition, but its rigid paradigm was to become that against which the scientific departments of these same institutions would, in due time, stage their revolt and from which they would declare their independence.

It was to this America that Catholics, many from countries in which religion and citizenship were two sides of one coin, came, at first to establish themselves and, later, to find their American identity in a nation whose culture was both rich in and rife with the elements of hard science and harsh religion.

Father Gillespie allows us to witness, through his admirable selection of themes and figures, the complex cultural scene that Catholic psychologists and psychiatrists entered and against the grain of whose own contradictions they had to identify and prove themselves as loyal Americans and competent scientists. The land itself was engaged in a larger, not dissimilar, process as its scientific pioneers in every field were breaking free of the strappings of literalist religion that, in its suspicion of, if not horror at, the evolutionary hypothesis, viewed science through a glass darkly as the enemy of belief.

Catholics were entering psychology—knowledge of the soul as it had been defined philosophically and, like a letter that needed no reply, had been filed in a Thomistic category—during the very period in which its leading theorists were attempting to fashion it into a science as strict, measure bound, and capable of prediction as physics and chemistry. As such, it made no room for the essentialist definitions of philosophical psychology but committed itself to operational definitions in which phenomena were described in terms of the operations by which they were measured. Intelligence thus became defined as an individual's score on a specific IQ test, and personality was rendered down into a cluster of scores on a psychometric test.

Father Gillespie opens for us, then, the double bind in which Catholics, naturally gifted with the curiosity that spurs all scientific inquiry, found themselves: They professed a faith whose psychological vocabulary was abstractly philosophical and whose understanding of the soul was uncompromisingly theological. Any approach, therefore, no matter how valid in itself, that contemplated these matters in other than these ways was dangerously secular and superficially reductionist. Experimental psychology, in its nineteenth-century infancy, was a bastard child not to be nourished at the Catholic breast.

Yet, as we learn in the anecdotes with which the author seasons his text, Catholics were drawn to their new psychology not because it set them at odds with their church, but because they sensed in it something profoundly Catholic—the attractiveness of truth that waits in the clearing beyond the forest wall and the inviting path of wonder, unlike any other portal, that leads toward it. These remarkable first Catholic citizens of psychology were

reflexively misunderstood by ecclesiastics because they intuitively understood that all paths, including the Catholic, finally converged into one
in the presence of truth. This psychological access to that truth by disciplined observation and measurement was one of many approaches that,
like spokes to a hub, led to the same central reality. These early experimentalists shared a profound and traditional Catholic belief in, and reverence
for, the irresistible magnetism of the truth.

These Catholic scientists confidently entered a developing scientific field
held under suspicion by many church leaders. Therefore, suspected in their
religious homeland they entered a universe whose leaders were also suspicious of them and of the possible medieval gods of Roman superstition
that, like the trinkets of Egyptian deities the Israelites smuggled away in
their sacks, might be concealed in their baggage.

These Catholics labored under multiplied stresses. They had to gain credentials in first-class training programs and join themselves to a profession
regarded dubiously by the institutional church. They then had to become
thoroughly committed colleagues while being regarded dubiously by institutional psychology. That they attained both goals testifies to the personal,
scientific, and religious integrity of Thomas Verner Moore, Edward Pace,
and their many followers. Indeed, all of them would have been puzzled
by any distinction between scientific, religious, and personal integrity. Integrity was as unitary as their approach to the truth of the world. Gillespie
quotes Moore's magisterial summation of the conviction that has guided
succeeding generations of Catholics in psychology and psychiatry: "I had
never encountered any established facts of science that were incompatible
with the doctrine of faith. The apostle in science, in order to interpret scientific facts with authority, must himself be a scientist, an original worker
contributing to progress in his field of research."

Nonetheless, well over half a century would pass before the Catholic
Church first struck an uneasy truce with and then tentatively embraced
psychology and psychiatry as genuine and helpful instruments of truth
and healing. Father Gillespie tells a story that, in its blind rejection of
modern thinking, remains too deep for tears a century later. In the first decade of the twentieth century, Pope Pius X, later declared a saint, roundly
condemned a vague aggregate of positions, lumped under the heading of
"Modernism," that he judged incompatible with church teachings. This
led to a long dark night of anti-intellectualism, well symbolized in the de-
struction of the then highly sophisticated faculty at the major seminary of
the Archdiocese of New York: The rector, an expert in Oriental studies, was
fired and replaced by the chaplain of the New York City Police Department.
While this is a larger story of years of strict censorship of the reading mate-
rial of priests and seminarians, it gives us the flavor of the decades during

which dedicated Catholic psychologists and psychiatrists, along with all colleague scientists, had to function almost as an underground community in totalitarian times.

This led to a climactic confrontation at mid-century between two views of reality, that of a church whose spokespersons condemned psychology and psychiatry, railing against Freudian pan-sexuality and wildly claiming that their therapies were intruding on and usurping the sacraments, especially that of Confession. The histrionic Monsignor, later Bishop, Fulton J. Sheen led the charge with claims so sweeping in their generality that they offended and roused the loyal Catholics in these fields. Sheen later made peace with the professions he had once derided. One of its celebrated moments occurred during a meeting, which we will revisit in a moment, of the National Guild of Catholic Psychiatrists, one of the numerous Catholic structures that led parallel lives with the main scientific associations that developed during the twilight years of suspicion. By belonging to such groups, Catholics not only demonstrated their own loyalty to the church but gradually educated church officials about the true nature of their work. At the same time, they were bridges to the American Psychiatric Association and the American Psychological Association on which Catholics could stand with their colleagues, not to contemplate the torrent below but all that they held in common. These organizations served a profoundly useful function in their time of beginning what would become an adult conversation between religion and psychology.

In the late 1950s, the mood of reconciliation between Catholic scientists and their church leaders, which played at least some part in preparing Catholicism to embrace the world once more in Vatican II only a few years later, had warmed considerably. At a gathering of the National Guild of Catholic Psychiatrists in Washington, D.C., the late Richard Cardinal Cushing signaled good will as he stood before a large crowd to speak on "A Cardinal Looks at Psychiatry." In his accent, flat and hard as New England marble, he put aside his text to say, "This gives psychiatrists a chance to look at a Cardinal." The echo of the laughter that filled the auditorium was the sound of an era coming amiably to an end. It was seconded in a dinner address by Sheen himself in which, as if he had never criticized psychology at all, he used a baseball analogy to illustrate his new viewpoint. "As I cannot speak of a great Catholic left fielder," he intoned dramatically, letting each audience member identify with his example, "but only of a great left fielder who is a Catholic, so I cannot speak of a great Catholic psychiatrist but only of a great psychiatrist who is a Catholic." Peace, it was wonderful.

These recollections arose for me as I followed Father Gillespie's skilled summary of those times and of those yet to follow, in which psychology and psychiatry, which, as one professional is quoted, regarded religion as "marginal," began to understand it as a serious and important dimension of human life.

When I entered the graduate program at the Catholic University of America, one could still feel the presence of Pace and Moore in the offices and seminar room, hardly changed from their time except for fresh varnish and still housing, in cabinets and on shelves, the brass instruments for sensory research that they had brought back from Wundt's European laboratory. By then, the department was headed by a priest whom the text honors but does not name. John W. Stafford, C.S.V., bustled about in his experimenter's jacket, teaching, managing, urging the best out of everyone, one of the most remarkable and generous hearted men I have ever known.

Let me conclude with other memories of that period and of some of the remarkable people that you will meet in these pages. Were it not for women like Virginia Staudt Sexton and men like William C. Bier, S.J., the final crucial recognition of religion as a central theme and legitimate subject for psychological research would have been long delayed or perhaps never taken.

That occurred when Psychologists Interested in Religious Issues, the successor group to the American Catholic Psychological Association, which Father Bier had established shortly after World War II, was voted by the general membership of the American Psychological Association into full membership as Division 36 of that scientific organization. I recall the modest pride of Father Bier and Doctor Sexton, who, in memory, stand for all those who go unmentioned but who had worked with them to achieve this goal. The silver-haired Father Bier, a canny New Yorker whose Manhattan inflections were not lost beneath his slightly throaty tone, did not take a moment to boast or to recall the battles of the past. Instead, he turned to all that was to be done in the future, getting back, in a sense, to work before the bells of celebration had stopped ringing. I see him still, as I saw him at so many meetings, thinking out loud, pausing to form his thoughts, searching, ever searching, for the right phrase and the right direction to take in addressing the next challenge.

Let him stand there as well for the reader as the symbol of every scientist and believer who has never compromised either identity but inhabited them comfortably, successor to Moore and Pace and many besides and progenitor of new and enthusiastic generations of men like Father Gillespie, whose chronicle of other centuries heralds the challenges of this new one.

EUGENE C. KENNEDY, PH.D.
Professor Emeritus of Psychology
Loyola University of Chicago

Preface

In the telling of a story there is often another story. This seems especially true for this scholarly telling of a story—or should I say stories? The story-telling in this volume has been a collaborative effort in which I have enjoyed the company and conversation of a wide assortment of individuals who have helped me to blend facts, ideas, and narratives. Many of these men and women were on the cutting edge of these narratives. As the reader will discover, many of these stories have up until now received little or no attention.

In one sense the story of the writing of this volume began with my dissertation under the guidance of Merle Jordan, Th.D., and Chris Schlauch, Ph.D., at Boston University, and Gerry Fogarty, S.J., Ph.D., at the University of Virginia. In another sense, this work started with my studies as an undergraduate at St. Joseph's College (now University) in Phila-delphia, where, as a psychology major, I was active in the department's Moore Psychological Society. (While I was curious about who Thomas Verner Moore was, I did not know anything about the person for whom this society was named.) During my undergraduate studies in psychology I began to want to understand my studies in light of my Catholic faith. This motivation became more acute when I attended graduate school at Du-quesne University's Department of Psychology, where I studied the works of Adrian van Kaam for the first time. The writings of van Kaam, a Dutch priest-psychologist, intrigued me and demonstrated that the disciplines of psychology could be integrated into the philosophical and theological tra-ditions of the Catholic Church. Such a conclusion is commonplace today; it was not so then, given the often agnostic airs of psychology during the 1960s. My undergraduate curiosity about Moore and my graduate study of van Kaam, however, led me to believe that the breath of the Spirit was guiding their respective labors in psychology.

Later my belief was supported by the Maryland Province of the Soci-ety of Jesus, which I entered in 1975 at the novitiate of St. Isaac Jogues in Wernersville, Pennsylvania. As discussed in chapter 10 of this book, the novitiate also housed the Jesuit Center for Spiritual Growth, whose staff was offering a steady program of workshops that incorporated psycholog-ical insights into Ignatian spirituality. My novitiate experiences under the tutelage of George Aschenbrenner, S.J., were enriched by these workshops, which further shaped my own integration of psychology and Catholicism. My Jesuit formation subsequently led me to studies in philosophy at St. Louis University and theology at the Jesuit School of Theology at Berkeley. They in turn broadened and deepened my appropriation of the Catholic tradition of relating faith and reason, religion and science, grace and nature. Following my ordination in 1986 and after two years on the Jesuit staff at Wernersville, I was offered the opportunity to further my professional integration of psychology and faith by attending Boston University for doctoral studies in pastoral psychology. The present work, built upon my dissertation research, represents the fruits of academic, clinical, and pastoral endeavors since my undergraduate days thirty years ago.

This story has indeed been a long one, one that has been supported emotionally and spiritually by family members and friends who have encouraged my pastoral identity as a priest and my professional identity as a pastoral counselor. Besides my parents, to whom this work is dedicated, I have been blessed by the support of siblings Mary Hauser, Rev. Fran Gillespie, S.J., Rev. John Gillespie, Eileen Johnson, and Kathleen Overturf. I am especially grateful to Kathleen for her editorial comments and to John, whose own search for the integration of psychology and Catholicism preceded and inspired my own.

There were also many spiritual companions along the way. My fellow Jesuits at Boston College, especially the Manresa House community, and at Loyola College of Maryland exhibited an engaging interest. Among the Jesuits at Loyola, Fr. William Davish and Fr. William Sneck offered constructive editorial advice.

During the sometimes dreary days of "dissertating" I experienced a real "holding environment" from my fellow doctoral students at Boston University. In addition, the faculty, staff, and students in the Pastoral Counseling Department have been helpful, especially Robert Wicks, Psy.D., who has been a generous and wise mentor throughout this process. Also encouraging have been spiritual guides, therapists, and special friends.

Much of the writing of this book took place during the spring semester of 2000, when I was on a faculty sabbatical made possible through the encouragement of Loyola College's academic dean, John Hollwitz. I spent this semester sabbatical at the Institute for Ecumenical and Cultural Research, St. John's University, Collegeville, Minnesota. There I enjoyed the scholarly and spiritual companionship of a community of Christian scholars: Angela Ashwin, David Schultenover, Brett Webb-Mitchell, Dale Cannon and his family, Loreen and Marc Herwaldt, John Jerry-Anthony Parente, and Karen Jacobson. I owe special appreciation to Maureen Barney, who shared so much of the Minnesota experience with me and has been a source of inspiration throughout this work.

Research for this book took me to more than a dozen archives around the country. Special thanks are due to archivists Rev. Gerard Connolly, S.J. (deceased), at Fordham University, Gabriella Earnshaw at the Henri J. M. Nouwen Archives and Research Collection of St. Michael's College, Br. Michael Grace, S.J., at Loyola University of Chicago, Br. David Klingeman, O.S.B., at St. John's University, Collegeville, Sr. Mary Kraft, C.S.J., of the Sisters of St. Joseph in St. Paul, John Popplestone, at the Archives of the History of American Psychology, Phillip Runkel, at Marquette University, and Sr. Margery Smith, C.S.J., at the College of St. Catherine.

Patrick Henry and Mark Massa, S.J., were most generous in their editorial comments on this work's drafts. Susan Muto provided valuable assistance with understanding the witness and work of Adrian van Kaam, as did Sr. Sue Mosteller for Henri Nouwen and Judy Roemer for George Schemel. Benedict Neenan, O.S.B., provided valuable insights and resources concerning Thomas Verner Moore. The editorial assistance of Paul McMahon and John Eagleson at Crossroad Publishing Company has proved invaluable.

Many of the historical accounts developed in this volume have been obtained through the oral history given to me by the men and women who engaged, sometimes at the expense of criticism, in the confluence of Catholicism and psychology. I am deeply grateful to these individuals who, during the five years in which the research was conducted, not only allowed me to interview them, but also gave me encouragement throughout the project: Joan Arnold, Sr. Rita Mary Bradley (deceased), Rev. William Barry, S.J., Walter Burghardt, S.J., Patrick Carey, Bessie Chambers, Sara Charles, M.D., Kathleen Clarke, James Connor, Godfrey Diekmann, O.S.B., Margaret Donnelly, Barry Estadt, Sr. Kathleen Gallivan, S.N.D., Eileen Gavin, Ph.D., Rev. James Gill, S.J., M.D., Rev. John Grimes, Sr. Ann Harvey, C.N.D., Rev. John Haughey, S.J., Sr. Pat Johnson, S.N.D, Eugene Kennedy, Claire Lowerey, Robert MacAllister, M.D., Rev. Dominic Maruca, S.J., John McCall, John McDargh, Rev. William W. Meissner, S.J., M.D., Sr. Sue Mosteller, C.S.J., Rev. Edward Nowlan, S.J., Sr. Mary O'Hara, C.S.J., John O'Malley, S.J., Mary Reuder, James Shannon, Michael St. Clair, Richard Sipe, Virginia Staudt Sexton (deceased), Gordon Tavis, O.S.B., Rev. Adrian van Kaam, C.S.Sp., and Rev. Richard P. Vaughan, S.J.

Finally I extend my gratitude to the men and women whose lives as professional psychologists and psychiatrists are related in this text. Recently, historians such as Philip Gleason (*Contending with Modernity*), Mark Massa (*Catholics and American Culture*), and Charles Morris (*American*

Catholic) have described how Roman Catholicism assimilated and in some ways accommodated to American culture during the twentieth century. In a somewhat similar vein this work hopes to offer a glimpse of American Catholicism by presenting the ways in which American Catholics encountered and appropriated psychology during the twentieth century. The creative and at times courageous ways in which they did so is a story worth telling.

Introduction

Once upon a Time...

What has Athens to do with Rome? What does Rome have to do with America? Such questions, one ancient the other recent, may be raised when considering the ways in which Roman Catholicism and American values have encountered one another in the coliseum of psychology. During the past decade a vast literature has sprung up dealing with themes pertaining to both religion and psychology. Much of this literature reveals efforts at seeking spiritual and psychological pathways to arrive at a contemporary sense of the soul. One need only notice the incredible sales of such bestsellers as *Care of the Soul* and *Chicken Soup for the Soul,* leading one to conclude that "soul" really sells.[1]

What is going on here? Perhaps there is genuine longing by Americans to get in touch with their souls through the literature of psychospirituality. Then again, might the fascination with soul be just another fad attributable to the swirl of meanings surrounding the end of one and the beginning of another millennium? While the successful selling of the soul may eventually wane in popular literature, the popularity of this marketing phenomenon suggests something more substantial than the "chicken soup" varieties offered by the market place.

Psychology, a word whose etymological meaning from the Greek suggests the "study of the soul," had until a century ago been identified with philosophy more than science. Then, toward the end of the nineteenth century, the experimental laboratories of Europe established psychology as a disciplined field of studies that sought entry into the school of the sciences. To gain entry the field had to develop objective methods of measurement that eventually led to psychology being understood as the "science of behavior." During the same period the emergence of psychoanalysis led to a clinical psychology that placed great emphasis on unconscious motivations, thereby relegating to second place the rational choices of the mind. The relatively quick emergence of this "new psychology" with its "science of behavior" and psychoanalysis with its emphasis on the "unconscious" led many adherents to wander from its philosophical understanding of soul and prompted the quip that psychology had first lost its soul and then its mind.

1

While seemingly simplistic, the remark suggests that the emergence of these new "schools of psychology" could lead many believers astray from "saving their souls." If psychology became a discipline more identified with behavior or the unconscious mind, then what was to become of soul? And what would become of religion if "soul" became less important than behavior or the unconscious? Such were some of the concerns as Roman Catholicism faced the emerging discipline of psychology.

For the Roman Catholic Church, the challenge to teach and guide the souls of the faithful has been one of the central mandates received from Jesus Christ.[2] Through its history and traditions the church developed a process of caring for souls (*cura animarum*) by means of a system of seven sacraments. The sacrament of penance with its practice of confession has been one of the most common disciplines through which the faithful allow their souls to be so cared for and thus receive a sense of God's mercy.[3] The emergence of psychology at the turn of the twentieth century, with the loss of its "soul" and its "mind," posed a serious threat to the church, especially coming at a time when Catholicism was attacked by other intellectual and political movements of the modern world.

The church's fears in some ways have proven warranted. Compared to fifty years ago only one-fifth as many of today's American Catholics seek solace in private confession.[4] At the same time, many Catholics, like many other Americans, find consolations in counseling and therapy. With the psychiatrist Karl Menninger one may wonder, "Whatever became of sin?"[5] Similarly, one may ask, whatever became of confession?

During the course of the last century the Roman Catholic Church has at times viewed the emerging disciplines of psychology as challenging its attempts to help individuals to come to an awareness and an appreciation of their relationship with God and hence the soul. Psychological disciplines, by enhancing human self-awareness, have necessarily invaded the territory once seen as under the jurisdiction of religion. As a result, the knowledge and values that have emanated from psychology have at times threatened the church's centuries-long mandate of *cura animarum*. Roman Catholic individuals and institutions in America have responded to the challenges posed by psychology. The individuals, ideas, and institutions that have comprised these responses make for a good story.

Previous Research

The Catholic Church has not been alone in trying to make sense of psychology within the spheres of faith. Issues concerning the relations between religion and psychology have been discussed from psychology's earliest efforts as a discipline to its present popularity. Since William James's

Varieties of Religious Experience in 1902[6] endeavors to define a relationship between religion and mental health have been one of psychology's most fundamental pursuits. In recent years a substantial body of literature related to the dialogue between religion and psychology has developed. Such studies have included the relations between religion and psychology,[7] the perennial problems involving the boundaries between religion and science,[8] the interface of religious ethics and pastoral care,[9] the significance of religious experiences in psychotherapy,[10] and the emerging literature concerning God-representations and psychoanalysis.[11]

The evangelical psychologist Stanton Jones notes that there have been three classic ways in which psychology has interacted with religion. The first mode has been in the form of the psychology of religion. That is to say, psychologists since William James have made efforts to study religion and religious variables scientifically. A second form of interaction has been the ways by which psychology has informed pastoral care by supplying it with information concerning human behavior. Third, there have been the critical ways by which psychological findings have been used to redefine and even dismiss religious beliefs. Jones notes that psychoanalytic, behavioristic, and humanistic psychologists have used constructs and theories to dismiss religion.[12]

At the professional level, questions persist as to the limits in the interaction between psychology and religion given their distinct identities. There appears to be some dispute about psychology's openness to religious concerns. For instance, a study done by Benjamin Beit-Hallahmi in 1977 found that psychologists viewed religion as marginal,[13] and a subsequent study by Ragan, Malony, and Beit-Hallahmi in 1980[14] and another by Bergin and Jensen in 1990[15] indicated that psychologists were less religious compared to the general population. Bergin and Jensen found that only 33 percent of clinical psychologists surveyed saw religious faith as the most important influence on their lives compared with 72 percent of the general population. On the other hand, more recent studies by Shafranske and Malony in 1990,[16] Derr in 1991,[17] Lannert in 1992,[18] and Shafranske in 1995[19] indicated that psychologists do consider spiritual and religious issues as relevant for their professional work.

In recent years there have been indications that psychologists have become more willing to entertain religious issues. Between 1995 and 2000 the American Psychological Association published four works dealing with issues pertaining to psychology and religion. One work, *Religion and the Clinical Practice of Psychology,* edited by Edward P. Shafranske, consists of twenty-one chapters dealing with such issues as the cultural and historical context of relations between psychology and religion, religion and mental health, and psychotherapy with religious clients.[20] The APA also published

A Spiritual Strategy for Counseling and Psychotherapy by P. Scott Richards and Allan E. Bergin,[21] which addresses the atmosphere of alienation between psychology and religion and offers suggestions for an amelioration between the fields in the counseling context.[22]

Another indication of psychology's movement toward religion can be seen in the fact that the *American Psychologist,* the flagship journal of the American Psychological Association, has published in recent years articles pertaining to the relations between psychology and religion. In 1988 Roger Sperry, a leading cognitive theorist, questioned religion's role in cognitive science.[23] The next year William O'Donohue discussed how a clinical psychologist may be conceived as a metaphysician-scientist-practitioner.[24] In 1991 Allan E. Bergin published in the same journal an assessment of values and the role they play in psychotherapy.[25] Then in 1992 Stanton L. Jones published an article in which he sought to increase awareness in the psychological community of religion's role in the professional objectives of psychologists. Citing studies that found clinical psychologists to be the least religious among helping professionals, Jones argued that psychologists need to become aware of the importance of religious belief in the lives of their clients. For Jones, "psychology could be enriched by a more explicit exploration of the interface of religion with its scientific and applied activities."[26]

An enlightening analysis of the relations between psychology and religion has been done by Donald Browning.[27] In a particularly penetrating presentation, Browning found that a mutuality exists between psychology and religion in the way each field serves the other.[28] On the one hand, religion contributes to psychology by acting as a "carrier" of morality and religious views upon which psychology's cultural tradition is based. Psychology's development as a discipline has been dependent upon the classics of history, many of which are religious classics. On the other hand, Browning considered that psychology serves the church in four ways: diagnosis, development, therapy, and ethics. Browning noted with caution, however, that an overreliance by religion upon the clinical psychologies can obfuscate the rich religious traditions of understanding and wisdom, and he noted:

> In the end I believe that these modern psychologies have little to contribute that our Jewish and Christian traditions do not possess already. On the whole, they help us to differentiate, refine, balance, and perceive more deeply the resources that we already have.[29]

Thomas Oden in *Care of Souls in the Classic Tradition* expressed similar skepticism toward some of the ways psychology has been appropriated by religious traditions. He found that Christian denominations in their pastoral practices have too readily accommodated themselves to psychology and neglected their own wisdom traditions. For Oden, "the fundament of Christian pastoral care in its classical senses has at best been neglected and at worst polemicized. So pastoral theology has become in many cases little more than a mimic of the most current psychological trends."[30] It is within the framework of such issues that the relations between the discipline of psychology and the attitudes toward some of its major tenets expressed by members of a particular religious denomination may be understood.

As our discussion will show there has been a great deal of literature focused on religion's appropriation of psychology. Important contributions have been made by Peter Homans, who published two works that present an overview of controversial issues between psychology and theology.[31] More recently, John McDargh has described ways in which Catholic and mainstream Protestant theologians have appropriated psychology.[32] James Gustafson[33] and Mark Poorman[34] have indicated ways by which moral theology has incorporated findings of behavioral empirical science.

Several accounts of the history of the *cura animarum* have been written. One of the most important is *A History of the Cure of Souls* by John McNeill, published in 1951. In this work McNeill presented an overview of the ways in which pastoral care evolved over the centuries in Judaism, Christianity, Hinduism, Buddhism, and Confucianism. Concerning Roman Catholicism's approach to the *cura animarum*, McNeill highlighted the sacramental tradition, especially the sacrament of penance and its confessional practices. From a theological perspective McNeill described how the Council of Trent responded to the Protestant Reformation by seeking to rid the Catholic Church of its abuse of the sacrament of penance. The principles underlying the need for the confessional were maintained and even further emphasized as "pastors were encouraged to excite people to confession and admonish them to examine their consciences."[35]

In his chapter on Roman Catholicism McNeill discussed further practices surrounding the *cura animarum*. He pointed out how a whole system of casuistry developed concerning confessional practices, led by Counter-Reformation Jesuits. While pedantic to some, such casuistry refined the church's sense of moral freedom and thereby enhanced the understanding of caring for the soul. McNeill recognized the French schools of spirituality inspired by the writings of such figures as Francis de Sales, Jane de Chantal, Vincent de Paul, and François Fenelon. McNeill suggested that there was an important distinction between the church's practices surrounding confession and those around spiritual disciplines. In this respect, there occurred a refinement in the ways in which pastors directed souls in spiritual disciplines. One not only saw a confessor to confess one's sins, but also saw a spiritual director to promote one's desire for further holiness.

A history of Protestant pastoral care in the United States by E. Brooks Holifield was published in 1983. *A History of Pastoral Care in America: From Salvation to Self-Realization* represented the first general survey of pastoral care in America.[36] Earlier, Paul Johnson[37] and Edward Thornton,[38] in *Professional Education for Ministry: A History of Clinical Pastoral Education,* described the emergence of clinical pastoral education and training programs in American Protestant seminaries that in turn led to the establishment of the field of clinical pastoral education (CPE). In a similar vein Charles Van Wagner traced the development of the American Association of Pastoral Counseling.[39]

Pertinent to the present work was the study done by Allison Stokes, who surveyed the impact that Freudian psychology and psychoanalysis had upon the practice of American Protestant ministry.[40] Her study revealed in historical detail the pastoral appropriation of psychological theory by liberal Protestantism. Among the early developments highlighted by Stokes were the efforts of Boston's Emmanuel Movement, the pioneering work of Anton Boisen in establishing clinical training for seminarians, and Flanders Dunbar's bridge-building between religion and medicine. Stokes also described the collaboration of the Protestant minister Norman Vincent Peale with the psychiatrist Smiley Blanton in establishing the Peale-Blanton clinic in 1937 and promoting cooperation between religion and psychiatry. The meetings of the New York Psychology Group (NYPG) figure prominently in Stokes's account. The group, which met monthly between 1942 and 1945, consisted of a core of about two dozen of the leading psychotherapists and Protestant theologians of the era. Such figures as Eric Fromm, Seward Hiltner, Rollo May, David Roberts, Carl Rogers, Ernst Schachtel, and Paul Tillich were regular participants. Interestingly enough, for reasons that this presentation will suggest, no Roman Catholics participated in these meetings.

For several decades the tension involved in acculturation to the American way of life has been a persistent theme among historians interpreting American Catholicism. In 1958 Robert Cross in *The Emergence of Liberal Catholicism in America*[41] described this tension, as did Thomas O'Dea in *American Catholic Dilemma.*[42] Both Cross's and O'Dea's works may be seen as responses to John Tracy Ellis's charge in 1956 that there was a paucity of substantial scholarship in the American Catholic community.[43] Ellis critically argued that up to that time American Catholic scholarship was too narrow in focus.

In the decades following Ellis's critique, arguments have reverberated within the American Catholic academic community. For instance, in 1980 William Halsey described American Catholic "romanticism" and "innocence" during the period between World War I and World War II.[44]

For Halsey American Catholicism found "safety, sanity and salvation" through its promotion of Thomism among its intellectuals and in its higher educational institutions.

More recently Margaret Reher in *Catholic Intellectual Life in America* contributed to the series "The Bicentennial History of the Catholic Church in America" by offering an overview of the various historical currents in American Catholicism's intellectual life. Reher concludes her historical survey by considering American Catholicism as having entered a more pluralistic phase.[45] Christopher Kaufman, meanwhile, as a contributor to the same bicentennial series, examined the rise of Catholic health care in the United States. He especially highlights the immense contributions of women religious through their Catholic hospitals and nursing schools and the social consciousness that grew from such institutions.[46]

The tension involved in acculturation has also been discussed by Philip Gleason. In *Contending with Modernity* he presents a comprehensive overview of the intellectual and institutional developments of twentieth-century American Catholicism. Gleason sees Catholic higher education's secular success in terms of Catholicism's "contending with modernity"; it has "accelerated the academic acculturation of American Catholic higher education" and led to greater "accommodation" and "assimilative tendencies."[47] For Gleason and other Catholic writers there exists the nagging concern that American Catholic colleges and universities may be traveling a route taken by Protestant universities a century earlier. Such a route has been described by George Marsden in *The Soul of the American University: From Protestant Establishment to Established Nonbelief.* Marsden, a non-Catholic colleague of Gleason at the University of Notre Dame, presents an account of the rise and fall of Protestantism's influence in American higher education.[48] His work has been highlighted by some Catholic educators as a possible forecast of the future of American Catholic institutions.[49]

Other significant studies of twentieth-century American Catholicism have been presented by Jay Dolan,[50] Gerald Fogarty,[51] James Hennesey,[52] William Leahy,[53] and David O'Brien.[54] Each of these studies has led to a greater understanding of the progress of the institutional and intellectual life of American Catholicism.

Approach and Method

The project of seeking to articulate a history of relations between professional psychology and American Catholicism represents an autobiographical endeavor, describing as it does some of the issues and people I have studied during the course of three decades of work in psychology. It is meant as a historical narrative. As such it attempts to compel the reader to recognize the challenges that faced American Catholic individuals and institutions as they sought to understand and make informed decisions concerning the attitudes and values made available by the emerging disciplines of psychology. The narrative thereby offers a lens into a portion of Roman Catholicism as it attempted to assimilate American values as they were informed by professional psychology during the twentieth century. As will be related, there was at times considerable tension as Catholicism attempted to appropriate the attitudes, insights, and methods of psychology without accommodating to the emerging secularization which many of psychology's leaders tended to promote. As a religious entity American Catholicism, of course, is not alone in its denominational efforts to appropriate psychology without accommodating to its sometimes secularizing values. Moreover, Roman Catholicism exists as a unique international entity, and stories could be related about how the church in other nations and cultures has attempted to appropriate psychology's attitudes without accommodating to all of its values. For convenience' sake, the phrase "American Catholicism" is employed in a recognition of the distinct manner in which Roman Catholicism in America (specifically the United States, with all due respect to Canada and Latin American) encountered psychology as it emerged as a cultural force. "Psychology" refers to the experimental and clinical disciplines whose central project revolves around understanding the mental states and processes.

With any narrative account there are biases and limitations. The reader may wonder why some events and people are emphasized while others are not. Indeed, the section on Sr. Annette Walters grew out of a critique by Dr. Mary Reuder, a leader in the American Psychological Association and a former student of Sr. Walters, who upon reading my dissertation commented that the research tended to emphasize events and figures from the East Coast. I recognize that this still may be the case although having interviewed several dozen people and used the archives of a dozen universities throughout the United States, I believe that I have arrived at a fair sampling of the significant leaders in the dialogue between American Catholicism and professional psychology.

Also one may notice a preponderance of white males and a dearth of females and minorities. Admittedly this may be viewed as a limitation of this work and a bias of the author. However, it may also be a fair indication that few women or members of minority groups were afforded opportunities to have a significant impact on the conversation between Catholicism and psychology. Indeed it makes the contributions of Magda Arnold, Virginia Staudt Sexton, and Annette Walters all the more significant.

It also should be noted that the study restricted itself to a few academic and clinical areas of professional psychology. Developments pertaining to related fields such as education, nursing, or social work are not presented. Certainly there have been contributions made and there are stories to be told by and about figures from these fields as well, but that is another project.

The topic itself emerged during my studies at Boston University. When faced with a dissertation project, I realized I had consistently been interested in looking for ways to integrate psychology's insights about human development with the tenets of faith. In considering the changes in professional psychology and in American Catholicism, I discovered that there was a story waiting to be told. More precisely, there were stories waiting to be heard, and so I set about engaging in an oral as well as an archival history.

During the course of five years of research for the dissertation and then this work I interviewed several dozen people. Some of them, such as Virginia Staudt Sexton and Sr. Rita Mary Bradley, kindly consented to tell their stories shortly before their deaths. I am immensely grateful for the joy and grace I experienced through listening to the stories of men and women who engaged in what was at times a dramatic dialogue not only between forces of professional psychology and American Catholicism, but also among the cultural forces of the times. Indeed this work, tracing American Catholicism since the turn of the century, tries to capture not just one but a series of evolving *Zeitgeists*. While by no means comprehensive, the effort, I believe, does give one a lens through which it is possible to glimpse how Catholicism both clashed and cooperated with the psychological forces in twentieth-century America.

Sequencing the Stories

This historical account may be read as a sequence of stories about the encounters between American Catholicism and professional psychology. As will be seen in chapter 1 the sequence is not meant to be ordered chronologically, but thematically. In presenting the serene setting of the 1954 St. John's Summer Institute and contrasting it with the tense public confrontation in the media between Bishop Fulton J. Sheen and leaders in the psychoanalytic profession, I intend to place the reader into what was at times an intense drama. For some such as Sheen it was no less than a battle for the human soul. Psychology, psychiatry, and especially psychoanalysis did not always have such a cooperative relationship with Catholicism as they more or less do today. Real antagonism existed, and so in the first chapter we read of a confrontation between one of the leading prelates of the Catholic Church and leading representatives of psychoanalysis. Later a series of papal addresses by Pope Pius XII to professionals in the health professions quelled the controversies. The pope's statement that psychotherapy shares in Catholicism's quest "for the knowledge of the soul" represented a significant movement from antagonism to collaboration.

Chapter 2 offers a sequential look at the birth of the new psychology, coming during a troubled period of American Catholic history. Buoyed by the papacy of Pope Leo XIII, many Catholic scholars and leaders confidently appropriated aspects of the progressive spirit during the gilded age. However, a series of dramatic events led to a perception of an "Americanist" heresy and, combined with the church's battles with the modernist trends of the era, to a more reactionary stance by many Roman Catholic leaders. Amid these battles, there were the extraordinary initiatives of Fr. Edward Pace, whose laboratory at the Catholic University of America and whose scholarship led him to become one of the early leaders of the new psychology in America.

The third chapter presents the contributions of several Catholic scholars as they sought to understand the insights and theories that emanated from the clinics and laboratories of the emerging disciplines of psychology. These theories included Freud's controversial psychoanalytic methods and conclusions. The life, writings, and witness of Pace's student Dom Thomas Verner Moore, as well as the writings of E. Boyd Barrett, Charles Bruehl, and Rudolf Allers had considerable influence in American Catholicism's gradual appropriation of psychology, although there was at the same time a marked concern about some of the basic tenets of "Freudianism."

Chapter 4 describes the establishment and professional contributions of the psychology departments at St. Louis, Loyola, and Fordham Universities. The personalities involved and the research projects with which they were engaged served to make the methods and theories of psychology more respectable in Catholic circles. Gruender and Severin at St. Louis, Fordham's William Bier and Virginia Staudt Sexton, and Loyola's Vincent Herr, Charles A. Curran, and Eugene Kennedy introduced programs and promoted projects that solidified psychology's separation from philosophical psychology and made distinct pastoral contributions to mid-twentieth-century American Catholicism.

The remarkable life and witness of Sr. Annette Walters, C.S.J., is recounted in chapter 5. Beginning with her exposure to the Sisters of St. Joseph and subsequent entrance in 1929 into the College of St. Catherine, perhaps the most intellectually astute Catholic college of the era, the chapter relates Walters's doctoral training at the University of Minnesota, where she began a life-long friendship with the behaviorist B. F. Skinner. This section also provides details of Walters's amazing energies and the influence she exerted in promoting psychology among women religious. Her rise and fall with the Sisters Formation Movement is also described.

The sixth chapter examines the intellectual life of American Catholicism before the Second Vatican Council. Significant ideological and institutional movements of transformation were afoot in American Catholicism well before the Second Vatican Council, at least with regard to psychology. The challenge to Catholic intellectual life set forth in 1956 by John Tracy Ellis was accompanied by Catholic thinkers entering into a more amicable relationship with psychoanalysis. In this respect, the figure of the convert Gregory Zilboorg looms large. Also noteworthy during this period were the birth and growth of two Catholic professional associations: the American Catholic Psychological Association (ACPA) and the National Guild of Catholic Psychiatrists. Their memberships, which included priests, brothers, and women religious, were instrumental in psychology's legitimation by Catholic professionals and within the larger sphere of American Catholicism. The chapter also describes in detail the St. John's Summer Institute, an annual summer series of seminars between 1954 and 1973 that brought together mental health clinicians and an ecumenical gathering of clergy and religious. The seminars enhanced Catholicism's appropriation of psychology and collaboration with the once suspected psychological professions. Moreover, the institute created new standards for interfaith dialogue.

Chapter 7 offers an overview of the paradigm shifts in both Catholic theology and American psychology during the 1960s. The spirit of *aggiornamento* of the Second Vatican Council combined with the humanistic forces of psychology furthered Catholicism's appropriation of psychology. Later some critics felt that religious bodies such as American Catholicism went too far in their absorption of psychological attitudes and methods and the accommodation to psychology's secular values.

The influence of three psychiatrists and three psychologists are examined in chapter 8. Leo Bartemeier, Francis Braceland, and John Cavanagh, by serving as members of the professional echelon of psychiatry and through their association with the hierarchy of the Catholic Church, helped alleviate the fears of Catholics toward psychiatry and psychoanalysis. The chapter also presents the contributions of Fathers Charles A. Curran, Adrian van Kaam, and William Meissner, each of whose writings offered ways by which the insights of psychology could be integrated into Catholic theology. By so doing they demonstrated the contemporary relevance of the medieval Thomistic axiom *gratia perfecta natura* (grace builds on nature).

The ninth chapter compares the life and legacies of Thomas Merton and Henri Nouwen as they relate to psychology. Merton, a monk who dabbled in psychology, and Nouwen, a priest-psychologist whose life manifested some of the ideals of monasticism, are significant figures in American Catholicism's dialogue with psychology.

Chapter 10 explores how Fr. William Barry, Sr. Joyce Rupp, and other contemporary Catholic authors have, through their psychological training, integrated themes pertinent to both psychology and spirituality. This chapter also includes a discussion of how constructs borrowed from Jung's analytical psychology and strategies employed in Freud's psychodynamic have been successfully employed by George Schemel and other spiritual directors, especially in the context of directed retreats.

Finally, a concluding chapter examines the major themes in American Catholicism's dialogue with psychology. Past issues and present patterns are summarized, and the respective roles of psychology and religion in the common quest for "the knowledge of the soul" are considered.

Chapter 1

From Two Spires
to One Banner

Antagonisms and Alliances

The two sparkling spires of the abbey's church soared above the vast Minnesota summer landscape as if to symbolize that beneath there gathered representatives from two separate worlds. Since the Enlightenment, scientific disciplines had more and more divorced themselves from religion. As a result Western culture had become accustomed to two disconnected streams of knowledge and inspiration. In the case of the relatively young science of modern empirical psychology, its methods and its clinical conclusions increasingly departed from the traditional wisdom offered by theology and Thomistic psychology.

But on that summer day of 1954 as dozens of priests and religious assembled at St. John College's monastic campus, a new relationship between psychology and religion, more specifically between clinical psychology and American Catholicism, seemed possible. Those who assembled that day had come to listen to leading psychologists and psychiatrists. The religious would be the first participants in the St. John's Institute for Mental Health. There would be three weeks of seminars that summer and the next twenty-two summers at St. John's. By 1973, when the last institute was held, some twenty-five hundred priests and nuns, ministers, and rabbis had engaged in classes and conversations with more than seventy leading psychiatrists and psychologists.

The topics at the seminars covered a wide range of psychological and religious concerns, from adolescence to paranoia, from aging to sexuality, from alcoholism to suicide. The institute was designed to address the salient issues at the interface between psychology and religion.

But at that time dialogue between psychology and Catholicism was not an amicable one. Like two separate spires psychology and religion were quite alienated, and debates stemming from distrust and ignorance had raged between them. The history of the arguments and the agreements, the competition and the collaboration, makes for a great story.

The New Century and the New Psychology

It has been said that as the young discipline of psychology departed from its philosophical and theological traditions and developed its experimental methods and behavioristic emphasis, it first lost its soul and then its mind. The bold movements undertaken during the late nineteenth century by experimentalists such as Hermann von Helmholtz and Wilhelm Wundt and clinicians such as Pierre Marie Félix Janet and Sigmund Freud led to the early discipline being branded as "the new psychologies." The experimental approach to psychology was accepted in the Catholic world largely due to the influence of Msgr. Desiré Mercier at Louvain and Fr. Edward Pace at the Catholic University of America. Indeed Pace, who had studied under Wundt, had one of the first psychological laboratories in America. But Catholicism's acceptance of Freud and his psychoanalytic counterparts was a different matter altogether. A few Catholic psychiatrists such as Dom Thomas Verner Moore, who for twenty-five years served as the chair of Catholic University's department of psychology and psychiatry, did find some value in the psychoanalytic method. But Freud's writings and psychoanalysis in general were for all intents and purposes anathema for Catholics. And Freud did not make dialogue with religion easy, as is evidenced by his work *The Future of an Illusion*.

Growth of American Psychoanalysis

Despite the misgivings of many religious leaders, psychoanalysis was an emerging force in American clinical training shortly before World War II due to the forced migration of many Jewish psychoanalysts from Europe. Later during the war the psychoanalytic strategy of catharsis proved effective in treating war neurosis.

Even before Freud died in 1939, psychoanalytic thought was showing significant signs of division and diversity that would influence the ways in which psychoanalysis saw itself and was seen by other disciplines. Such differences within the psychoanalytic field involved both theory and technique and would eventually enable an easier and fuller acceptance and assimilation by religious bodies such as the Roman Catholic Church.

In a comprehensive study, Nathan G. Hale described the various perceptions that Freud's psychoanalytic technique and theory have had in the twentieth century in the United States.[1] At first Freud and his followers were seen as iconoclasts who challenged the foundations of civilization and religious belief. The fact that most psychoanalysts were Jewish did not readily endear psychoanalysis to American intellectual and institutional establishments, many of which had anti-Semitic biases. With the rise of

Nazism in Germany, many Jewish psychoanalysts were forced to flee, and by 1942 the United States had become the center of psychoanalysis. In cities such as Boston, Chicago, New York, and Washington refugees helped to enhance the reputations of psychoanalytic institutes.[2]

Meanwhile psychiatry in the United States incorporated the biological approach of neuropsychiatrists and the biosocial approaches led by Adolf Meyer. With the onset of the war and its host of demands, the United States Department of Defense turned to psychiatry and psychology for testing and evaluating recruits and for treating soldiers traumatized by combat. According to Hale, it was in such areas that psychoanalysts made a particular contribution. For instance, two psychoanalysts, Roy Grinker and John Spiegel, described their experiences of the Tunisian campaign in a small text entitled *War Neurosis*. Their analysis proved so poignant and relevant that forty-five thousand copies of the text were distributed to service personnel treating such soldiers.[3]

Psychiatric understandings and strategies contributed immensely to the war effort, with psychoanalysts doing more than their share. As Hale writes:

> The psychoanalysts not only supplied key personnel, whose influence far outweighed their numbers. They also developed theories, classifications, systems, and methods of treatment for the war neuroses. They contributed significantly to the training of the young physicians who made up the majority of the Army's psychiatrists.[4]

The psychoanalytic contribution to the preparation and assistance of soldiers in combat led to a wider acceptance of psychoanalytic thought. As a result, in the years immediately following the end of the war, psychoanalytic institutes were flooded with requests. Hale reports that between the years 1948 and 1951 more than four thousand psychiatrists sought psychoanalytic training. In addition, the National Institute of Mental Health generously contributed to psychoanalytic institutes. As Hale again notes, from 1948 to 1967 such institutes received $1,121,030; the Menninger Clinic in Topeka, Kansas, alone received $881,584. The development of psychoanalytic training centers led to psychoanalysts' holding major administrative positions in related disciplines. For instance, by 1961 in the Boston area, psychoanalysts and candidates held 70 percent of the psychiatric teaching positions in the schools of social work, more than 75 percent of the professorial positions in the psychiatric departments of the area's medical schools, and more than half of the staff positions in Boston's general hospitals and in the psychiatric services at the Veterans Administration hospitals.[5] Such success helped to make psychoanalytic training the dominant force in American clinical psychology. For some American

Catholic leaders such a force was a threat and needed to be critiqued forcefully. Their views of psychoanalysis demonstrated the church's ambivalence concerning psychoanalytic thought. The ambivalence came to the public eye in disputations concerning psychoanalysis rendered by the most visible Catholic prelate of the era, Fulton J. Sheen.

Fulton J. Sheen's Challenges to Psychoanalysis

Having received his philosophical training at Louvain, Sheen was well acquainted with Catholic efforts to develop psychology within Thomistic guidelines. His dissertation was entitled "God and Intelligence in Modern Philosophy," for which he received the Cardinal Mercier Prize for International Philosophy. He then went to Catholic University, where for twenty-five years he held the chair of apologetics. It was as an apologist that Sheen claimed responsibility for challenging the secularist forces encroaching upon American society. For Sheen, psychoanalysis was one such force.

Sheen's most public attack against psychoanalysis, one that created considerable controversy, occurred shortly after the war when psychoanalytic thought was experiencing the beginning of its popularity boom.[6] The controversy began on March 9, 1947, when Msgr. Sheen attacked psychoanalysis from the pulpit of St. Patrick's Cathedral in New York City. He criticized "a particular type of psychoanalysis called Freudianism which is based on four assumptions, materialism, hedonism, infantilism and eroticism."[7] Sheen stated that he believed such criticism of Freudianism necessary "to the extent that it denies sin and would supplant confession."[8] Sheen furthermore asserted, "There are no more disintegrated people in the world than the victims of psychoanalysis. Confession gives you the standard of Christ, the perfection of personality."[9] Sheen's criticisms were motivated by the belief that many Catholics were coming to view psychoanalysis as a substitute for the confessional, and that for them sublimation supplanted absolution.

Controversy over the sermon became pronounced several months later when on May 27, 1947, Dr. Frank Curran, a leading Catholic psychiatrist, resigned his position as the chief psychiatrist at St. Vincent's Hospital in New York City because of what he saw as the failure of the Archdiocese of New York to repudiate or clarify Msgr. Sheen's comments. Dr. Curran was particularly perturbed by the report that Sheen was critical of psychiatry as well as of psychoanalysis. Three weeks later columnist Albert Deutsch began a series of articles about the controversy. On June 17 Deutsch reported an interview he had with Dr. Leo Bartemeier, who responded to Sheen's attacks by stating:

It is most unfortunate that one who enjoys Msgr. Sheen's prestige would allow himself to give voice to such grievous errors. Tolerance and charity are fundamental tenets of both Catholicism and psychoanalysis. There is no contradiction between Catholicism and psychoanalysis, which is aimed at the understanding of people in trouble in order to bring about more wholesome personal, family and community relations.[10]

Deutsch also referred to rejoinders made by Dr. Lawrence Kubie, a leader in the New York Psychoanalytic Institute, who responded to Sheen's attack point by point:

Neither in philosophy, purpose or technique is psychoanalysis "hedonistic, infantilistic or erotic." Freud himself was an ascetic in his personal life, and repeatedly emphasized in his writings the importance of curbing unbridled pleasure-seeking. He refers to this not as the restriction of the "pleasure principle," but the "reality principle" in life.[11]

The day after Kubie's remarks Deutsch ran another article, in which he interviewed Sheen and informed him of Bartemeier's and Kubie's replies to his attacks. Voicing his displeasure at how he was misquoted by the press, Sheen added fuel to the controversy. Learning of Bartemeier's view that the sermon contained "grievous errors," Sheen replied, "The fact that Dr. Bartemeier is a Catholic doesn't make him immune to racketeering proclivities so common among psychoanalysts. Catholics can be racketeers too. Look at Mike Quill."[12]

The storm over Sheen's sermon took on an added dimension when Dr. A. A. Brill, a leading New York psychoanalyst, addressed a summer institute of rabbis and denounced Sheen's attacks. Brill contrasted Sheen's view with those of Rabbi Joshua Liebman. Brill noted that Liebman, in the best-selling book *Peace of Mind,* presented one of the first examples of how psychology and religion can find common ground and how clergy and psychologists can work together. Since Brill's presentation was at Union Hebrew College and his audience consisted of some eighty rabbis, the reference to Rabbi Liebman's successful use of psychoanalytic insights seemed an even sharper critique of Sheen's position. Brill asserted that Sheen refused to discuss his criticisms with psychoanalysts, including Catholics. He added: "In brief, Msgr. Sheen is entirely governed by the 'omnipotence of thought' which is characteristic of primitive thinking."[13]

Deutsch once again used his column to report that prominent Catholic psychiatrists had launched a counteroffensive against Sheen by issuing a joint statement. Besides Bartemeier and Curran, Dr. Edward Strecker, a former president of the American Psychiatric Association, and Dr. Francis Gerty, the chief of the Illinois Neuro-psychiatric Institute, defended their profession against Sheen's attacks. Bartemeier questioned Sheen's authority when he noted, "Through his many radio broadcasts and public speeches, he has left a widespread and erroneous impression that he is the official spokesman for the Catholic Church."[14]

Finally, on Sunday, July 20, Sheen sought to set the record straight in a letter to the *New York Times* that received added coverage in the *Times* on July 21. In his letter Sheen pointed out some distortions in the press coverage: he was not critical of psychiatry or of all forms of psychoanalysis. He even mentioned that he was sympathetic to the views of Jung and Adler. In his letter Sheen listed the following two points:

> The point of discussion is not the Catholic Church and science, nor have I ever presented myself as the spokesman of the church on the subject of psychiatry except to praise it when it remains within the limits of the scientific. Catholics in psychiatry do not make Freudianism Catholic any more than Catholics in physics make atomic bombs moral. I am, however, a spokesman of the Catholic Church when I say that any positive denial of sin on the part of Freudian psychoanalysis renders that science inadequate for the handling of the problems which affect the whole man.

With Sheen's clarification about psychiatry and his qualifications of his criticism of psychoanalysis some of the controversy abated.

Pope Pius XII and Psychotherapy: "For the Knowledge of the Soul"

In 1952, a chain of events occurred that was to redefine relations between Catholicism and psychoanalysis. The key figure of the series of events was Pope Pius XII. For most American Catholics of the time Pope Pius XII was a popular and revered leader. But for some he represented a source of both freedom and repression for Catholic institutions and intellectuals as they encountered the postwar world.

In his approach to the modern world Pius XII presented the church's principles and tradition in a way that seemed both to encourage and to warn. This approach was evident in two public addresses he made pertaining to psychotherapy. These addresses became almost necessary when Msgr. Pericle Felici, an official of the diocese of Rome, published a statement saying that he considered Catholic practitioners of psychoanalysis and their patients to be committing mortal sin. The statement was printed in April 1952 in the *Bulletin of the Catholic Clergy of Rome,* the official voice of the Roman Vicariate. Felici further asserted that the real effectiveness of psychoanalysis had been greatly exaggerated and that "the psychoanalytical school can easily become a school of corruption."[15]

A storm of controversy ensued. A few months later the Vatican officially responded when Pius XII alluded to psychoanalysis before three hundred surgeons at the First International Congress on the Histopathology of the Nervous System. The pope strongly asserted his arguments against psychotherapeutic treatments that seek to unleash the sexual instinct for seemingly therapeutic reasons. The psychoanalytic technique of free association was perceived as one such treatment. For Roman Catholics Pius XII's statement set a moral limit on how far psychoanalytic techniques aimed at unleashing sexual repressions may go. Then seven months later the pope made another statement that appeared to be more accepting of certain forms of psychoanalytic and psychotherapeutic work. On April 13, 1953, he gave an address to the Fifth International Congress of Psychotherapy and Clinical Psychology. In his address the pope, while noting several concerns about determinism and materialism espoused by many psychotherapists, invoked a blessing upon his listeners and asserted:

> Be assured that the Church follows your research and your medical practice with her warm interest and her best wishes. You labor in a terrain that is very difficult. But your activity is capable of achieving precious results for medicine, *for the knowledge of the soul* [emphasis added] in general, for the religious dispositions of man and for their development.[16]

The pope's statements reflected developments in Catholic thought concerning psychoanalysis. The fact that the meeting was held in Rome was due to the organization's president, Dr. Leo Bartemeier, Fulton Sheen's former nemesis.

The pope's two statements concerning the mental health professions served as a catalyst for both controversy and exchange. His statements on the moral limits of psychoanalysis and his condemnation of "pansexualism" served to support the arguments of Fulton Sheen and others. On the other hand, his support for psychotherapy in general augmented the movements in the church for greater awareness of psychology.

From Antagonisms to Alliances

The following pages will trace the history of antagonisms and alliances between psychology and American Catholicism. As this introductory chapter suggests, there were times of acrimony and antagonism. However, recent years have seen more collaborative efforts, such as were seen during those summer days at St. John's in 1954. And suitably in a visit to St. John's monastic campus one would see, rather than two spires, a magnificent banner thrusting boldly into the sky. Perhaps the difference suggests the new relationship between psychology and Catholicism; the division that once existed between science and religion, between psychology and Catholicism, is no longer so pronounced. As a consequence two spires of inspiration, two forces of knowledge and wisdom, once separate, now collaborate in the construction of a solid banner of wisdom. Today psychologists and theologians, psychotherapists and spiritual directors are allies rather than antagonists. They have become a united force with a more holistic understanding of the care of human beings—our behaviors, our minds, and our very souls.

Chapter 2

The Turn-of-the-Century Immigrants

Catholicism and the New Psychology

In 1892 when Edward Pace founded one of the nation's first experimental laboratories of psychology at the Catholic University of America, both American Catholicism and American psychology were heavily dependent upon European influences for direction and guidance.[1] At the end of the nineteenth century, American Catholic intellectual life and the emerging science of psychology were, in effect, emigrants from the rigorous academic schools of Europe. Catholicism relied heavily not only upon Roman institutions, such as the Jesuit-run Gregorian University, but also upon the revitalized school at Louvain. Psychology, meanwhile, in seeking to achieve a more scientific identity, and in so doing separate itself from philosophy, established first experimental and then clinical institutions. By the dawn of the twentieth century, American institutions had inherited the new psychology from Europe and were enthusiastically adapting its methodology to their own questions. The present chapter will describe the developments surrounding the emergence of the new psychology and how American Catholicism's responses, while initially optimistic toward the new psychology, became suspicious and timid.

The empirical psychology emigrating from the laboratories of Europe in the late nineteenth century was called the "new psychology" to distinguish it from the "old" or "armchair" psychology based in both the medieval and modern philosophical traditions.[2] While the latter traditions saw psychology as a way to rationally explore what constitutes the mind or soul, the new psychology empirically asked what the mind does and how it acts.

Figuring most prominently in the birth of empirical psychology was Wilhelm Wundt (1832–1920), who established the first psychological laboratory in Leipzig in 1879. His research and teaching as well as his voluminous publications led to his being given the title "father of experimental psychology." Wundt studied under Johannes Müller (1801–58), the "father of experimental physiology." He also collaborated with another empirical physiologist, Hermann von Helmholtz (1821–94), and read the

21

innovative psychophysics of Ernst Weber (1795–1878) and Gustav Fechner (1801–87). Wundt incorporated his understanding of the works of his fellow Germans into an experimental method for dealing with problems of the mind. Spanning several decades of research and writing, Wundt's experimental psychology was noteworthy for the ways it used psychophysical instruments to explain perception and sensation as well as reaction processes. This approach led Wundt to conceive of the goal of psychology as "the analysis of mind into simple qualities."[3] His approach was labeled "elementalism."

Unlike many of his students and successors, Wundt saw himself as a philosopher as well as a psychologist and later bemoaned psychology's movement away from philosophy. It was, however, his experimental approach that created the impetus to move psychology away from the study not only of the "soul," but also of the "mind," and eventually to the study of "behavior." It was not long before claims were made that psychology had first lost its soul, then its mind, then consciousness, but it still had behavior. As new psychology laboratories sprung up in universities in Europe and the United States,[4] the "new psychologists" found philosophical discussions increasingly irrelevant as the emerging experimental discipline became estranged from its metaphysical underpinnings. As a consequence, the emerging discipline was suspect to the Catholic Church in America, which was at the time trying to find its own identity.

The Catholic World at the Turn of the Century

The nineteenth century was a tumultuous one for Roman Catholics, especially in Europe. The century began with many movements hostile toward the Catholic Church that had earlier been unleashed by the French Revolution. As the century progressed, the Vatican in its fight for survival took, for the most part, a reactionary position toward the state and the culture at large. This was especially evident during the thirty-two-year papacy of Pope Pius IX (1846–78). In Germany, for instance, beginning in 1872 with the rise of Bismarck, the *Kulturkampf* challenged the church's role and rights in German society and subsequently led to the emigration of millions of Germans to America and elsewhere. In Italy, meanwhile, in the face of Italian nationalism the Vatican went through a series of conflicts that ultimately led to the devastating loss of the Papal States by 1870.

With the security of the Vatican state threatened, the church often took a defensive attitude toward social change and theological issues. As a result, the church was viewed by its critics, within and without, as creating a siege mentality. This mentality was demonstrated in the ultramontanist papacy of Pope Pius IX, whose suspicion toward the democratic movements and the liberal spirit of the age was pronounced. This suspicion was evidenced in his 1864 document known as the *Syllabus of Errors,* a list of statements that the pope deemed erroneous. For instance, he declared to be erroneous the statement that "the Roman pontiff can, and ought to, reconcile himself and come to terms with progress, liberalism and modern civilization."[5]

Anything suggesting "liberalism," consequently, was seen as anathema by the great majority of Roman Catholic leaders. Given that so many of the church's institutions had been destroyed or stolen by the French Revolution and its "liberal" mind-set, any kind of "liberalism," whether political, economic, or theological, was perceived as a threat to the papacy and therefore to the church. Opponents of liberalism coalesced into a political force known as ultramontanism, which under Pope Pius IX created almost an "idolatry of the papacy."[6]

With the death of Pius IX in 1878 the European world was percolating with the hope that the new pope would provide more positive relations between the Vatican and the Western world. The early days of Pope Leo XIII's pontificate offered just that. In 1879 the pope published his third encyclical, *Aeterni Patris,* or *On Restoring Christian Philosophy.* By means of this encyclical the new pope inaugurated what many believed was a renaissance in Catholic philosophical and theological thought. *Aeterni Patris,* among other things, challenged Catholic scholars to acquaint themselves with the changes that the emerging sciences had presented in this historical epoch. Such a challenge signaled the beginning of a new era in the relations between science and Catholicism, as it marked a turn from many reactionary stances that the church had held since the dawn of the Enlightenment.

In issuing *Aeterni Patris,* then, Pope Leo XIII seemed to offer ways of reconciling the church with the modern world. One area needing reconciliation was the relationship between religion and science. Leo XIII recognized the monumental progress of science during the nineteenth century, and he believed that an adequate Catholic response could be made only through a revitalization of philosophy, especially Thomistic philosophy. Leo wrote:

> We exhort you, venerable brethren, in all earnestness to restore the golden wisdom of St. Thomas and to spread it far and wide for the defense and beauty of the Catholic faith, for the good of society, and for the *advantage of all the sciences* [emphasis added].[7]

In effect, the pope challenged the Catholic intellectuals of his day, mostly philosophers and theologians, to pay attention to the advances made by science and to progress with them rather than react against them. He asserted that "every wise thought and every useful discovery, wherever it may come from, should be gladly and gratefully welcomed."[8] In this respect the pope was restating the words of St. Thomas, who believed that every truth should be loved for its own sake.

Since the second half of the nineteenth century the revival of Thomistic thought, with its rational psychology, was one of the responses of Roman Catholic thinkers to the modern era. Indeed, even before he became Pope Leo XIII, Gioacchino Pecci was one of the leaders in the Thomistic revival. As a seminarian at the Roman College, Pecci had become enamored of the synthesis offered by Aquinas and had found the post-Cartesian approach of French scholars and the post-Kantian efforts of Germans severely wanting for the promotion of the Catholic faith. Later, as archbishop of Perugia, Pecci and his brother Giuseppe invited Dominicans, the order to which Aquinas had belonged, to turn the diocesan seminary into a Thomistic center. It was not surprising, therefore, that on assuming the papacy Pecci set about spreading Thomistic thought throughout all Catholic seminaries.

To enhance the scholastic renaissance the pope turned to the ancient University of Louvain in Belgium to become the center of the Thomistic revival. His choice was not surprising, since he had become well acquainted with Louvain during his days as papal nuncio to Belgium during the 1840s. In 1880 the pope encouraged the Belgian bishops to establish a university chair in Thomistic philosophy. They agreed and chose Fr. Desiré Mercier to assume the position.

Mercier, with doctorates in both philosophy and theology, since 1877 had held the chair of philosophy at a Belgium diocesan seminary when he assumed his new role in 1882. In preparing for the position Mercier met with the pope, and they concurred that the best means for updating Catholic thought and confronting idealism and materialism was through a strong curriculum grounded in the concepts and principles of philosophy. Mercier's efforts eventually led to the creation of a special institute of Thomistic philosophy at Louvain that was to be the flagship of neo-Thomism.

Mercier did not restrict himself to philosophy alone, however. He shared Leo XIII's Thomistic belief that "every wise thought and every useful discovery, wherever it may come from, should be gladly and gratefully welcomed." As a result Mercier engaged the new psychology that was emerging in the clinics and laboratories of Europe. He went to Paris to study with Jean Martin Charcot and became well versed in the writings of Wilhelm Wundt, Alfred Binet, and William James. Then in 1891 he organized a course and laboratory in experimental psychology at Louvain. He saw this effort as furthering the integration of the revival of Thomistic principles with the emerging science of psychology. He wrote:

Psychology is undergoing today a transformation from which we would be blameworthy to remain aloof.... Here is a young, contemporary science, which is in itself neither spiritualistic nor materialistic. If we do not take part in it, the psychology of the future will develop without us, and there is every reason to believe against us.... We must prepare workers who will produce their own works, original experiments, which no one can overlook without ceasing to be familiar with the science.[9]

Mercier, in effect, became a Catholic apologist for both the rational psychology of Thomism and the empirical psychology of Wundt. Given the heightened suspicion of his day and the strained relations between religion and science, this was not always an easy matter. Mercier, however, had the confidence of Pope Leo XIII and his successors, as was evident in his being made archbishop of Malines, Belgium, in 1906 and then a cardinal in 1907. A few years later Cardinal Mercier's spiritual stature sustained the Belgian people through the First World War and the agonizing ruin of their nation.

Mercier's reputation, however, could have been made elsewhere. In 1889, toward the end of his studies, he was invited by the Catholic University of America to help inaugurate the new psychology in the United States. The person who invited Mercier was Fr. Edward Pace. Ironically, Mercier's refusal of Pace's offer meant that it would be Pace rather than Mercier who would lead American Catholicism into dialogue with the new psychology. Still, Mercier kept abreast of developments in psychology until he assumed his responsibilities as archbishop. He published three books, *Psychologie* (1892), *Les origines de la psychologie contemporaire* (1897), and *La psychologie experimentale et la philosophie spiritualiste* (1900). Through these works Mercier created guides for the early Catholic psychologists to navigate the waters between the "old" and the "new" psychology. Mercier's philosophical psychology, of course, was Thomistic, and he concurred with Wundt and James that the new psychology must remain related and relevant to philosophical questions. At the same time Mercier argued that Catholic philosophers who were termed "spiritualistic philosophers" and who distrusted the new psychology needed to become cognizant of the findings of experimental psychology. As he noted:

Neither the work nor the method of experimental psychology is opposed to the principles of spiritualistic philosophy.... Experimental psychology widens the road of progress for true philosophy and furnishes it with valuable information.[10]

As a Thomistic philosopher, Mercier found this confluence between psychology and philosophy expressed in Aristotelian metaphysics, and thus he deplored the work of those such as Alfred Binet, who viewed experimental psychology and metaphysics as distinct. The history of psychology would later prove Binet more prophetic than Mercier on this point. On the whole, however, Mercier's pioneering efforts, coupled with the papal blessing of Pope Leo XIII, encouraged European and later American Catholic psychologists to engage and assimilate much of the new psychology. Future textbooks of Catholic philosophical psychology and even morality would have to take into account the findings of the new psychology. Mercier's groundbreaking efforts in developing psychology in Catholic circles planted seeds that would someday be harvested throughout the Catholic world.

American Catholic Higher Education at the Turn of the Century

At the beginning of Pecci's papacy the Thomistic revival had hardly caught on in America. The reason was simple. The United States had no real center for Catholic theological training. While there were a number of seminaries scattered throughout the nation, none of them was of high quality. In those days if a Catholic priest wished to study theology at an advanced level, he would have to travel to Europe and enroll in a theology school. As a consequence, Roman Catholicism was readily viewed by American intellectuals as a foreign influence just like the millions of immigrants who streamed to American shores. Indeed, at the time the American Catholic Church was a church of immigrants whose resources were few and whose needs were overwhelming. At the end of the nineteenth century and well into the twentieth, American Catholicism could be most clearly defined in terms of immigrants and their assimilation. In 1910 the foreign-born population in the United States consisted of 2,311,000 immigrants from Germany, 1,352,000 from Ireland, 1,343,000 from Italy, and 846,000 from Austria.[11] Since the majority of these immigrant populations were Roman Catholic, their arrival placed an incredible strain on the church's already limited financial resources. Given the inundation of immigrants into the United States, in 1908 the Vatican proclaimed that the United States as a nation no longer deserved missionary status.

The immigrant identity of American Catholics led the church to give an increasing priority to education, especially to parochial elementary schools. In 1880 there were 2,246 Catholic grade schools with 405,234 students. Within thirty years the number of grade schools more than doubled to 4,845 and the number of students tripled to 1,237,251.[12] At the level of higher education, there were some seventy Catholic colleges sprinkled mostly around the nation's Northeast and Midwest. They had, however, adapted their educational program from the seminary model and as a result were limited in their preparation of lay Catholic students.

For several decades the need for a Catholic university having a national stature had been seen and addressed by a number of bishops. The first significant effort occurred in 1884 at the Third Plenary Council, a national legislative assembly of the bishops, held in Baltimore. On this occasion John Lancaster Spalding, bishop of Peoria, cast a strong appeal for a national Catholic university. In words indicative of his scholarly temperament, Spalding stated:

> In whatsoever direction we turn our thoughts, arguments rush in to show the pressing need for us of a center of life and light such as a Catholic university would be. Without this we can have no hope of entering as a determining force into the living controversies of the age; without this it must be an accident if we are represented at all in the literature of our country; ... without this we shall be able to offer feeble resistance to the false theories and systems of education which deny to the Church a place in the school.[13]

With the ecclesiastical support of Cardinal James Gibbons of Baltimore and the financial assistance of the young heiress Mary Gwendoline Caldwell, Spalding's dream of a first-rate university under Catholic auspices took its first steps toward becoming a reality. On November 13, 1889, in Washington, D.C., Catholic University opened its doors. However, Spalding's vision of projecting a quality Catholic university into the American academic landscape would soon suffer from ecclesiological and financial difficulties. In its first decade of life the young university would lose considerable prestige both within and outside the Catholic community when some of its administrators and faculty met ecclesiastical disapproval.

In its early years, the ideal and the reality of fulfilling Spalding's vision for the Catholic University were entrusted to some of American Catholicism's best and brightest minds. For its friends the young university represented "the headquarters of the assimilated elite of Catholic America,"[14] while among its enemies, especially those in Rome, it was seen as "a true fortress of Catholic intellectual liberalism and, as such, subject to continuous criticism by those who were opposed to such ideology."[15] These criticisms coalesced around the new university, the consequences of which were to set a conservative tone for decades not only at Catholic University but throughout American Catholic intellectual life.

As noted above, the new university was believed to have been blessed with some of American Catholicism's best and brightest minds. Its first rector, Bishop John Keane, could be described as a man ahead of his times as he worked fearlessly for a better integration of Catholicism and American culture. Keane was a close friend and disciple of Fr. Isaac Hecker, a convert to Catholicism who later became a Redemptorist priest before founding the Paulist congregation in 1858. Having grown up under the influence of New England transcendental thought, Hecker had as a vision for his new congregation to work toward better relations between the Catholic Church and American culture. Hecker died in 1888, but, as will be considered below, his Paulist biographer, Walter Elliott, stirred up a great controversy in Europe about what was seen as the lax and liberal attitude of certain American Catholic leaders. Throughout the 1890s a progressive mood swept American Catholicism. Influential members of the church's hierarchy, including Bishop John Keane, Bishop John Lancaster Spalding, Cardinal James Gibbons (archbishop of Baltimore), and John Ireland (archbishop of St. Paul), as well as Msgr. Denis O'Connell (rector of the North American College in Rome), interpreted what they believed to be signals from the Vatican and entered into greater dialogue with American culture. Gibbons, the senior American Catholic prelate, struck up friendships with American presidents while Keane promoted an ecumenical spirit unheard of in its times. For instance, he conversed with university presidents G. Stanley Hall at Clark, Andrew White at Cornell, and Charles Eliot at Harvard.[16] Eliot even invited Keane to give the prestigious Dudleian Lecture at Harvard. Keane's vision of the Catholic University led him to promote quality scholarship and research, and several members of his faculty were significant contributors to their respective fields. Fr. Edward Pace was one of those. Another was John A. Zahm, whose book *Evolution and Dogma* published in 1896 opened the doors for Catholics to consider accepting evolutionary theory.

This progressive spirit in American Catholicism lasted for two decades and was even beginning to be shared by sympathetic Europeans. Such progressive movements on both continents, however, would soon succumb to a series of Vatican pressures. One of the first occurred in 1892 when Archbishop Francisco Satolli arrived in Washington as Leo XIII's representative to the Chicago World's Fair. At first Satolli gave indications that he supported the progressive overtures. When the pope appointed Satolli, however, as his permanent representative to the United States, more than a few bishops protested for fear of future Vatican interventions in American Catholic affairs. Their fears were warranted. In 1895 the pope in the apostolic letter *Longinqua Oceani* praised the growth of the Catholic community in the United States, but had serious misgivings about the American model of separation of church and state as an ideal for other nations.

The pope's letter was followed by a critical letter to those bishops and priests who participated in interdenominational congresses such as the World Parliament of Religion held in Chicago. It was also in 1895 that Msgr. O'Connell was asked to resign his position as rector of the North American College in Rome. Apparently O'Connell's sympathies for the controversial views of Bishop Keane and Archbishop Ireland led to his resignation under pressure from the Congregation for the Propagation for the Faith, the Roman department to which American Catholic ecclesiastical leaders reported until 1908.

The next year Satolli, who by that time had returned to Rome as a cardinal, found Keane's views too progressive and as a consequence asked for Keane's resignation as rector of the Catholic University. The cardinal was reported to have sought the censoring of Archbishop Ireland and the removal of three of Catholic University's progressive professors, among them Edward Pace.[17] Such policies were never enacted, but the rumor gave ecclesiastical ammunition to conservative Catholic leaders and weakened the progressive positions of Catholic liberals.

The greatest controversy of the period, however, came in 1899 when the pope issued the apostolic letter *Testem Benevolentiae,* in which he challenged certain doctrines that he considered heretical and to which he gave the name "Americanism." Much of the controversy stemmed from the French translation of Walter Elliott's biography of Isaac Hecker. As read by certain French conservatives, the biography seemed in certain places to contradict church teachings.[18] Catholic leaders such as Gibbons and Ireland defended the book and saw the problem in terms of a translator's interpretation. The encyclical, nevertheless, was another setback for the progressive spirit of American Catholicism. It served to diminish the influence of Bishops Keane and Ireland and more significantly created a cautious tone among Catholic scholars and writers.

With the death of Pope Leo XIII in 1903 an even stricter policy toward liberal thinking was ushered in with the papacy of Pope Pius X. The new pope saw a variety of potential heresies brewing in the works of several European authors. Prominent among these were the French biblical scholar and priest Alfred Loisy, the French philosopher Maurice Blondel, and the British spiritual writers George Tyrrell and Baron Friedrich von Hügel. The writings of these men did not have a great deal in common, but the spirit with which they raised questions was so similar to the "modernist" spirit of the times that they were labeled "Catholic modernists." According to Halsey, one consequence of this spirit at a time when Thomism was undergoing a revival was that Tyrell made Thomas Aquinas appear as a modernist.[19] As Halsey further noted, on both sides of the Atlantic among Roman Catholic thinkers such as Pace there existed "an adventuresome quality of mind."[20] This openness among a certain number of Catholic scholars led to their engaging in dialogue with such non-Catholic thinkers as philosopher and educator Josiah Royce. But, with the death of Pope Leo XIII, Royce warned:

> But will Catholic officialism ... permit the new Catholic scholarship liberty to develop on these lines? Will not the new pope ... undertake to bring to a pause the evolution of these tendencies towards a reform of Catholic philosophy, and towards an era of good feeling between Catholic and non-Catholic science and scholarship? I confess to a good deal of doubt upon this subject. I confess also that I am rather disposed to anticipate a reaction against all this natural, but, as I fancy, unexpected growth that has taken place in the world of Catholic scholarship within the last two decades.[21]

Royce was right: the new pope and his lieutenants departed from the dialogical openness generated by Leo XIII. Instead, some of Pope Pius X's initiatives created a new era of suspicion, as demonstrated in 1907 through two statements. The first, promulgated in July, entitled *Lamentabili Sane,* was another papal syllabus of errors. This one was directed specifically toward modernist thinking. Among the sixty-five statements listed as errors were the following:

2. The Church's interpretation of the Sacred Books is by no means to be rejected; nevertheless, it is subject to the more accurate judgment and correction of the exegetes.

57. The Church has shown that she is hostile to the progress of the natural and theological sciences.

64. Modern Catholicism can be reconciled with true science only if it is transformed into a nondogmatic Christianity; that is to say, into a broad and liberal Protestantism.[22]

Two months after the *Syllabus* the pope issued *Pascendi Dominici Gregis.* The content and the tone of the encyclical were highly critical of modernism, considered to be a "synthesis of all heresies."[23] Moreover, its scope went beyond condemning modernism, for the encyclical had the adverse effect of slowing most creative scholarship in the church. Because of *Pascendi* the Holy Office initiated a crackdown on progressive thought among Catholics by instituting the following policies: priests were required to pronounce an oath against modernism; numerous books were added to the *Index of Forbidden Books;* committees were established to be vigilant for teachings and teachers that were potentially heretical. Such committees were officially established by dioceses, but networks known as the "Sapinere" were also formed that further enhanced the atmosphere of fear and suspicion among American Catholics.

While the papal pronouncements were meant to counteract the liberal tendencies of European thinkers, they had a significant influence in the United States. For example, the *New York Review,* a progressive Catholic journal founded in 1905, was seen as having modernist sympathies, and as a consequence became defunct within only a few years. Moreover, American Catholic scholars became much more cautious in their writings, and even the rector of the New York Archdiocese's Dunwoodie Seminary, James Driscoll, was dismissed for being too progressive. Consequently, for many scholars the Catholic Church once again fell into a state-of-siege mentality that was a throwback to the era of Pope Pius IX. In the coming years this mentality was lifted only slowly and had considerable influence on the way psychology and psychoanalysis were perceived.

This mentality, while building a system of intellectual unity among Catholic scholars, had a dreadful downside. For decades American Catholic scholars were limited in the avenues of thought open to them. For many their encounter with secular scholarship was often apologetic and antagonistic. There was a dearth of meaningful dialogue between American Catholic scholarship and the modern American intellectual spirits of pragmatism and progressivism represented by John Dewey. Instead, a form of separatism grew between Catholic scholars and their American counterparts. Several decades later one commentator described American intellectual life as having "two hostile camps," one "occupied by liberals of various descriptions, the other by the Catholic and non-Catholic disciples of Thomas Aquinas."[24]

According to the church historian John Tracy Ellis, no better description of the Roman Catholic Church's general state of affairs at the beginning of the century was given than that of the archbishop of Albi, Euodoxe-Irenee Mignot. In a widely quoted letter addressed to Domenico Ferrata, cardinal secretary of state to Pope Benedict XV, Mignot wrote:

> In this doctrinal reaction, have not some of the underlings gone a good deal too far? Have they not sometimes given an enmity to sincere and impartial research? There is no doubt of this. And in consequence there is a real wave of anger against authority among scholars and thinkers everywhere. The Church has lost some of the prestige which was hers under Leo XIII. Within the bosom of the Church, discouragement has seized upon intellectual and social workers. Denounced, spied upon, abused by the papers of the occult power (the *Sodalitium Pianum*), held in suspicion by those who, deceived by false reports, suspected the honesty of their intentions, they

found their work grown very difficult. Many a man withdrew once and for all from the lists who might have won many a victory for the Christian cause. This sense of unrest has made itself most unfortunately evident in many major seminaries, in religious houses of study and in university centers. Upon this, testimony is unanimous: our young men have lost the sacred passion for intellectual labor, and it is very difficult for their professors to stimulate it.[25]

Edward Pace and Experimental Psychology

In the American Catholic world the first seeds of psychology were planted by a native Floridian, Edward Pace. Born in 1861 and educated in Jacksonville, Florida, and then at St. Charles College in Catonsville, Maryland, Pace quickly developed an educational background that would serve him well in the future. When he was nineteen Pace was sent to Rome where, at Propaganda University, he received a bachelor's degree in sacred theology in 1883 and a doctorate in sacred theology in 1886. He was ordained a priest in 1885.

During his studies in Rome, Pace drew the attention of his religious superiors, who were impressed by his eloquence and knowledge. With the support of Bishop John Keane, the first rector of Catholic University, Pace was encouraged to go further with his studies. In 1888 he was again sent to Europe, this time to study philosophy, but he soon discovered psychology to his liking. In 1889 he enrolled at the University of Leipzig to study psychology under Wilhelm Wundt. In 1891 Pace received a doctorate from the University of Leipzig. Prior to this, Pace had done graduate studies in theology at Louvain, where he met Mercier. With his advanced degrees in philosophy, psychology, and theology, it is not surprising that the influence Pace would have on American Catholic thought would prove considerable.

In 1891, after completing his studies in Europe, Pace returned to the United States. He brought with him equipment to do experiments on sound and reaction time and set up a laboratory that immediately established him as a leader in the emerging field of psychology. In 1892 Pace became one of the first five psychologists elected to the American Psychological Association by its charter members. As he set about serving the needs of Catholic University, Pace assumed the position of professor of psychology. Then in 1894 he was made professor of philosophy, a position he would hold until he retired in 1936.

Since a department of psychology had not yet been established, Pace's early courses in psychology were offered in the department of theology. The initial courses included: Experimental Psychology, Rational Psychology, and General Psychology. Two years later, in 1893, two other courses were added: Psychological Academy and Theory of Mental Evolution and Abnormal Study. In 1896 a course entitled Psychology Laboratory was taught.[26] It was not until 1905, however, that a department of psychology was established, although psychology remained affiliated with philosophy in the person of Pace, who taught both psychology and philosophy.

Over his many years at Catholic University, Pace, besides being a professor of philosophy, served as dean of philosophy (1906–14, 1934), general secretary (1917–25), and vice-rector (1925–36). Pace's reputation enabled him to assume roles beyond the Catholic University. He was cofounder of the American Philosophical Association (1893), cofounder of the Catholic Philosophical Association (1926), cofounder and first editor of *Catholic Educational Review* (1911), cofounder and coeditor of the journal *New Scholasticism* (1926), and editor of Catholic University's proprietary publication *Studies in Psychology and Psychiatry* (1926). Between 1907 and 1912 he was one of the leading editors of the fifteen-volume *Catholic Encyclopedia*. Furthermore, Pace made significant contributions in the emerging fields of education. He was founder and first director of the Catholic University's Institute of Pedagogy (1899), which later became its Department of Education. Under Pace's administrative tutelage, this became one of the leading departments at Catholic University. In 1925 he became president of the American Council on Education, and in 1929 he was appointed by President Hoover to the National Advisory Committee on Education. Finally, Pace made a significant contribution to Catholic involvement in social action when at the end of World War I he drafted a national pastoral letter promulgated by the Catholic bishops on national issues facing the church at that time.[27]

It is not surprising, then, that in 1914 Pace received a papal award from Pius X. What is surprising and indicative of the controversies in the church at the time is that earlier certain Catholic leaders viewed Pace with suspicion. During his tenure at Catholic University there was a rumor that Cardinal Satolli wanted him removed. While this might be pure conjecture, it is true that in 1896 he was perceived by Bishop Sebastian Messmer of Green Bay, a former fellow faculty member, as "a dangerous liberal." At first the bishop was not going to allow him to speak in his diocese. He later consented but wrote to Pace stating the conditions:

> We finally compromised by instructing [Zahm, a professor at Notre Dame University] to inform you . . . and to state clearly that we shall consent to your lecturing at our session only on the clear understanding that you will not treat or bring up any matter or question in

connection with your subject, which might give rise to dispute and unpleasant objections.[28]

The suspicion in which Catholic bishops such as Messmer held Pace had to do with their concern about the new psychology in contrast to the rationalistic psychology of scholasticism. Such apprehensiveness perhaps was best expressed by the Jesuit historian Thomas Hughes, who in an article published in the *American Catholic Quarterly Review* in 1894 attempted to demonstrate that the emerging psychology should be seen as suspect. Like many others, Hughes saw psychology as the "science of the soul" and as such could not be subjected to experimental investigation, for "its nature exempts it."[29]

Hughes presented his argument in the form of proofs reflecting the common Catholic rationalistic approach to psychology, which was in contrast to the new experimental discipline. He wrote:

> If these authorities mean by their psychometry to measure physical motion or vibrations in the nerves we wish them well. But, if they or any one else shall pretend to measure physiological functions, as though sensation consisted of motions running up to the brain and down again, we beg to submit that the notion is a philosophical absurdity. And if they really mean to subject psychological activity to laboratory investigations, as though the soul could in any way be measured or weighed, we do not scruple to call the whole enterprise a theological impiety.[30]

Hughes recognized the ensuing estrangement of psychology from its classical tradition and went on to criticize the new discipline for considering itself emancipated not only from the Christian faith, but also from such disciplines as logic, ethics, biology, and anthropology. Hughes even questioned whether the then Msgr. Mercier would like to be viewed in the company with people such as G. E. Müller, Hugo Munsterberg, William James, Oswald Külpe, and George T. Ladd. On the other hand, given their psychological training, priests such as Mercier and Pace would probably have wanted to be numbered alongside these great early psychologists.

From the vantage point of history, Hughes's perspectives on the new psychology seem quite narrow, but were fairly typical of Catholic attitudes. The fact that his lengthy essay was published in the *American Catholic Quarterly Review,* one of the leading Catholic journals of the time, meant that Hughes's remarks would carry a great deal of weight.

For the purpose of disputation, in the same issue of this journal Pace published an article defending the new psychology. In the article, entitled "The Growth and Spirit of Modern Psychology," Pace took great pains to inform the reader what the subject matter of psychology is and what it is not. Anticipating the views of Hughes, Pace began his essay by asserting, "'Psychology without a soul' is a phrase often misused to brand, and presumably to crush, the audacious offspring before it is old enough to speak its defence."[31] Pace presented an overview of the history of the discipline from Aristotle to Kant. He then focused on the work of Fechner and Wundt and showed how their worldview represented both continuity and innovation. Furthermore, Pace recognized limitations of the new discipline. To those who argue that the mind cannot be quantified as other sciences quantify objects, Pace replied:

> Now it is true that we cannot grasp the mind and hold it up to external agencies as we hold a mirror before a candle. We can, however, shift the candle about, that is, we can vary the objective impression and catch its reflection in the judgment pronounced by the mind and note how far impression and judgment coincide.[32]

Pace then considered five problem areas where progress had been made in the new psychology: analysis of sense-perceptions; the study of attention; the succession of mental states; the time sense; and feelings and emotions. All in all, Pace expressed great optimism about the new psychology, citing the rapid growth in the psychological literature and in psychology laboratories, his own included. He also observed trends toward specialization that he saw as necessary if psychology was to become a mature science. He added a caveat, however, that "the specialist in psychology or in any other science cannot afford to lose sight of those relations which, on a higher plane, bind all branches of knowledge to unity, or to dispense with that broader education which makes his after-building secure."[33] In this way Pace recognized the important role that philosophy still had in psychology. This was to be a theme throughout the rest of Pace's long career.

Pace concluded his article by recognizing that psychology as a discipline was still young and dependent on other disciplines. He foresaw a time, however, when psychology would mature and eventually be given its rightful place. He added:

> Further results will doubtless prove that the experimental study of mind may be turned, indirectly, at least, to the profit of all the sciences, and that whatever psychology owes them may, in time, be amply repaid. In rendering this practical service, based upon exact and painstaking research, the new psychology not only helps us to know the mind but also helps the mind to know. In both respects it has progressed; in neither can it be blamed for being modern.[34]

Like Mercier, Pace was to work in the field of psychology for a while and to argue for its identity as an authentic discipline, but would then focus his attention on philosophy. It was as if their work was to till the soil and plant the seeds but leave to others to nurture the growth. In the American Catholic world, then, it remained for Pace's students, and in particular for Fr. Thomas Verner Moore, to develop the new psychology in American Catholic culture. With his courses and his labs Pace sketched the blueprints for the discipline, and in his various roles as administrator at the university and as public leader he provided vision for the enterprise. As we shall see, however, Moore provided the professional initiatives that enabled an emerging Catholic student population to explore psychological knowledge both in the laboratory and in the clinic. In this way the new psychology would be integrated into American Catholicism.

Chapter 3

The New Psychology

Footholds in American Catholicism

Thomas Verner Moore and the New Psychology

Thomas Verner Moore was born in 1877 in Louisville, Kentucky. He was a grandson of Thomas Verner Moore, a prominent Presbyterian minister who had served as a pastor in Richmond during the Civil War. In 1877 his son, John Neuton Moore, married Charlotte McIlvain, a devout Catholic, and they gave birth to three sons, Banks, Thomas, and Stuart. When Thomas was four years old his father died, leaving his wife to raise their three sons. When he was eight years old, Thomas began to sense his religious vocation. In his later years Moore noted:

> Perhaps the first point of importance in my life was my determination to become a priest. This was made when I was about eight years of age, and was never changed. Just how it came about I do not know. But it was made suddenly after a period in which I persistently said I would not be a priest. I remember being in a group of altar boys who were saying, "They are not going to make a priest out of me," and I chimed in vigorously with the rest of them. When the idea came to me, I at once went to the parish priest, who smiled and showed me a copy of Homer in Greek, and said: "Look here, Tom, see what you will have to learn first." I replied, "I will start right away." That day, or the next, I went to visit a kind old priest who was chaplain at St. Mary and St. Elizabeth's Hospitals on the outskirts of the city and asked him to teach me Greek. He gave me a grammar and a dictionary and we went to work immediately.[1]

Such determination at an early age demonstrates a pattern with which Moore approached many of his future endeavors. In 1896 he set out to realize his dream when he entered the Paulist Fathers at Catholic University. After several years of studies Moore was ordained a Paulist priest in 1901, but he would not remain a Paulist.

Shortly after entering the Paulists, Moore's career in psychology began when during the summer of 1896 he met Pace and began a collaborative relationship that would last forty years until Pace's death. Before Pace would accept him as a doctoral candidate, he required that Moore attain a firm background in physics, chemistry, mathematics, and biology. Moore did so and went on to write a dissertation under Pace that led to a publication entitled *A Study in Reaction Time and Movement*.[2] Moore received his doctorate in 1903 and began teaching at Catholic University in Pace's new Institute of Pedagogy. Shortly thereafter Moore received permission to go to Leipzig to study under Wundt. Pace himself, no doubt, one of Wundt's first American students, had something to do with Moore's being accepted into such a prestigious program. Moore's time in Leipzig, however, was cut short by tuberculosis after only three semesters. He spent nearly a year in a sanatorium in Germany's Black Forest.

Upon his return to the United States in 1906, Moore went to the University of California at Berkeley to serve as a chaplain in the Catholic Newman Center, where he built a chapel before leaving in 1909. During his tenure at Berkeley he served part-time on the faculty and managed to finish the research he had begun under Wundt, which he published in 1910 under the title "The Process of Abstraction: An Experimental Study."[3] The teaching, research, and ministry justified Moore's reasons for entering the field of psychology. He followed in the Thomistic tradition of relating faith and reason and, in modern times, religion and science. As he wrote:

> While looking upon a scientific career as an apostolic field, it seemed to me that an effective apostolate in science could not confine itself to what had direct and immediate value in apologetics. I felt that the conflict between science and religion was due to the fact that for some centuries most of the research work in science had been done by men outside the Church who knew little or nothing about fundamental theological principles. While knowing little of religion, they were often hostile to the Faith and interpreted scientific facts in a spirit of hostility to theological principles. It seemed to me that if scientific facts were interpreted objectively and by minds sympathetic with religion, there would not be found any conflict between science and the dogmas of faith. For I had never encountered any established facts of science that were incompatible with the doctrine of faith. The apostle in science, in order to interpret scientific facts with authority, must himself be a scientist, an original worker contributing to progress in his field of research.[4]

Such a statement resonates with the thought of Pope Leo XIII in *Aeterni Patris*. It aptly summarizes one of the central motivations for Moore's career in psychology. His finding no incompatibility between the facts of science and the doctrines of faith, at a time when the clouds of conflict between religion and science filled the air, reflects Moore's long pattern of approaching science in a manner consistent with the principles of Thomistic philosophy and theology.

But Moore's interest in psychology was not to be confined to the experimental realm. As psychological insights began to be applied in the practical world of American society, a new impetus emerged at psychological clinics. The first such clinic was established at the University of Pennsylvania by Lightner Witmer in 1896. In December of 1909 Moore visited Witmer's clinic and was taken by its work with feeble-minded children. "It became my ambition," Moore said, "to start such a clinic at the Catholic University."[5] Since the profession of clinical psychology was not really developed at that time, Moore chose to pursue a medical degree. As he noted, "It soon became evident to me that without a medical education it would be impossible for me to conduct an effective clinic for the mental problems of childhood."[6]

In 1910 Moore began medical school at Georgetown University. After two years he received permission from his Paulist superior to continue his medical studies in Germany, where he attended courses with Emil Kraepelin on psychiatry, Georg Elias Müller on neurology, and Oswald Külpe on imagery. It was in Külpe's course that Moore was able to pursue his apostolic goal of approaching certain psychological issues from a philosophical perspective. His research with Külpe was later published as a monograph entitled "Imagery and Meaning in Memory and Perception."[7] The work served as a basis for subsequent research and synthesis as demonstrated in his 1939 work *Cognitive Psychology*.[8]

The First World War forced Moore to interrupt his medical studies in Germany, and in 1914 he returned to the United States, where he studied under the great psychodiagnostician Adolf Meyer. He completed his medical training at Johns Hopkins in 1915. Upon receiving his degree he immediately set about fulfilling the ambition sparked at the Witmer Clinic, namely, to establish a clinic. On January 15, 1916, Moore opened the first psychiatric outpatient department in Washington at Providence Hospital near Catholic University. Moore's first patients were emotionally disturbed children, although the department later accepted adults.

In 1918 Moore's apostolic endeavors led him to France and the battlefields of the First World War. Joining the army as a military physician, Moore used his psychiatric training in the service of traumatized soldiers. The competence and compassion with which he discharged such duties was recognized, and by the end of the war he had been promoted to the rank of major. On the basis of these war experiences Moore undertook a study of emotions from the perspective of the traumatic shock suffered by soldiers in combat. He later published his observations in an article for the *Psychoanalytic Review*,[9] a journal which at the time was almost anathema for a Catholic to read, much less for a priest to submit an article for publication.

The First World War led Moore to take steps toward a new vocational identity. He found his life as a Paulist priest to be without sufficient structure, and so he began to consider entering a monastic order, either the Carthusians or the Benedictines. He made a retreat at the famous English Benedictine Abbey in Downside, to which he subsequently decided to apply in 1920. His application was rejected when the Downside's abbot learned from Moore's brother, Stuart, that his sibling had earlier had a bout with tuberculosis. Moore was indefatigable in his desire to enter a Benedictine community. Consequently, in 1923 with the support of Washington's Archbishop Michael and together with a band of other American scholars, Moore was accepted by the Benedictine community at Fort Augustus, Scotland. In 1924 they returned to the United States and established St. Anselm's Abbey in Washington, D.C. Moore's vision for the abbey was that it be a community "where the fullness of liturgical observance would be maintained, while the special work of at least some of its members would be scientific research for the good of religion and the welfare of man."[10]

Moore remained at this abbey until 1947 when, upon his retirement from Catholic University, he again changed his religious order and joined the Carthusian community in Miraflores, Spain. The Carthusians observe one of the strictest monastic rules of the Catholic Church. For Moore, entering the Carthusians was the final fulfillment of the dream he had as a boy. In his words:

> The idea of a contemplative solitary life has been in my mind for many years. In the family library was a little book on the Fathers of the Desert, and it created within me the desire to seek God in some lonely spot of nature, but I could see no possibility of doing so. Some time after a retreat made in 1913 at the Carthusian house at Parkminster in England, I wrote asking for admission but was refused. For years I have prayed that in some manner I might end my days in a contemplative life of prayer. . . . And it is now time for me to accomplish by prayer things that I failed to do by action in the years that passed.[11]

Moore and the Possibility of a Catholic Psychology

In 1924, as it became clear that he was to succeed his mentor Edward Pace as the director of the psychology department at Catholic University,

Moore developed a grand scheme for the future of the department. While undergoing his Benedictine novitiate year at Fort Augustus, he wrote to the university's rector, Bishop Thomas Shahan, and outlined his vision in three areas.[12] He saw it as important first to continue the department's empirical investigations in "pure psychological theory" and into human faculties, especially as they related to intelligence. He also believed that through the department's well-equipped laboratories it was possible and indeed necessary "to develop the more modern field of investigation where psychology comes in contact with education."[13] Moore placed great emphasis on this goal: "This is necessary for the sake of Catholic students of education, lay and clerical, to say nothing of the Sisters in the Sisters College and the Summer School."[14]

Finally, Moore believed that the university had an obligation to develop medical psychology. Referring to the fact that up to that time he had been the only faculty member at the university working in this area, Moore saw the great need for training competent clinicians to deal with children, especially those who were emotionally disturbed, delinquent, or suffering from mental illness. Moore, moreover, argued for training clinicians who would treat Catholic adults:

> It is vitally necessary that Catholics verging on a mental breakdown should have some place to go for treatment, particularly in view of the fact that many modern psychiatrists regard their trouble as originating in a conflict between their religious principles and the driving forces of nature, and attempt to effect a cure by analyzing away their faith. There are at present very few Catholic mental clinics and very few Catholic physicians who attempt to treat mental cases.[15]

Moore put forth several recommendations for ways the archdiocese could respond to the psychological needs of Catholics, especially children. He believed that the archdiocese should sponsor (1) a clearing house for juvenile delinquents, (2) a home for feebleminded children, and (3) manual training classes in parochial schools for mentally retarded children and other students with learning disabilities.[16]

In the same letter Moore made a strong argument for the psychological training of priests. From his experience in the fields of psychology and psychiatry, Moore was convinced that such training would be increasingly necessary for Catholic clergy:

> The day is past when moral guidance was left to the clergy. It is being taken up now by the psychological clinic. When a child gets into trouble in many of our cities his general confession is heard, not by a priest but by a psychologist, who is often positively antagonistic to

religion. The child's future is then settled by the psychologist without any recourse to the principles of moral theology or the demands of Christianity. Unless something is done on the Catholic side the moral guidance of the next generation will to a large extent pass away from the priesthood.[17]

The need for Catholic clinicians to treat Catholic clients, in that pre-ecumenical age, was a central concern throughout Moore's professional ministry. In a 1936 letter to the rector of Catholic University, Bishop Joseph Corrigan, Moore reiterated this concern, stating that every Catholic college and parochial school system should have persons with psychological training, and that one of the primary purposes of the university's psychology department was to provide priests, sisters, and the Catholic laity with such training.[18] Moore furthermore felt that one of the unique contributions that students of psychology could make in the American Catholic context was to see the discipline's relationship to philosophy:

> Though modern trends in psychology are definitely towards practical problems, psychology is essentially linked very closely with philosophy, and only one with some insight into philosophy and scientific training and a knowledge of modern psychology could give the synthesis which is required in order that psychology might make the contribution to theory and philosophy which it should make.[19]

Moore's influence extended throughout many levels of the American Catholic world. As Neenan describes in his dissertation, Moore as a "psychiatrist, educator, and priest" touched many segments of American Catholic society, from the emotionally disturbed children with whom and for whom he spent much of his clinical ministry to his engaging and cajoling university administrators and bishops in debate and with requests.[20] Moore frequently gave addresses on psychological issues to Catholic organizations and published numerous articles in Catholic publications. In an article entitled "The Clergy and Mental Hygiene," Moore addressed issues surrounding the mutual distrust between priests and psychiatrists. On the one hand, he admonished Catholics for their prejudice against dealing with psychiatrists. On the other hand, he cautioned against allowing the governance of morality to pass from the church to medical science:

> Our clergy should be alive to the fact that movements are afoot which consciously or unconsciously aim at a more or less complete medicopsychiatric control of ethical problems. This movement is now actually taking over to a very large extent the guidance of the child in the more or less serious moral conflicts of youth. Adults also who have mental problems find that fundamental ethical principles

are involved in their conflicts. To whom can they go? The confessor tells them to consult a physician. The physician first approached is often a general practitioner. He says consult a psychiatrist. A psychiatrist is found and it frequently happens that he at once commences to attack the patient's religion. The fact that this attack by psychiatrists is so common is no doubt one reason why many pastors get the idea that psychiatry itself is essentially antireligious. They find it hard to realize that the strange word is only the modern term for the science of emotional disorders; and that, therefore, an antireligious psychiatrist is no more an argument against the practice of all psychiatry than the existence of an antireligious school of education would justify anyone in advocating the abolition of all education.[21]

Moore, however, did not limit himself to the Catholic world. Perhaps because his own family was ecumenical and his family's legacy was well ensconced in American society, he did not exhibit some of the defensive attitudes that were common among so many of his Catholic peers. It should be remembered, however, that a high percentage of American Catholics at that time either were immigrants or had parents or grandparents who were immigrants. As a result, Moore's ministry took place amid an American Catholicism that could be characterized as trying to define itself in American society. It should be remembered from the previous discussion of the early history of Catholic University that certain experiments at adaptation to American culture had been challenged by Roman authorities, which made such progressive thought suspect.

Moore did not seem to be impeded by such qualms. His propensity for pushing ahead with scientific ideas was rarely admonished and was often rewarded, as shown by an $85,000 grant from the Rockefeller Foundation in 1939 that enabled him to enlarge the Department of Psychology and Psychiatry at Catholic University. As a priest and a monk, Moore was able to rub shoulders with Catholic bishops and intellectuals alike, a role that enabled psychology to become ever more acceptable in the American Catholic context. In addition, Moore's reputation as a scientist and as a scholar had become well established. Besides Pace, Wundt, and Külpe, Moore had some association with other scholars of his day, among them the structural psychologist E. B. Tichener, the statistician Charles Spearman, the psychiatrist Adolf Meyer, and the psychoanalyst Gregory Zilboorg.

Moore's work and writings have some controversial points. Many of these relate to the fact that he was a religious priest responsible to a church that at the time was still very suspicious of the modern world and its new approaches to science. At the same time, as a psychologist and a psychiatrist Moore was well acquainted with the hostility that these emerging sciences showed toward religion. In this respect it may be said that he encountered a constant conflict between his career and his ministry.

One manifestation of this conflict was his dispute with the Social Service Department at Catholic University. Members of this department held that clients with religious problems should be referred to a parish priest since religious concerns were not the responsibility or the expertise of social workers. Moore argued strongly against this approach, believing that when necessary and appropriate a social worker should be prepared to give religious advice. Moore was not afraid to tackle religious leaders who found his psychological approaches inconsistent with Catholic philosophy. As Neenan says, Moore's book *Cognitive Psychology* was criticized by Robert Edward Brennan, O.P., author of *Thomistic Psychology,* for ignoring neo-Thomistic categories and creating confusing scientific terms and approaches.[22] Moore later responded by charging Brennan with ignorance of some of the contemporary movements in psychology and psychiatry.[23]

Perhaps the best instance of Moore's defense against criticism of his approaches to his scientific discipline occurred in his response to Msgr. Fulton J. Sheen in 1945. Sheen, who at the time was on the Catholic University faculty, publicly criticized the way psychology was being taught in Moore's department. In response Moore shot back a letter in which he wrote:

> If you have serious misgivings as to what is going on in my department, I should much prefer that you lay the matter before the Bishops rather than your students. If my teaching is false the Bishops will inform me and I shall gladly lay aside this office of teacher and make such amends as they may suggest.[24]

Moore did remain on friendly terms with Sheen, but, as we saw earlier, Sheen became the most prominent American Catholic critic of psychology, especially of psychoanalysis. Moore, like other Catholic writers, was critical of Freudian psychoanalysis, but instead of dismissing Freud's insights completely, he recognized both their assets and their limitations. In his first book, *Dynamic Psychology,* published in 1924, Moore spent an entire chapter carefully commenting on Freud and psychoanalysis. Given his psychiatric training, Moore's observations are presented with greater breadth and depth than those of other Catholic critics of Freud. For example, he speaks of his own use of psychoanalysis and finds psychoanalysis limited by the mentality of the patient, the amount of time required, and the type of disorder.[25]

Moore nevertheless found value in Freud's contributions. In an article published in 1937, Moore made a fuller evaluation of Freud's work and specifically found valuable Freud's interpretation of the unconscious, his development of the theory of dreams, and his insights into the mental mechanism of psychoneurotic patients. On the other hand, he found wanting Freud's tendency to make generalizations without warrant, for example, to consider all dreams as wish fulfillments, to disregard some of the principles of scientific evidence as seen in claims made in *Totem and Taboo* (1913), and to disdain the demands of morality and religion.[26]

The thought and writings of Thomas Verner Moore undoubtedly had a major impact on the gradual acceptance and transformation of psychology among American Catholics. The sheer quantity of Moore's productivity gives evidence of the breadth of his influence. From 1922 through 1947, when he retired from Catholic University, Moore published more than sixty articles and twelve books, including *Dynamic Psychology* (1924), *Cognitive Psychology* (1939), *The Nature and Treatment of Mental Disorders* (1944), *Personal Mental Hygiene* (1944), and *The Driving Forces of Human Nature and Their Adjustment* (1948).[27] Later as a Carthusian monk he wrote *The Life of Man with God* (1956) and *Heroic Sanctity and Insanity* (1959).[28] Moore's greatest influence on American Catholic psychology, however, was in the classroom; he taught several generations of men at Catholic University and women at its related institutions: the Sisters College, Trinity College, and the National Catholic School of Social Service. Many of these students taught at Catholic institutions and became the intellectuals and professionals who fostered a greater understanding and use of psychology by American Catholics. By the time Moore retired from Catholic University, other psychology departments at Catholic colleges and universities had been established, some by students of Moore. At Boston College, for example, Fr. James Moynihan, S.J., went directly from his studies with Moore to found the psychology department in 1947. At Fordham, Fr. Walter G. Sommers, S.J., established the psychology department in 1934. As we shall see later, Fr. William Bier, S.J., another student of Moore, helped to lead the department to international prominence.

E. Boyd Barrett's Critique of Psychoanalysis

One of the first Catholic publications to consider the new psychology was written by Jesuit psychologist E. Boyd Barrett. Born in Ireland and trained at Louvain, in 1911 he wrote an article titled "Some Modern Psychologists" for the popular English Catholic periodical *The Month*.[29] In this article Boyd Barrett presented for a readership consisting mostly of priests in Great Britain and America observations on the influence of Wundt and James, and on the current work of psychologists sympathetic to Catholic scholastic philosophy, namely, Oswald Külpe and A. Michotte. On the whole Barrett's tone is complimentary toward developments of the new science. A decade later, in 1921, Barrett published another article in *The*

Month in which he tackled a question that had become important for
Catholics, namely, the relationship between psychoanalysis and Christian
morality.[30] At the end of the article Barrett draws three critical conclusions
about psychoanalysis. First, he believes that there is nothing really new in
the psychoanalytic method. Second, he states that, though he sees nothing inherently immoral in the Freudian method of dream interpretation,
free association, and hypnotism, he still is convinced that it has immediate
moral dangers. Barrett apparently was not aware that early in his practice
Freud had abandoned hypnotism. Finally, Barrett criticizes the materialism
of the Freudian approach as well as its "sex-obsession."

In a subsequent article on psychology published in the *Irish Ecclesiastical Record* and entitled "Pathological Psychology," Barrett saw the need for
priests to have a knowledge of "pathological psychology" for their ministry. While critical of the materialism maintained by many psychologists
and neurologists of his era, Barrett nevertheless noted that "even pagan
wisdom can be utilized and employed in spiritual work."[31] A year later in
an article entitled "Studies in Practical Psychology" published in the Jesuit
periodical *America,* he further addressed the need for a priest as a director
of souls to become familiar with the findings of "practical psychology,"
especially those involving the psychopathologies of scruples and delusions
that are often encountered in a priest's ministry.[32] Barrett's observations
are among the first indications that psychology had some wisdom to contribute to the ways in which Catholic priests approach the *cura animarum.*
A few years later, in 1925, Barrett, by this time a professor at Georgetown
University, compiled his views on psychology and psychoanalysis in a book
entitled *The New Psychology.*[33] In this work he presented a comprehensive
overview of some major developments in the new psychology as they related to a Catholic mind-set. One of his basic intentions in the book was to
answer some questions raised by Catholics about whether seeing a psychoanalyst was immoral. Given the success of psychoanalysis in curing "nerve
troubles," some Catholics were beginning to turn to psychoanalysts. Religious leaders and writers such as Barrett, however, had their reservations
about the determinism and materialism inherent in the Freudian approach.
They were also opposed to Freud's attacks on religious ideas and practices,
particularly those expressed in his essay "Obsessive Actions and Religious
Practices" (1907) and *Totem and Taboo* (1913). Freud's statements in *Totem
and Taboo* concerning the origin of religion in the resolution of the Oedipus
complex were quite disturbing for religious believers. Consequently, it was
not surprising that Freud and his theories would be attacked by religious
writers. Barrett was one of the first Catholics to do so, but he certainly
would not be the last.[34]

In his book *The New Psychology* Barrett intended to show how psychoanalytic thought is complemented or contradicted by scholastic psychology. He admitted that psychoanalysis had enhanced the understanding of hysteria, scruples, and other obsessions that priests often encounter in their flock. Yet Barrett continued to take issue with some major tenets of Freud's psychoanalytic theory that had by then become quite popular. Having argued throughout the last chapter of his book against Freud's approach to religion, Barrett concluded:

> We have dealt at length with the Freudian sex-theory of religion, not, as we have said, on account of any inherent subtlety or difficulty in it, but because it has been spread broadcast in books and has led many astray. It is, from first to last, a narrow, unscientific theory. It does violence to psychology, history and common-sense. It is, moreover, stupid and degrading. It would reduce mankind to a sub-bestial tribe of beings, so infatuated with sensuality and so disgustingly hypocritical as to elevate the indulgence of their lowest instinct into a holy and sacred pursuit. In fine, it is a theory which makes a mockery of God and man; it mocks God by making Him a mere symbol, and man by making his intellect the degraded slave of his senses.[35]

Barrett's strong views against the Freudian approach to religion were to become quite common among Catholic leaders and writers. Several Catholic writers, despite seeing the value of the Freudian innovations in theory and technique, voiced strong criticisms of some of Freud's major principles regarding religion and sex. Indeed one commentator, Charles Menig, went so far as to discount such complex psychoanalytic strategies as abreaction, catharsis, and sublimation as simply techniques that have for centuries been practiced in the sacrament of penance. In an article in the *Ecclesiastical Review* Menig states:

> If there is a particle of truth in psychoanalysis it throws new light on some of our Catholic practices. It proves especially the healing power of sacramental confession, which not always has been appreciated. Confession induces man under the guidance of grace, to dig down into his past, analyzing his soul and tracing the disturbing elements which as complexes may be infesting his psychical life. There is genuine abreaction in the purpose of amendment, true catharsis in the regained purity and peace of conscience, and highest sublimation in the sublime ideals placed before him by Christ and the Church. Of another psycho-analysis normal man has no need.[36]

By the end of the 1920s the battle lines between Catholicism and psychoanalysis were beginning to be drawn. In the ensuing decades more critics and more controversies would follow.

Charles Bruehl's Pastoral Applications

During the 1920s psychoanalytic literature grew in popularity in American literary circles so that, despite their reservations about Freud, American Catholic priests were exposed to what Catholic authors saw as the positive aspects of psychoanalytic thought.[37] There were indications that psychiatry and psychoanalysis had something important to say regarding *cura animarum.*

This became evident during the 1920s in articles published in one of the American periodicals most widely read by American priests, *The Homiletic and Pastoral Review.* Founded in 1901, the *Review,* which continues to be widely read to this day, originally was a forum for helping priests with their sermons and catechetical issues. As years passed, the *Review* expanded its concerns and developed a section entitled "Pastoralia" written by Rev. Charles Bruehl. Born and raised in Germany, Bruehl later studied under Mercier at the University of Louvain, where he received his doctorate in theology. As a result, Bruehl was quite familiar with intellectual movements in Europe, and from his position as a professor at St. Charles Seminary, outside Philadelphia, he saw the need to acquaint present and future priests with such movements because of their relevance for their ministry. His articles in the *Review* were a means of disseminating his views on psychoanalysis to a wider audience.

The October 1921 issue of the *Review* launched Bruehl's pastoral reflections, and by the November issue Bruehl was arguing that priests should appreciate insights from emerging fields of "applied psychology" and use them in their care of souls.[38] Bruehl observed that while there exists a considerable Catholic literature in pastoral theology, he found in his research no systematic treatise on pastoral psychology. He argued that the works on pedagogical psychology were insufficient in helping priests deal with the pastoral needs of adults. He voiced his concern about a gap in the theological literature of his day:

> In our mind, a serious gap exists which accounts for many deplorable blunders that might have been avoided with better knowledge of the psychology of the fallen man. The mistakes of priests are rarely due to ill will; they result from a lack of vision, particularly an insufficient appreciation of the psychological consequences which their actions may have owing to the exaggerated sensitiveness and the disturbed emotional equilibrium caused by original sin.[39]

Later, in the June 1922 issue of the *Review* in an essay entitled "Cura Afflictorum," Bruehl showed how the attitudes toward mental anguish have changed. For Bruehl, priests, though they are not expected to be psychotherapists, should nevertheless acquaint themselves with psychological knowledge:[40]

> In many ways, then, such information may be profitable. In the confessional and at the sickbed it is absolutely necessary. In his own behalf it will be advisable to acquire some information concerning these things; for he will then be better able to avoid what is becoming increasingly frequent in our days—a collapse in the best years of manhood, a so-called nervous breakdown that may render him useless for many years or will at least greatly impair his efficiency.[41]

Bruehl considered the scrupulosity encountered by many priests in the confessional to be compulsions. Though Bruehl's remarks about such compulsions were in his own estimation "fragmentary," they were nevertheless one of the first indications by an American Catholic writer of the great pastoral need for priests to educate themselves to address the mental health concerns of their flock.

A few years later Bruehl presented a series of essays designed to provide a systematic overview of several major psychological topics and to focus their relevance for the pastoral care of souls. In the March 1925 issue Bruehl began a series dealing with abnormalities, adjustments, conflicts, and the unconscious. In the first essay, "The New Psychology Applied to Pastoral Problems," he argued that findings of the emerging field of psychology should be used by the "director of souls." Contrasting the classical rational psychology of scholasticism with Freudian psychoanalysis, Bruehl believed that there need not be any fundamental conflict between the two. Recognizing the materialistic and deterministic tendencies of the new psychology, Bruehl nevertheless found that this was the result of the personal biases of the proponents of psychology and not inherent to the field itself.

In the same article Bruehl considered how the two psychologies can complement each other in the study of the will. He considered classical psychology to have established the existence of freedom in the spirituality of the will whereas the new psychology studied the nature and the motives of the will. Bruehl noted, however, that classical psychology says nothing about the various pathologies that afflict the will. In this respect, he saw psychoanalysis as "coming to the rescue":

> Those who are familiar only with the classical psychology are somewhat inclined to overlook the actual impediments the will encounters in concrete instances. Acquaintance with the new psychology will broaden their views and make them judge the terrific struggles of their fellow-men more sympathetically. It will also induce them to take a more lenient attitude toward their lapses. All in all, the new

psychology makes for a better and more thorough understanding of man in the concrete. And it is with this man we have to deal in our daily ministrations.[42]

In the *Review*'s next issue Bruehl continued his discussion of the new psychology, and even suggested that there was a "grain of truth in the Freudian theory that all nervous disorders are of sexual origin and due to misdirected sex energy." He discussed Freud's pleasure-principle and reality-principle, a noteworthy presentation given the general Catholic suspicion toward Freudian theory. In the June issue Bruehl discussed a pastoral application of Freudian theory by considering the unconscious. While noting his reservations toward Freud and his followers and their extreme deterministic and materialistic interpretations of the unconscious, Bruehl nevertheless accepted the substance of the psychoanalytic findings about the unconscious. He asserted that such findings needed to be used in education and even in spiritual direction.

Bruehl's introduction of psychoanalytic thought into the Catholic pastoral world continued during the next several years. In subsequent issues he treated various relevant psychological topics in articles entitled "The Sources of Mental Abnormalities," "Abnormal Characters," "Fear and Guilt," "Religion and Mental Hygiene," "The Therapeutic Value of Religion," "Religion and Psychic Health," "Types of Personality," "Differences of Temperament," "Temperaments and Their Pedagogical Treatment," and "The Modern Classification of Mentality." Bruehl later wrote a series of essays on the psychological aspects of conversion. Bruehl's "Pastoralia" section was published in the *Review* until 1930; the author had contributed 102 articles, of which 21 explicitly treated a psychological topic.[43]

It is difficult to assess the impact that Bruehl's articles had upon Catholic priests and their application of psychological insights and strategies to their *cura animarum*. The articles themselves indicate that some aspects of the new psychology were beginning to penetrate the American Catholic culture. Still there is no record that any of the clinical aspects of the new psychology were taught in Catholic seminaries. The stigma of "modernism" was easily attached to Freudian views. It would be some years before their wisdom would overcome Catholicism's suspicion toward Freudian thought and psychology in general.

Rudolf Allers's Critique of Psychoanalysis

One of the most influential Catholic psychiatrists of the era was the Austrian immigrant Rudolf Allers. Allers received his medical training at the University of Vienna and was a member of the last class taught by Freud at the medical school. Allers later became an instructor in psychiatry at the medical school of the University of Munich and after the First World War assumed a similar position at the University of Vienna. He subsequently came under the influence of the Italian priest-psychologist and psychiatrist Agostino Gemelli and pursued a doctorate in philosophy at Sacred Heart University in Milan.[44]

In 1938 Allers came to the United States and taught at Catholic University and then, beginning in 1948, at Georgetown. With such an extensive psychiatric and philosophical background, Allers through his teaching and publications was to have a considerable impact on the ways in which American Catholic professionals accepted psychology. Widely read among Catholics were his books: *The Psychology of Character* (1932), *Practical Psychology in Character Development* (1934), *Sex Psychology in Education* (1937), *Self Improvement* (1939), and *Character Education in Adolescence* (1940).[45] The last was a refinement of his articles published in the *Homiletic and Pastoral Review* in 1939. In 1942 Allers published in the *Review* a series of essays dealing with issues surrounding abnormality and morality. These essays, in addition to an article published in the *Ecclesiastical Review* (1938) analyzing the priest-psychiatrist relationship, went a long way toward defining the boundaries between the psychiatrist and the priest as well as psychology and Catholic morality in general.

Rudolf Allers's reputation in the American Catholic Church was not limited to one intellectual arena. As noted above, Allers's training was not only in psychiatry but also in philosophy. With such a background Allers felt it necessary to evaluate the growing influence of Freud's psychoanalytic theory and technique. More forcefully than Moore, he was highly critical of Freudian and psychoanalytic thought.[46] His criticism was expressed in two publications, *The New Psychologies* and *The Successful Error.*

In *The New Psychologies* (1933), Allers attacked Freud's theory and method along five fronts.[47] He found that psychoanalysis, with its psychoenergetic conception of libido, based its theory on purely biological principles. Second, Allers saw psychoanalysis as essentially materialistic when it explains mental phenomena as capable of being broken down into distinct and quantifiable psychic energies. Allers viewed the ethics espoused by Freudian psychoanalysis as hedonistic. Its theory of motivation conceives of drives as seeking satisfaction and pleasure, especially sexual pleasure. The fourth problem Allers had with Freud's position was its determinism. Allers believed Freud's construction of the human personality left no room for freedom or the objectivity of values. Finally, Allers argued that psychoanalysis with its materialistic position left no place for the existence of a substantial soul.

In *The New Psychologies* Allers contrasted the Freudian approach with that of the individual psychology of Alfred Adler, which he believed to be more acceptable in its theory and method. He saw the Adlerian approach, with its greater emphasis on character and social relations, as capable of being supported by and further developed through a Christian philosophy of education. Indeed in an earlier work, *The Psychology of Character* (1932), Allers used Adler's theory to develop a Thomistic approach to character development.

Allers's most comprehensive critique of Freud was articulated in *The Successful Error*, published shortly after Freud's death in 1939. In his preface, Allers stated that his work represented a multifaceted attack on Freud. He believed that Freud's influence had infected not only the discipline of psychology, but also the fields of education, sociology, and most especially religion. One of the reasons for the forcefulness of Allers's attack on psychoanalysis was that, unlike Moore and others who simply had reservations about psychoanalysis, Allers was convinced that Freudian theory and practice were inexorably linked.

After showing some logical fallacies of psychoanalysis and evaluating critically its axioms on sexuality, Allers spent several chapters on the distortion of psychoanalysis in the fields of psychology, medicine, philosophy, education, and religion. Concerning religion, Allers asserted:

> A philosophy which denies free will, ignores the spirituality of the soul, and with shallow materialism, without any attempt as a proof, identifies mental and bodily phenomena, knows of no other end than pleasure, is given to a confused but nevertheless obstinate subjectivism, is blind to the true nature of the human person; such a philosophy cannot have even one point in common with Christian thought. It is its perfect opposite.[48]

Allers furthermore argued that psychoanalysis could be considered heretical in that its major principles of materialism, determinism, and hedonism were derived from positions that the Catholic Church had declared to be heresies. Allers saw psychoanalysis as a form of neopaganism having a more pejorative effect than the pre-Christian paganism of the ancient Greeks whom Christian thinkers have well used. Allers saw no room for Catholics to compromise with such a theory or its technique. Toward the end of his book, Allers wrote:

> Psychoanalysis is a thoroughly materialistic conception. It stands and falls with its materialism. Whosoever feels incapable of accepting the philosophy of materialism cannot but reject psychoanalysis. Because of its materialism, the philosophy of Freud and his school is, in what regards ethics, a simple hedonism. It is addicted to an extreme sub-

jectivism which even blinds the eyes of the psychoanalyst to obvious objective facts and truths. Because of its subjectivism it is impersonalistic and ignores the essence of the human person. Its philosophy, therefore, is based on ideas which not only a Catholic, but every man believing in a higher principle existing above matter and dominating it, cannot but reject.[49]

Allers's attacks on Freud's positions, while severe, did not descend into ad hominem assaults nor did he reject everything that Freud and his psychoanalytic thought espoused. Allers paid deference to Freud by listing several of his achievements. For instance, Allers gave Freud credit for inaugurating the movement of medical psychology and for emphasizing the importance of childhood experiences for later development. For Allers, Freud's greatest accomplishment was demonstrating how mental treatment is capable of healing certain maladies: in this way Freud freed medical science from its overreliance on biology.

Within the American Catholic context the overall impact of Allers's critical review of Freud's psychoanalytic theory and technique was monumental. From his position as a professor first at Catholic University and later at Georgetown, Allers was well acquainted with Catholic leaders and highly regarded by bishops. Moreover, as a member of the Catholic University philosophy faculty, he shared the company of a future bishop, Msgr. Fulton J. Sheen, who was to become the best known Catholic critic of Freud and psychoanalysis. Allers's ability as a teacher no doubt enhanced his influence. Among his many awards, he was honored toward the end of his life with the Cardinal Spellman–Aquinas Medal, the highest honor presented by the American Catholic Philosophical Association.

Chapter 4

From Rational to Clinical Psychology
Three Jesuit Universities

Established in the heart of their respective cities, three Jesuit universities—
Fordham (New York), Loyola (Chicago), and St. Louis—offered the best
that Catholic higher education had to offer in the early and mid-twentieth
century. For decades the backbone of their bachelor's degrees was the required courses in philosophy and theology. As was the custom in Jesuit
liberal arts education, undergraduates had to take as many as thirty-six
credits in these two fields, generally taught with a Thomistic emphasis. So,
when faced with the new psychology, each school was at first wary of the
attendant currents of secularism.

St. Louis University

In 1926 St. Louis University became the first Jesuit institution to formally
establish a department of psychology. However, as far back as 1883 graduate classes in rational (Thomistic) psychology had been taught. In 1885,
Fr. Thomas Hughes taught a graduate course, "Body and Mind," that included theories of physiological psychology. Other courses incorporating
some aspects of physiological psychology followed over the next several decades. Despite these forays, it was not until 1912 that the new psychology
was formally introduced at St. Louis University when Fr. Hubert Gruender taught a class in experimental psychology. Gruender had by then begun
graduate study in psychology that would take him to Columbia University to work with the experimentalist Robert S. Woodworth and to the
University of Bonn, where he obtained his doctorate in 1919.

Gruender was a "renaissance" Jesuit. His advanced training in philosophy and music, in addition to psychology, allowed him to broaden and
deepen his psychological understanding. In experimental psychology he
did significant research in the areas of aphasia, color blindness, and stut-
tering. During almost three decades of work at St. Louis, Gruender wrote
six texts. Their titles suggest his attempt to place experimental psychology
within the framework of the Thomistic system of knowledge: *Free Will,*

Psychology without a Soul, An Introductory Course in Experimental Psychology, Problems in Psychology, A Textbook of Rational Psychology, and *A Compendium of Scholastic Philosophy.*

After Gruender obtained his doctorate in 1919, the number of classes in psychology at St. Louis gradually increased. By 1925 there were eight courses. Gruender taught six—three of them in Latin! "Sentient Life" and "Intellectual Life," taught in Latin, were heavily laden with Thomistic themes, while "Experimental Psychology," "Color Sensation," and "The Visual Perception of Space" were offered in English with an empirical emphasis.

In 1926 Gruender was called upon to organize a psychology department that offered classes at both the undergraduate and graduate levels. Eleven courses were offered for the undergraduate degree; the master's degree required twenty-four credits as well as oral and written exams and a thesis. Three other professors collaborated with Gruender in establishing the department, including Gruender's Jesuit colleague Fr. Raphael McCarthy.

McCarthy, who later served as president of Marquette University (1937–44) and Regis College (1947–53), directed St. Louis's psychology department from 1927 to 1936 and again from 1944 to 1947. In his training and in his professional life as a Jesuit psychologist, McCarthy had a versatile career. After his philosophy and theology studies, he attended the University of London, where he earned a combined doctorate in psychology, philosophy, and physiology. He served as editor of the Catholic intellectual periodical *Thought* and wrote a number articles in psychology as well as two books, *Training the Adolescent* and *Safeguarding Mental Health*.[1] McCarthy was sought after for lectures throughout the American Catholic world. He frequently spoke on the subject of mental health or, as it was popularly referred to in those days, "mental hygiene."

Two other figures at St. Louis played leading roles in American Catholicism's relationship with professional psychology: Dr. Walter Wilkins and Fr. Francis Severin. Wilkins, who gained a national reputation as a clinical psychologist, became the department's first lay director in 1949 and remained in the position until 1960. He had a significant role in the establishment of the American Catholic Psychological Association in 1948.

Fr. Frank Severin, who did graduate studies in psychology at the university's medical school and at the Catholic University of America, began teaching at St. Louis in 1940. His career spanned four decades during which he aided greatly in the assimilation of psychological perspectives into American Catholicism. Severin also had a hand in the formation of Division 32 (Humanistic Psychology) of the American Psychological Association.

In subsequent decades the department expanded its program for undergraduate and graduate students alike, but it was not until 1964 that St. Louis University formally established a doctoral program in psychology. However, the department did grant a Ph.D. in psychology in 1933 to Fr. Charles Ignatius Doyle. In addition to his psychological training, most of it at St. Louis, Doyle spent a year studying philosophy at Louvain and had served four years as an associate editor of *America,* the Jesuit periodical. Shortly after receiving his degree Doyle was sent to Chicago to establish a psychology department at Loyola.

Loyola University of Chicago

When Charles Ignatius Doyle arrived at Loyola in 1934 and was given the charge of establishing a psychology department, he faced the issue of the emerging discipline's identity within a Catholic institution. He had to find a way to differentiate experimental and clinical psychology from Thomistic rational psychology, while at the same time he had to provide a means for psychology students to relate to the Thomism pervading the school. First it was necessary to grasp the insights of Thomism's rational psychology and, second, to see how it can support rather than hinder training in experimental and clinical psychology. As we have seen, Pace and Moore at Catholic University and Gruender and McCarthy at St. Louis, all with extensive training in both Thomism and the new psychology, were able to integrate Thomism into the emerging fields of psychology and to engage easily in dialogues between Catholic philosophers and professional psychologists. Doyle had a similar background, and he used it well at Loyola. He had assistance from Loyola's philosophy department in recruiting majors. It did not take Doyle long to develop a solid psychology department taught by an astute faculty.

During the early 1940s Doyle organized the Chicago Society of Catholic Psychologists. The society attracted a wide range of professional psychologists, Catholic and non-Catholic alike, and the organization served as a model for the institution of the American Catholic Psychological Association in 1948. Moreover, like Moore at Catholic University, Doyle founded a child guidance clinic, the demands of which led him in 1945 to surrender the reins of the department to his Jesuit colleague, Fr. Vincent Herr.

Herr, like Gruender, McCarthy, and Doyle, was a multitalented Jesuit. Besides receiving extensive philosophical and theological training in his Jesuit formation, he took summer psychology courses at the University of Michigan and at the University of London, spent a year studying at the University of Vienna with the gestalt psychologists Charlotte and Karl Buhler, and obtained a doctorate from the University of Bonn, as Gruender had done earlier. Herr's doctorate was in psychology and philosophical anthropology. With such an extensive empirical background Herr was able to guide generations of students into professional psychology and attract a wide range of competent faculty. It was under Herr's departmental leadership from 1945 to 1965 that Loyola, through its faculty, graduate students, and their projects, became a major catalyst for American Catholicism's appropriation of professional psychology.

In the early 1950s Loyola began to hire faculty of significant stature, who not only enhanced Loyola's reputation as a department, but also played important roles in bringing psychology into the Catholic world. Among such luminaries was Dr. Magda Arnold, who was later described by her Loyola colleague Eugene Kennedy as "a wonderful old world type psychologist."[2]

Arnold was born near Vienna in 1903 and went to Canada in 1928. She obtained her doctorate in psychology from the University of Toronto and taught there until 1947, when she moved to the United States and assumed a position as a professor in the psychology department at Wellesley College. In 1949 Arnold took the position of chair of the psychology department at Bryn Mawr College. In 1950, inspired by her commitment to the Catholic faith, Arnold resigned her position at Bryn Mawr and began teaching at Barat College in Lake Forest, Illinois, and a few years later joined Loyola's psychology department.[3]

During her long and distinguished career Arnold held Fulbright and Guggenheim fellowships, which helped establish her as one of the foremost authorities on the psychology of emotions. Her books *The Human Person* (1954) and *Emotion and Personality* (1960) were major contributions to the field. A later work to which she contributed, *Screening Candidates for the Priesthood and Religious Life* (1962), made the instruments of professional psychology available to those responsible for the formation of Catholic clerics and religious. In addition, her book *Story Sequence Analysis* enhanced the use of such instruments.[4]

After retiring from Loyola in 1970 Arnold assumed a position at Spring Hill College in Mobile, Alabama, where she continued to do experimental work and through a grant from the National Institute of Mental Health wrote her final book, *Memory and the Brain* (1984).[5]

Another illustrious faculty member, Dr. Frank Kobler, arrived at Loyola in 1946 and had a significant impact on the department's reputation for clinical research and training. A "crack clinician,"[6] he published in 1964 *Casebook in Psychopathology.*[7] He also directed several Loyola projects, including one on the psychology of American Catholic bishops. During his years at Loyola, serving under Herr and later Ron Walker, Kobler was seen as "the power behind the throne."[8]

Also on the faculty at that time were two priests, Charles A. Curran and

William Devlin, whose astute clinical training drew national attention to the department. Curran came to Loyola in 1954 after teaching for twelve years at St. Charles Seminary in Columbus, Ohio. In a subsequent chapter of this book, Curran's influence and writings will be examined in detail. For now it is important to note that Curran arrived at Loyola after working closely with Carl Rogers at Ohio State. He is credited with introducing to the American Catholic culture Rogers's client-centered approach with its emphasis on empathy and freedom that was congenial to Catholic pastoral practices.

William Devlin was the first American Jesuit priest-psychiatrist. After his Jesuit training in philosophy and theology, Devlin earned a master's degree in social work at Catholic University. With the encouragement of Thomas Verner Moore, Devlin continued his studies at Catholic University, earning a doctorate in clinical psychology in 1943. Moore intended that Devlin be his replacement as the chair of the department. This did not happen, but Devlin did follow Moore's path in psychiatry by enrolling in Loyola University's medical school, where he was awarded his medical degree summa cum laude in 1946. The next four years Devlin served as intern and then as resident in psychiatry and neurology. Finally, at age forty-five he had achieved his goal of becoming a priest-psychiatrist.

Devlin's clinical and ministerial identities made his advice, like Moore's, widely sought by bishops and physicians alike. His reputation grew, and in 1959 he was featured in a book, *God and Freud*,[9] the summary of which was a feature article in *Look* magazine.[10] Leonard Gross, the author of the book and the article, had established a friendly relationship with Devlin. While Gross was complimentary of Devlin's clinical practice and his priesthood, the author's journalistic flair apparently so upset Devlin (as well as some of Devlin's superiors) that a controversy ensued and nearly resulted in a lawsuit against Gross and *Look* magazine. The controversy was indicative of the sensitive nature of Devlin's profession in the American Catholic subculture at the time.

In consenting to have an article written about his unique pastoral and professional identity, Devlin understood that he would have final say over what Gross wrote. There was no paper trail, however, and a series of letters between Gross and Devlin seeking to clarify the issue proved ineffective. Devlin considered bringing Gross to court and their friendship was fractured. Shortly before the article appeared in January 1959, a graduate of Fordham University working for *Look* saw the galley proofs of the article. He thought them controversial and alerted a New York Jesuit superior about the contents. It was felt that several statements by Devlin could be misconstrued. The Jesuit superior in New York contacted Devlin's superior, Fr. James Maguire, who was also the president of Loyola. Maguire spoke with Devlin about his concern as well as with some lawyers. A lawsuit against *Look* and Gross was considered by Maguire on behalf of Devlin, but that was rejected as creating even more controversy. Maguire instead advised Devlin to write a letter to *Look* indicating his concerns about the article. He did so, but *Look* refused to publish it, considering it an unfair statement of what had transpired in the communication between Gross and Devlin. The magazine also cited the principle of a journalist's freedom not to be censored in denying Devlin's request for final approval of the article. Devlin's disapproval, nevertheless, was made public in the *Chicago Sun-Times* in a book review of *God and Freud,* which appeared the same week that the *Look* magazine piece was published. In the *Sun* article Devlin stated: "I vigorously disapproved the text as well as its publication on the grounds that (1) his [Gross's] out-of-context quotations amounted to outright misrepresentation of my position, and (2) his treatment of abstruse moral and psychological problems was quite superficial."[11]

Shortly before the *Look* article appeared, Fr. Maguire alerted several leading American archbishops and all of the American Jesuit provincials about the article and noted that Devlin had written a letter in protest.[12] While the whole scenario seems like "much ado about nothing" to the contemporary reader, such concern about Devlin's image as a priest, as well as his reference to another priest in connection with homosexuality, was indicative of the Catholic Church's heightened sensitivity at that time about issues pertaining to psychology in general and sexuality in particular. Within a few weeks the controversy subsided.

Devlin worked virtually around the clock. He regularly saw more than a dozen patients each day and at the same time maintained responsibilities as a clinical instructor in psychiatry at Loyola's medical school and as an associate professor in the psychology department. In addition, Devlin served as a consultant to organizations such as Catholic Charities, the Clinical Institute of Juvenile Research, and the Research Board of Hypnosis in New York. He did all of this while maintaining a regular sacramental ministry as a priest. Psychiatrists later would describe Devlin's intense style as a Type A Personality. Sadly, this temperament may have contributed to his sudden death from a heart attack in 1962 when he was fifty-five years old.

In the early 1960s Eugene Kennedy joined the department's faculty and brought considerable attention to Loyola through his research and writings. Kennedy, who received his doctorate from Catholic University in 1962, became a prominent figure in American Catholic psychology. In 1965 he coauthored with Paul F. D'Arcy, his departmental colleague and fellow Maryknoll priest, *The Genius of the Apostolate,* a significant contribution toward understanding the vocation of the priest and the religious from a psychological perspective.[13] From 1968 to 1972 Kennedy directed an extensive psychological study of the American priesthood, supported by the American Catholic bishops and described in further detail below.

Kennedy went on to write numerous articles and more than forty books, in many of which he appropriated the insights of professional psychology for the American Catholic world. His writings include *What a Modern Catholic Believes about Sex and Marriage* (1971), *Believing* (1974), *A Sense of Life, a Sense of Sin* (1975), *Sexual Counseling: A Practical Guide for Non-Professional Counselors* (1980), *The Now and Future Church: The Psychology of Being an American Catholic* (1984), and *Authority: The Most Misunderstood Idea in America* (1997).[14] Perhaps more than any other American Catholic psychologist Kennedy popularized the insights of psychology for American Catholics and many others.

Kennedy also was a significant influence in the American Catholic Psychological Association as it shifted from being primarily a fellowship of Catholic psychologists to becoming a more ecumenically inclusive organization, known as Psychologists Interested in Religious Issues (PIRI). In 1975 PIRI was accepted as Division 36 of the American Psychological Association, and Kennedy was elected the division's first president. His leadership and his acquaintance with prominent psychologists, ranging from the behaviorist B. F. Skinner to the existentialist Rollo May, were instrumental in attracting a host of members, Catholic and non-Catholic alike. He also created the division's William James Award, an annual honor bestowed on the psychologist who best promoted the dialogue between psychology and religion. For over five decades Eugene Kennedy has helped to make the psychological world credible for skeptical Catholics and the Catholic world more acceptable to incredulous psychologists.

Loyola Research Projects

In 1956 the National Institute of Mental Health, concerned about the controversies and misunderstandings between clergy and practitioners of mental health, approached Loyola, Harvard, and Yeshiva Universities about conducting three major research projects. Representing Catholics, Protestants, and Jews respectively, the three universities were awarded a combined grant of $435,000 to conduct studies that would "(a) develop a rapprochement or synthesis between theology and the principles of psychoanalysis and psychiatry; (b) prepare a curriculum or some broad outlines of studies concerning mental health which would embrace new knowledge from the disciplines of psychiatry and psychology and the other behavioral sciences, together with the social sciences."[15]

The NIMH grant funded a series of research projects at Loyola that undertook psychological investigations on samples of seminarians, then priests, and finally bishops. The project on seminarians (1957–62) was co-directed by Herr and his fellow Jesuit Devlin. According to Herr, they were interested in "(a) the role of the Roman Catholic priest in dealing with emotional health; (b) research in the area of possible relationships between religion and health; and (c) the preparation of a basic content curriculum for Roman Catholic Theological Seminaries."[16]

During the course of the five-year project 980 seminarians and 200 priests agreed to respond to Loyola's battery of surveys. Before the project was launched few Roman Catholic seminaries offered courses in pastoral counseling. By the end of the survey more than a hundred were offering classes in pastoral counseling and mental health.

In 1967 the National Conference of Catholic Bishops approached Loyola to do a similar in-depth and extensive examination of the life and ministry of the Catholic priest. Directed by Eugene Kennedy and Victor Heckler, the study was carried out from 1969 to 1972, a time when the reverberations of the Second Vatican Council were decimating the ranks of American priests. Utilizing the tools of psychological assessment, interviews, and clinical judgment, the researchers evaluated a total of 271 diocesan and religious priests in a process that involved thorough psychological interviews as well as psychometric tests. In 1971 the results were published by Kennedy and Heckler in *The Catholic Priest in the United States: Psychological Investigations*. Their findings pointed to the need for a dramatic overhaul in the formation of priests, raising serious questions about the emotional maturity of a substantial number of American Catholic priests:

> In summary, the ordinary men who are American priests are bright, able, and dedicated. A large number of them are underdeveloped as persons with a consequent lack of fully realized religious and human values in their lives. They are not sick; they are not fully grown. They seem to need a broader, deeper, and genuinely freer experience of life to overcome this lack of development. There seem to be minimal risks in increasing the active options in their lives and, therefore, increasing the areas in which they must become more fully responsible for themselves and their work. The priests of the United States are clearly adequate in their function; they could be far more effective personally and professionally if they were helped to achieve greater human and religious maturity. The basic therapy for this kind of problem is the opportunity and encouragement for a deeper and freer participation in life itself.[17]

The study of Catholic priests was followed a few years later by another psychological study of American Catholic clerics, this time of the bishops.

With the remaining funds from the NCCB grant, several related studies were carried out by two Loyola doctoral students, Sr. Mary Sheehan and Fr. James Schroeder, under the direction of Dr. Frank Kobler. Overall the study surveyed a sample of 81 active and retired American bishops from a population of 298, including archbishops and cardinals. Twenty of the bishops agreed to a two-hour taped interview concerning their psychological development. Using the same psychometric instruments as were used with the priests, Schroeder reported that bishops showed significantly more "trust, successfully formed identity, self-esteem, positive affectual experience, expressiveness and comfort in social contexts."[18] He also found that in comparison to priests, bishops were "not more mature in faith, showed significantly less individualistic expressivity and were less self-actualized." Sheehan and Kobler reported a statistically significant finding that the "bishops showed more psychological development than the priests."[19] They concluded their study by noting:

> As would be anticipated, there are some really outstanding men among the American bishops. They may be characterized by their immense drive, their strong social consciousness, their great confidence in and identification with the mission of the Church and their great personal warmth and concern with the individuals who come under their care and jurisdiction. In many others, this personal warmth and concern is notably absent. Most of the bishops tend to lead happy, busy lives. They are seldom lonely. Most of them have had personal difficulties with the problems of human intimacy that the acceptance of celibacy usually brings in its wake. For some, only a distant, ritualized relationship with other people, especially with women, is noteworthy. For most of the bishops the gratification provided by their own work and by their own role has more than compensated for this loss.[20]

While the results might not be surprising, the very fact that the National Conference of Catholic Bishops financially supported a major psychological study of priests and then of themselves indicates that the techniques and tools of psychology had become not only accepted but institutionalized by American Catholicism's leadership. Loyola's studies of American Catholicism's leaders in the 1970s suggest that the days of American Catholic's suspicion of psychology were long gone.

Fordham University

Fordham's psychology department was established by Fr. Walter Sommers in 1934. While he never earned a psychology degree himself, his background in physics and physiology made him knowledgeable about experimental psychology research (he is credited with developing the first lie detector test). During Sommers's leadership as the director, enrollment in the department grew from a mere handful of students to over a hundred within four years. Sommers initiated clinical programs with hospitals in the New York area. Unfortunately, his time as director of the department was brief; he died in 1938 at age forty-eight. Despite his brief tenure, Sommers was an inspiration to faculty colleagues and students alike. Among his students were Margaret Donnelly and Virginia Staudt Sexton, among the first female graduate students in psychology at Fordham, who both went on to distinguished careers in academic and professional psychology. Sexton in particular played a major role in transforming American Catholic attitudes toward psychology as well as the attitudes of professional psychologists toward Catholicism.

Born in New York City in 1916, Sexton attended Hunter College, where she graduated with a major in classics in 1936. After several years of teaching at a Catholic elementary school, she attended Fordham, earning a master's degree in psychology in 1941 and a doctorate in experimental psychology in 1946. Sexton went on to teach at Notre Dame College of Staten Island, where, besides teaching psychology and serving as a guidance counselor, she established the psychology major and a laboratory. In 1952 she resigned from Notre Dame and taught at her alma mater, Hunter College. She remained at Hunter until 1968, having attained full professor status. From there she moved to Herbert H. Lehman College of the City University of New York, where she taught until her retirement in 1979.

Sexton's reputation among American Catholic psychologists was established when together with Henryk Misiak, a Polish-born Catholic priest who served as a faculty member in Fordham's psychology department, she wrote *Catholics in Psychology: A Historical Survey* (1954). This landmark historical work allayed many Catholic fears about psychology by demonstrating the extensive work done by Catholic psychologists in Europe and in the United States. Sexton and Misiak also collaborated on three other books, *History of Psychology: An Overview* (1966), *Phenomenological, Existential, and Humanistic Psychologies: A Historical Survey* (1973), and *Psychology around the World* (1976).[21] Sexton authored more than one hundred articles and three other books and served on several journals, among them *Journal of Mind, Journal of Phenomenological Psychology, Journal of Professional Psychology: Research and Practice,* and *Humanistic Psychologist.* She was associate editor for *Psychological Abstracts* and editor of the History and Systems of Psychology Section of the *International Encyclopedia of Neurology, Psychoanalysis, Psychiatry, and Psychology.*

Besides her scholarly endeavors, Sexton influenced the profession of psychology through her leadership in the American Psychological Association. A member of fourteen divisions of the APA and a Fellow of nine of them, Sexton was president of Divisions 1 (General), 24 (Theoretical and Philosophical), and 26 (History). She served as chair of the Fellows Committee of Division 35 (Psychology of Women) and was a member of its Governance Committee. Her presidencies also included the International Council of Psychologists, the Eastern Psychological Association, and Psi Chi, the National Honor Society for Psychology. Given her leadership roles in the ACPA, PIRI, and the APA, as well as her numerous scholarly contributions to psychology, Sexton can be credited as having done more than any other woman in closing the gaps of misunderstanding between psychology and American Catholicism.

Fr. William Bier, S.J.

When William Bier was born in New York City in 1911, his future mentor, Thomas Verner Moore, was beginning his medical career. After completing high school, Bier entered the Society of Jesus in 1928. He received his baccalaureate degree and master of divinity degree from Woodstock College and in 1939 a master's degree in psychology from Fordham University. Following his ordination in 1940, Bier studied at Catholic University and came under Moore's tutelage. It was Moore who inspired Bier to seek ways of relating psychology and religion. In 1948 Bier successfully defended his dissertation entitled "A Comparative Study of a Seminary Group and Four Other Groups on the Minnesota Multiphasic Personality Inventory." This successful integration of psychology and religion led to the development of psychological methods for screening candidates for the religious life. Until then, such psychometric screening had been vigorously eschewed because of the Catholic Church's suspicion toward psychology.

In 1946, while still a teaching fellow at Catholic University, Bier began speaking with a group of Catholic psychologists about the possibility of a Catholic psychological organization. The next year Catholic psychologists were contacted by mail and asked about the possibility of forming such an organization. As Misiak and Staudt noted, there followed some discussion:

> When the actual planning started, there was considerable dissension among Catholic psychologists as to the advisability of such a special organization. Many feared that the new group would serve only to emphasize differences, making Catholics a separate group in the profession. Every attempt was made to dispel this notion of separatism then, and in the constitution and policies thereafter, and to demonstrate that the proposed group was intended as a supplement

to, and not a substitute for, the parent organization, the American Psychological Association. From the beginning, even in the planning stages, membership in the (latter) organization was set as the requirement for full membership in the new group. Several prominent non-Catholic psychologists were consulted in order to appraise their attitudes toward the proposed association.[22]

On September 11, 1947, during the annual meeting of the American Psychological Association in Detroit, 110 psychologists, through Bier's coordination, attended a meeting at Mercy College. A committee consisting of thirteen participants from eight Catholic colleges and universities was formed to further develop the organization. Bier was named chairman. The next year the APA met in Boston and the new organization met at Boston College, where Bier gave an update on the committee's work. In 1949 the American Catholic Psychological Association was formally established, and Bier was named its executive secretary, a position he held until 1970. The goal of the new organization was twofold:

1. To interpret to Catholics the meaning of modern psychology, and to advance its acceptance in Catholic circles.

2. To work toward the integration of psychology with Catholic thought and practice.[23]

Bier would often summarize such purposes: "to bring psychology to Catholics and to bring a Catholic viewpoint into psychology."[24]

In 1948 Bier became an instructor in psychology at Fordham University, and for the next twenty years he was associated with the department, becoming a full professor in 1966 and the department's chair from 1958 to 1968. In 1968 Bier was appointed Fordham's academic vice president, a position he held until his sudden death in 1980. Besides his work with ACPA, Bier also served as a leader and first president of Psychologists Interested in Religious Issues (PIRI), the offspring of ACPA, which later became the present-day Division 36 (Psychology of Religion) of the American Psychological Association.

Bier's articles were for the most part published in religious periodicals, including *America, Bulletin of the National Guild of Catholic Psychiatrists, Bulletin of the National Catholic Educational Association, Journal of Religion and Health, Pastoral Psychology, Review for Religious,* and *Theological Education.* In 1967, Bier wrote an essay, "Pastoral Psychology," for the *New Catholic Encyclopedia.* Beginning in 1955, he directed the biennial interdisciplinary symposiums on pastoral psychology held at Fordham and edited the series published by Fordham University that was the product of the symposiums. Volumes in the series are as follows (year of publication in parentheses):

1955 and 1957: *Personality and Sexual Problems in Pastoral Psychology* (1964)

1959: *Problems in Addiction: Alcoholism and Narcotics* (1962)

1961: *The Adolescent: His Search for Understanding* (1963)

1963: *Marriage: A Psychological and Moral Approach* (1965)

1965: *Women in Modern Life* (1968)

1969: *Conscience: Its Freedom and Limitations* (1970)

1971: *Alienation: Plight of Modern Man?* (1972)

1973: *Aging: Its Challenge to the Individual and to Society* (1974)

1975: *Human Life: Problems of Birth, of Living, and of Dying* (1977)

1977: *Privacy: A Vanishing Value?* (1980)

Many clergy, psychologists, and social workers attended these symposiums. The conferences and the subsequent series of books became major avenues for introducing Catholic clergy and laity to psychological approaches and insights for dealing with common pastoral concerns.

Bier was a leader in introducing and promoting the psychological testing of religious candidates. As early as 1936 Moore had advocated such testing.[25] Moore's advocacy was a major influence leading to Bier's recognition of the need and his subsequent dissertation research. Upon receiving his doctoral degree, Bier set out immediately to implement testing among candidates who had applied to the New York Province of the Society of Jesus, of which Bier was a member. Bier's work at first met with some skepticism. Indeed, some of Bier's first recommendations were not followed, and several young men had mental breakdowns during their religious formation, as Bier had predicted.[26] After five years of such testing, Bier presented his findings, which were later published in two consecutive articles in *Review for Religious*.[27] The articles alluded to Bier's success with such testing as well as his suggestions on how such programs should be professionally administered. Bier pointed out that other orders and other Jesuit provinces in the United States had begun to implement his testing design.

Bier's leadership as a Catholic psychologist was not without controversy. One dispute occurred over an article that Bier wrote in 1956 for the Jesuit periodical *America* entitled "Sigmund Freud and the Faith."[28] Bier concurred with much of the Catholic Church's reservations about Freud but indicated various steps toward reconciliation between psychoanalysis and religion, including the St. John's Institute workshops and the statements by Pope Pius XII discussed earlier. Shortly after Bier's article appeared, Bishop Fulton Sheen made a critical reference to it on his evening television program. The subsequent confrontation between Bier and Sheen on this matter[29] suggests that psychology still had a way to go before being assimilated by the Catholic Church and many of its leaders. A year later, in 1957, Bier experienced another indication of such resistance and of suspicion toward ecumenical efforts. At an address he gave for New York's Postgraduate Center for Psychotherapy in a symposium on "Religion, Psychiatry, and Freud," he shared the podium with Dr. Roy Stuart Lee, an Episcopal canon and author of *Freud and Christianity*.[30] Bier had considered publishing his address but received a letter from his provincial advising him against doing so:

> The New York Chancery would have to give the permission for the publication of your remarks as part of the Symposium on Religion, Psychiatry and Freud in which the principal speaker was the Episcopal clergyman, Roy S. Lee.
>
> I am absolutely sure that permission would not be granted especially in view of the fact that "Religion" occurs in the title and you are discussing the subject with a non-Catholic clergyman. I think that it is better that we do not even request the permission of the Chancery. I know you will be able to excuse yourself graciously.[31]

Bier did not publish his remarks, but he was not afraid to assert himself. His persistent and steady leadership of the ACPA demonstrated his special combination of administrative and psychological skills. Under his guidance from 1949 until the early 1960s, the ACPA experienced steady growth from an initial membership of 231 to 642 by 1960.[32] During his career at Fordham, Bier helped to shepherd the ACPA toward maturity by editing the association's quarterly newsletter. From 1950 until 1963 the newsletter was a bimonthly publication of eight pages. It described developments in the growing number of psychology departments at Catholic higher educational institutions. Bier kept track of such developments by means of surveys. For example, in 1955 he conducted a survey of Catholic colleges and universities to determine the number with courses in psychology. He found that of the 190 institutions replying, 30 percent offered a psychology major, and 24 percent offered a psychology minor; 40 percent offered some psychology courses and only 6 percent had none.[33] These findings helped Bier demonstrate the emerging enthusiasm for psychology in American Catholicism; his career went a long way toward building alliances and reducing antagonisms between religion and psychology.

Summary

As we have seen in this chapter, American Catholicism gradually gained enthusiasm for the new psychology. Through the efforts of outstanding individual faculty members at higher educational institutions, psychology was accepted and appropriated by mainstream Catholicism. This process was not always an easy one. Indeed it took the dedicated labors of many professionals in Catholic psychology departments—like those at St. Louis, Loyola of Chicago, and Fordham—for psychology to be integrated with Catholic thought and practice.

Chapter 5

Sr. Annette Walters, C.S.J.
Psychologist and Prophet

In the Twin Cities two religious edifices boldly punctuate the horizon and serve to demonstrate Catholicism's contribution to the area. Early in the twentieth century, Archbishop John Ireland authorized the construction of two cathedrals that placed indelible marks on both cities' landscapes. In downtown Minneapolis Ireland built St. Mary's, later to become America's first basilica. Completed in 1914, its majestic structure makes a statement to resident and tourist alike about Catholicism's past and present power in the region. Across the Mississippi, on St. Paul's most prominent hill and one mile from the state capitol, sits Archbishop Ireland's other cathedral, St. Paul's, where the first Mass was celebrated in 1915. It too suggests the significant influence that Catholicism has in the area. As if to confirm Archbishop Ireland's intention that Catholics integrate their Roman faith with their American citizenship, the road connecting the cathedral to the capitol bears the name Archbishop Ireland Boulevard.

Ireland's imprint can also be found in the two institutions of higher education that he founded in St. Paul, St. Thomas College (first degrees conferred in 1910) and the College of St. Catherine (first degrees conferred in 1913). St. Thomas at the time it was founded was for men, St. Catherine's for women.

Noted for his American assimilationist views toward education, Ireland sought to foster the education of Catholic laity, men and women alike. What made the College of St. Catherine distinct was the advanced education that the Sisters of St. Joseph's, the college's faculty, soon achieved. The mother superior of this congregation was Archbishop Ireland's own sister, Ellen (Sr. Seraphine, C.S.J.). The archbishop and mother superior coordinated sending forth one sister after another to the best universities. In 1903 two sisters were sent to Europe; in 1905 two attended summer school classes at Harvard. By 1917 twelve sisters had obtained master's degrees. Probably the best educated of them all was Sr. Antonia McHugh, who received two bachelor's degrees in 1908 and a master's degree in history in 1909 at the University of Chicago. She later became the college's president.

During her administration (1926–36) ten sisters earned doctoral degrees at such prestigious universities as Chicago, Columbia, Michigan, the Catholic University of America, Louvain, and Munich.[1]

The College of St. Catherine became one of the outstanding Catholic institutions in the country. Probably no other American Catholic college for men or women could boast of such high quality among its religious faculty. This excellence was demonstrated in 1937 when the College of St. Catherine became the first Catholic college in the United States to apply for and receive a Phi Beta Kappa chapter.

Walters's Education and Formation

It was into such a highly charged Catholic academic setting that the adolescent Annette Walters entered in 1927. Baptized Lutheran and having attended public schools most of her young life, in her junior year of high school Annette transferred from West High school to St. Margaret's Academy in Minneapolis, which like St. Catherine's was administered by the Sisters of St. Joseph. Her exposure to the sisters would motivate her not only toward Catholicism but also toward religious life. When she entered college Walters wanted to become a doctor. Shortly before entering St. Catherine's, she had become a Catholic, and within two years her career dreams had shifted from doctor to the Sisters of St. Joseph. Her decisions were no doubt inspired by the dedication to excellence in education exemplified by her Sisters of St. Joseph mentors. These were not just holy and dedicated women; they were women of keen intelligence who had pursued and obtained outstanding degrees. Within the American Catholic world they were women ahead of their time. February 14, 1929, Annette Walters chose to become a woman religious who would continue that tradition.

In 1933 Sr. Walters graduated from "St. Kate's" with a B.A. in chemistry. With the encouragement of her superior and mentor, the college president Mother Antonia, she changed her field of study and entered the University of Minnesota in the fall of 1933 as a graduate student in psychology. She earned an M.A. in educational psychology in 1935 and her doctorate in experimental psychology in 1941. The degrees themselves were certainly a personal achievement, but for a woman religious of that era to earn such a degree in experimental psychology, much less at a state university, was rare indeed. At that time many women religious had studied educational psychology, and there were women religious who had pursued graduate studies in psychology at Catholic universities such as the Catholic University of America, Fordham, and St. Louis. But Sr. Annette was probably the first nun to receive a doctorate in experimental psychology at a public university.

At times Walters's identity as a woman religious could have negative consequences. As she was entering into her professional career as a psychologist, she was considered for membership in Sigma Xi, the distinguished society of the leading researchers in science. In the 1940s very few women were invited to join. So while Walters's abilities as a candidate compared favorably with those of another woman in the university's psychology department, it was believed that as a Catholic nun Walters would not need such a prestigious membership to enhance her career. She was not accepted. Years later this professional and prejudicial slight was corrected through the initiative of a former student, Dr. Mary Reuder, and the support of B. F. Skinner.[2]

During her graduate studies Sr. Annette supplemented her education by taking courses at the University of Chicago in 1936 and 1939 with an Education Board Fellowship. In the summer of 1940 she took theology and psychology courses at the Catholic University of America, where she met Dom Thomas Verner Moore. But it was at Minnesota that Sr. Annette found her career path. At that time the university's psychology department was quite renowned due in large part to the work done by Starke Hathaway, who developed the Minnesota Multiphasic Personality Inventory (MMPI). Sr. Annette got to know Hathaway as well as other psychology luminaries, including Richard Elliott and a young professor, B. F. Skinner. As we will see, Walters's acumen and enthusiasm, combined with her religious witness, made an early and lasting impression on Skinner, and a lifelong friendship developed.

Friendship with B. F. Skinner

Walters's relationship with Skinner dated back as far as 1933, when she began her graduate studies at the University of Minnesota. It seems that Skinner was taken with the irony of a woman entering the secular world of experimental psychology clothed in the ostentatious sacred dress of a religious habit. Walters's intelligence and professional manner no doubt impressed the budding behaviorist and, while they disagreed about matters of faith and freedom, the friendship that formed during the 1930s was reinforced throughout the next four decades. Walters was known to visit the Skinner family and even babysit the children. Their friendship was especially evident during the 1960s and 1970s when both Walters and Skinner were well-known figures in their respective worlds. In 1964, for instance, upon reading about Walters's work with the Sisters Formation Conference in *Time* magazine,[3] Skinner wrote her:

> It was nice to see your picture in Time and to read about your current activities. As a matter of fact, I have been hearing about them from

various Sisters I have run into during my travels in the past two or three years. Somehow or other our paths have not crossed at the Annual Meeting. Since I know you are above the sin of pride, I can tell you that I have been told that you are the most powerful woman in the Catholic hierarchy. If that doesn't send you dashing off to Confession, here is another that may. When Eve (Yvonne to you) saw your picture she said, "As beautiful as ever."

Quite seriously, I am very proud of you as a student, and wish you the very best in this most important activity.[4]

Several years later Walters, along with her friend Sr. Ritamary Bradley, visited Skinner and his wife, Eve, in Boston, at the time of the annual meeting of the American Psychological Association in Boston. A month before the meeting Skinner had written Walters a letter in which he humorously chided:

I will be at the APA... and will look for you, no matter how inconspicious you may be. I take it from the fact that you still sign yourself Sister Annette that you have not "gone over the wall."[5]

Walters's sharp wit with her former professor was in turn evidenced in a letter that she wrote in 1970 inviting Skinner to present a lecture at St. Ambrose College:

I am in sackcloth and ashes at the thought that I may be taking you away from your important work for even one day in March. But inveterate sinner that I am, I am hoping against hope that you will be able to speak to a Quint-City group one evening this year.

She concluded:

If anyone is writing your biography these days, have him check with me. I would like to contribute to "The Portrait of the Behaviorist as a Young Man," or at least to a lighter sketch, perhaps to be entitled "Teaching ping-pong is for the birds."[6]

Another demonstration of their friendship occurred in 1974 when the noted Catholic psychologist and writer Eugene Kennedy published an interview with Skinner. During the interview the behaviorist mentioned his admiration for Walters:

I have many Catholic friends. One of my closest is Sister Annette Walters, who teaches psychology. She was a former student of mine. When she last came to visit me, she was out of her religious habit, and I suddenly realized that she has a new kind of power, that the strength of her own personality and intelligence showed through because it was not obscured by that habit and by the need to relate to people in terms of the role it defined. This is the kind of thing that is going on in the Catholic Church; people are walking away from bad uses of power and discovering how strong they can be when they do it.[7]

Concerned that he might have said too much, Skinner wrote to Walters and enclosed the page from Kennedy's book where the statement appeared. At the time Walters was sharing a house at St. Ambrose College with her fellow religious, Sr. Ritamary Bradley. In closing his letter Skinner wrote: "Christian love to you and Rita Mary. Cordially, 'Brother Fred.'"

Walters's response to Skinner is quite revealing of her affection for him and expresses her distaste for the backlash that he had to endure because of his behaviorist positions as explained in his controversial bestseller *Beyond Freedom and Dignity:*

My Dear Brother Fred,

You dear sweet man! Of course I don't object to what you said about me to Eugene Kennedy nor to his printing of it. I love it. I lap it up eagerly, delightedly, avidly, gratefully. Such kind words can never be dished out in servings too big for me to swallow. So much for humility.

I am deeply touched by the realization that you value my friend-ship—perhaps almost as much as I do yours. You have been an important person in my life for more than a third of a century in ways that you cannot possibly know. For many years I prayed for you daily. When and why I stopped I do not know.

Last year one of my students turned in a comprehensive report of reviews of *Beyond Freedom and Dignity* and I found myself close to tears as I read how rejecting many of them were. What troubled me was not that people took exception to your ideas and research conclusions but that they so often endowed you gratuitously with horns and hoofs. This saddens me profoundly.

What my students remember most about your visit to St. Ambrose is "that wonderful Skinner, the man." You came through to them as an extraordinarily kind, warm, and charming person...

Again thanks, dear Brother Fred, for all that you have done for me and all that you have been to me over the years.

Affectionately and gratefully,
Annette[8]

Their friendship carried into 1978 during Walters's last illness. Upon learning that she was dying Skinner tried to call her but could not get through. He then wrote a short note in which he stated, "At times like this I envy you your faith." After Walters died Skinner wrote to Sr. Ritamary:

> Annette did indeed live a wonderful life and she apparently left it with the same courage and dignity with which she lived it. Mathilde told me that she once said of me, "What a Christian he would have made!" and I know of nothing that has pleased me more. Last January we were in Paris and went to Notre Dame and after hearing of Annette's death I told Eve that if I go there I shall light a candle for her. Eve was rather startled. I should not do it, of course, thinking that Annette's soul needs any help from me. It just seemed like a fitting way to express my love for her.[9]

Skinner added:

> Annette Walters was one of the wisest, bravest, and most beautiful of my students. She championed her beliefs as strongly as she felt them. Her continuing friendship through the years, in spite of differences, gave me added confidence in the principles we held in common. She was a great woman and all women have gained because she lived.[10]

Professional Life

Sr. Annette's abilities as an experimental psychologist impressed Skinner and others. Her dissertation dealt with experimental optics. She published a monograph based on it, "A Genetic Study of Geometric-Optical Illusions."[11] But Walters did not remain confined to experimental psychology. In 1941 when Walters assumed a full-time position at St. Catherine's as a psychology professor, she immediately brought her experimental acumen into the classroom. Her courses in introductory and experimental psychology introduced to her students and colleagues alike how the new psychology could be applied and be made acceptable. One former student recalls how she inspired enthusiasm for experimental psychology by having teams of students perform separate experimental studies and then inform the class of their projects' method and results.[12]

She also responded to the need for clinical psychologists. In 1948 she became a licensed dilpomate in clinical psychology and was elected vice president of the Upper Mississippi Psychological Association. In 1949 when the American Catholic Psychological Association was formally established at Regis College in Denver, Walters became a charter member. For some years she was active in the organization, and in a multitude of ways, both as a professional psychologist and as a nun, she lived out its purpose: "to bring psychology to Catholics and Catholics to psychology."[13] By 1953

Walters had given some 230 lectures to a host of civic and parish groups and professional societies. She also had been included in the publication *American Men of Science.*

In 1952 Walters was awarded a Fulbright fellowship and spent the 1952–53 academic year in Belgium at Louvain University. It was there that she took classes in existentialism, phenomenology, and psychoanalysis and opined in her own words, "There is a breadth of view and an intellectual atmosphere unlike anything that I have seen in America."[14]

Walters's exposure to the currents of continental philosophy and psychology broadened her perspective and deepened her commitment to appreciating psychology's philosophical and even theological roots. This integration became clear in her book *Persons and Personality,* which she wrote in collaboration with her philosophy colleague Sr. Kevin (now Sr. Mary L.) O'Hara. Close to seven hundred pages long, the book served as an introductory text to the whole field of psychology. As indicated by the title of the final chapter, "Science, Philosophy, and Theology in the Study of Man," the work sought to integrate psychological insights about personality with Catholicism's classical understanding of the person in philosophy and theology. As the authors noted, the book was intended as a means "for beginning a synthesis of our scientific, philosophical, and theological knowledge of man."[15] In the book's preface the authors state that the book is fairly partisan in nature, as can be seen in its major objectives:

1. To present the data of scientific psychology in such a way that the person rather than isolated mental functions is at the center of interest...

2. To relate scientific psychology wherever feasible to relevant theological and philosophical considerations.[16]

The authors intended to address the concerns of their students, most of them Catholic, who were perplexed about how to reconcile the wisdom stemming from the sacred with that coming from the secular currents of the time:

> The Christian student in his study of psychology raises many questions that do not occur to the non-Christian student. He wants to know, for example, if it is true that miraculous cures are nothing more than suggestive psychotherapy. He is often disturbed by the seeming disharmony between psychological science and Christian principles. He finds it difficult to reconcile the amoral points of view adopted by psychologists with the moral view inculcated by his religion. He is confused by the implicit philosophy of popular books that tell him how to win friends and develop his personality. If he has studied phi-

losophy, he is confused by the different meanings that philosophy and psychology sometimes give to the same term and he wants to know which is "right." The present textbook attempts to answer or to help the student find the answers to these and to similar questions.[17]

The book was an instant success in Catholic psychological circles and was cited as an excellent example of how Catholic thought can interact with appropriate insights and methods of experimental and clinical psychology.[18] The book sold over twenty thousand copies, most of them to students at Catholic colleges and universities. Published by Appleton-Crofts in its distinguished Century Psychology Series, the text enjoyed wide circulation. The editor of the series was Dr. Richard M. Elliot, a prestigious psychologist from the University of Minnesota who knew Walters from her days as a graduate student.

The versatility and depth of Walters's intellectual capacity were further demonstrated in her edited work *Readings in Psychology,* published in 1963, which makes available 121 readings, divided into the following thirteen categories: the Science of Psychology; Nature and Nurture; Growth and Development; The Human Organism; Emotion and Motivation; Personality, Adjustment, and Mental Health; Sensation and Perception; Learning, Retention, and Thinking; Individual Difference; Abilities and Aptitudes; Volition; Trends and Viewpoints in Psychology; Psychology and Religion. The vast array of articles offers one of the most comprehensive series of psychology readings ever complied.[19]

The excerpts are from the leading psychologists of that period, including Theodor Adorno (Authoritarianism), Gordon Allport (Personality), Edwin G. Boring (Nature of Psychology), John Dollard (Frustration-Aggression), Viktor Frankl (Logotherapy), Sigmund Freud (Psychoanalysis), Eric Fromm (Ethics), Karen Horney (Psychoanalysis), Abraham Maslow (Enculturation), Rollo May (Freedom), Ashley Montagu (Animal Development), O. Hobart Mowrer (Learning), Gardner Murphy (History of Psychology), Vance Packard (Advertising), and B. F. Skinner (Operant Conditioning).

At the same time, Walters offers passages from the writings of leading Catholic thinkers of that time: Magda Arnold, Anne Anastasi, Charles Curran, John C. Ford, Agostino Gemelli, George Klubertanz, Johann Lindworsky, Noel Mailloux, Dom Thomas Verner Moore, Robert Odenwald, James E. Royce, Alexander Schneiders, Karl Stern, and James VanderVeldt. The last of the book's selected readings is the address Pope Pius XII gave to psychotherapists in 1953. It should not be surprising that Walters chose to conclude her book with this passage since it is a crucial statement by the pope supporting the work of psychotherapists and even, within certain guidelines, the work of psychoanalysts. Moreover, she begins the book with a statement from the pope to Catholic intellectuals and students:

> You must indeed take part, whenever there are conflicts in the world of thought, now that the minds of men are attempting to face the problems of man and nature in the new dimensions in which they will confront us from now onwards. . . . If you are to make your share in this work . . . are you not obliged indeed to establish yourselves at the very core of the intellectual movement of today after the pattern of Christ?[20]

Walters considered psychology the "very core of the intellectual movement of today." The book's introduction and editorial comments reveal a great deal about her approach to psychology. She asserts the classical Thomistic position that there is no incompatibility between the truths of science and those of religion. There had been, nevertheless, since the Enlightenment, considerable conflict between science and religion. And as we saw earlier in this book, the emerging science of psychology had more than its share of battles with Catholicism. Cognizant of these controversies, Walters asserts, and her work demonstrates, that psychology had become a multifaceted discipline. Its complexity and its maturation as a discipline had made it less easy a target for theologians. At the same time, however, throughout her work she raises questions and points out the limitations of some of the selected theorists and their writings.

Mental Health Institutes

Walters was on the board of the St. John's Mental Health Institute from 1954 to 1971 and served as a seminar director during the summers of 1954 and 1956. Interestingly enough, no women were allowed to attend the seminars until 1971. Walters had something to do with the change. In a note to the director she voiced her strong views on the subject: "It seems to me that the Institute *must* catch up with the dynamics of women's liberation as well as with socio-cultural changes that make much of its traditional subject matter hopelessly passé and middle class."[21] Within two summers the majority of the participants at the Institute were women.

In the late 1950s Walters and her community at St. Catherine's profited from the relative proximity of the St. John's Summer Institute in Collegeville. For several years she would invite the speakers who were attending the Institute to spend some time at St. Catherine's as well. Under Walters's direction such figures as Leo Bartemeier, Gregory Zilboorg, and others presented seminars similar to those offered to the clergymen eighty miles up the road at St. John's. As a consequence, mother superiors, formation directors, and other influential sisters gained psychological insight into religious life. Later in the summers of 1961, 1963, and 1964 she coordinated workshops at Marquette University for administrators of religious formation programs for religious sisters. These programs and institutes helped to seed the ground for the major changes in the lives of American women religious that came within a few years.

Professor and National Presenter

While considered throughout her career to be a demanding teacher, Walters was also popular with students and a skilled motivator. Several former students describe her as having been challenging as well as creative, at times using "offbeat" teaching methods. Walters absorbed ideas from many disciplines and enthusiastically expressed them in her classes. One former student described her:

> An avid reader, she sometimes came to class carrying several books that seemed unrelated, initially, to the course. One might be a novel; another a recent tome in political science; a third might be in the visual arts. She seemed to have read everything. She would often deliver monologues on what she was reading, report on projects on which she was working. She lighted up the classroom and your mind by her brilliance and intellectual stimulation.[22]

She would describe current topical books and encourage students to go to the library and read them. One student noted that when she did so, Walters had already taken them out![23] An energetic and engaging speaker during her more than fifty years of professional ministry, Walters gave an estimated four hundred lectures, seminars, and workshops.[24] Her audiences ranged from the professional to the imprisoned, from the institutional to the institutionalized. Early in her career, as Walters moved into her profession, her talks chiefly occurred in the classroom and university setting. Her reputation soon spread. Her professional credentials as an experimental and a clinical psychologist were rare among Catholic women, much less women religious. What made Walters all the more special was her charismatic energy; she was even asked to host her own television show. During an era when Bishop Fulton Sheen commanded a large national audience on network television, Walters had a series of television programs that introduced psychology to a viewing audience in the Twin Cities. With a grant of $35,000 from the Ford Foundation Walters pioneered televised classes in psychology in 1958 and 1959. The courses "Psychology of

Mental Health" and "First Course in Psychology" allowed interested view-
ers to receive academic credit from several colleges. The show succeeded
in bringing psychology into the living room and also into the convent.
Through television and tapes as well as institutes and professional speaking engagements Walters introduced psychological concepts and insights
into religious communities of sisters around the nation.

In 1959 Walters spoke at a summer gathering of religious women superiors at the University of Notre Dame along with psychologists Fr. William
Bier, S.J., and Fr. Charles Curran and psychiatrist Fr. William Devlin, S.J.
She addressed the topic "The Superior and the Personal Development of
the Subject-Religious." During the six-day conference Walters gave a presentation each day on the theme of "Conditioning Environmental Factors:
The Constructive and Destructive Influences in the Religious, Professional,
and Related Areas." Her presentations brought contemporary psychology
into dialogue with religious life and impressed upon her listeners the significance of incorporating psychological constructs into religious formation.
For example, Walters used Abraham Maslow's construct of "hierarchy of
needs."[25]

These and other talks brought Walters into increasing national prominence among American Catholic women religious. In 1960 she became the
executive secretary of the Sisters Formation Conference.

Executive Secretary of the Sisters Formation Conference

Walters's four-year tenure as the executive secretary of the Sisters Formation Conference (1960–64) gave her enormous influence on religious life
during a time of seismic transition in the life of women religious and the
Catholic Church in general. The Conference itself began as the Sisters Formation Movement during the late 1940s, when the expansion of American
Catholic education brought with it the demand for better education of its
teachers, most of whom were sisters. Pope Pius XII spoke to this need in
1952 at an international conference of the leaders of women's religious
communities when he called for an *aggiornamento,* that is, a renewal and
updating of religious life. In 1953, when it was established as a committee in the National Catholic Educational Association, the "Movement" was
renamed the Sisters Formation Conference.

When *aggiornamento* was widely encouraged by Pius XII's successor,
Pope John XXIII, and the Second Vatican Council which he had called,
Walters was in a unique position to initiate programs for renewal and
updating of religious life. As the executive secretary she set up and coordinated regional and national gatherings of women's religious throughout
the United States. She corresponded with and met a host of leaders of

women religious communities as well as promoted dialogue with Episcopalian communities of women religious. In addition, together with her colleague and friend, Sr. Ritamary Bradley, she visited women's religious communities in Latin America.

What her friend B. F. Skinner had heard was not an exaggeration. "I have been told you are the most powerful woman in the Catholic hierarchy." Some of her liberal leanings were not without controversy. This became especially evident in 1964 when several religious authorities succeeded in moving the Conference out of the jurisdiction of the Washington-based National Catholic Educational Association into the Vatican-based Conference of Major Religious Superiors. This meant that the Conference would have to have its actions and writings approved by Vatican authorities. Walters and Sr. Ritamary Bradley (the editor of the Conference's newsletter) believed they could not abide such interference from Rome and left their leadership positions in the Sisters Formation Conference.[26] The loss of two of the Conference's leaders signaled a major shift in the Conference's approach to issues, and it became less progressive. Moreover, the manner in which Srs. Annette and Ritamary were singled out for criticism by some of the superiors of women religious communities was shrouded in secrecy. Her departure from such a prominent position must have been a difficult transition for Walters. She returned to St. Catherine's for the academic year 1964–65. Her sudden departure and return to St. Catherine's were accompanied with speculation that she had experienced a nervous breakdown. The rumor was later denied in writing by her religious superior.[27]

Walters's responsibilities during her leadership years with the Conference moved her more deeply into the changes happening in religious communities of women in the United States and elsewhere. They also required her to restrict her professional activities in academia and in clinical psychology, and consequently she lost touch with some of the currents and trends emerging in professional psychology. After she returned to St. Catherine's, she spent a sabbatical year reentering the academic and clinical world of psychology. Then in 1966 she was invited to establish a psychology department at another women's college, St. Ambrose College in Davenport, Iowa.

At St. Ambrose Walters followed closely the emergence of the feminist movement and become a strong advocate for many of its principles for women in the Catholic Church. Her activism led her to became a leader in the National Coalition of American Nuns, to advocate the ordination of women in the Catholic Church, and to identify herself as a member of the noncanonical Sisters for Christian Community, which she did without relinquishing her vows as a member of the Sisters of St. Joseph, which canonically she could not do. Her progressivism led some to criticize her influence and leadership.[28]

During her years as a professor at St. Ambrose (1965–77), Walters also followed closely the growing research on values formation and religious development. Together with her colleague Sr. Ritamary, Sr. Annette published an article on religious behavior and motivation.[29] In 1977 she received a grant from the Quinlan Foundation to write a book on values development. Intending to write the book at Yale University, she applied for a sabbatical from her responsibilities at St. Ambrose in 1976 when she turned sixty-five. Her request was denied. Perceiving the denial as an instance of ageism and sexism, she challenged St. Ambrose's decision in court. The court procedures began in January of 1978. By this time Walters had been diagnosed with a cancer that some say was brought on by the stress surrounding the adverse decision and the case.[30] A month after the trial started Walters was hospitalized and died on February 22, 1978. After several years of appeals the case of *Walters v. the College of St. Ambrose* was decided in her favor.

Sr. Annette Walters as a woman religious, as an educator, and as a psychologist bore witness to her Catholic faith with great intelligence. From her days as a young woman who chose to become a Catholic and then to enter religious life through her days of studying experimental psychology with some of the great minds of the era, Walters's life may be seen as a trajectory toward greater influence and involvement in some of the important concerns of her day. Organizing and participating in numerous psychological conferences and institutes, using television to communicate psychological principles, teaching several generations of college students, promoting new ideas among American women religious during an era of major changes, all of this led her to be identified as an advocate for justice and civil rights whether for others or for herself. She died as she had lived, courageously engaged in the intellectual and social challenges of her faith and American culture.

Chapter 6

Signs of the Times

American Catholicism
before the Second Vatican Council

The period between the Second World War and the Second Vatican Council has often been viewed as a conservative era for American Catholics. With the papacy of Pope Pius XII dominating most of those eighteen years, and with the leadership of such archbishops as Cardinal Spellman of New York, Cardinals Dougherty and O'Hara of Philadelphia, and Cardinal McIntyre of Los Angeles, Roman Catholics in the United States were expected simply to pray and obey. It would be a superficial analysis, however, to conclude that only conservative currents flowed during these years in which the social and economic lives of American Catholics changed considerably. The Second World War and its aftermath brought significant changes in the ways American Catholics fit into American culture. In sheer numbers American Catholics had become a major force. James Hennesey notes that between 1912 and 1962 the number of American Catholics nearly tripled from 15,015,569 to 43,851,538, and during the nation's baby boom there was an increase of 12 million between 1954 and 1963.[1] Moreover, the Catholic contribution to the successful war efforts diminished prejudices toward Catholics and served to further their assimilation into American culture.

At the start of the twentieth century Catholic institutions of learning, from elementary schools to universities, set their course largely in response to the needs of an immigrant population. As the century progressed, Catholic institutions improved and multiplied. With fewer Catholic immigrants entering the United States than at the turn of the century and with the previous immigrants more assimilated into American culture, the Catholic institutional focus shifted toward education, including higher education. In addition, the GI Bill provided necessary financial resources for Catholics to attend colleges and universities. Consequently, as noted by Gleason, between 1940 and 1960 the number of Catholic colleges and universities increased by one-fifth from 193 to 231, their faculties went from 13,142 to 24,255 (more than an 80 percent increase), and enrollments almost tripled from just less than 162,000 to more than 426,000.[2] Like many other veterans of World War II and later of the Korean War, thousands of American Catholics used the GI Bill to attend college and graduate schools. The influx of students was seen also in the increase of doctorates awarded by Catholic universities, which by 1954–55 had risen to 252 (an increase of almost 150 percent from 103 in 1939–40).

Catholic University with its sizeable population of priests and nuns awarded the most (77), followed by Fordham (57), St. Louis University (38), Notre Dame (32), and Georgetown (24).[3] In graduate psychology, Catholic University maintained its premier position among Catholic graduate schools and on February 1, 1948, was one of the first clinical programs in the nation to receive accreditation from the American Psychological Association. Fordham University received the accreditation three weeks later, and its department would eventually supersede Catholic University's in reputation among graduate psychology programs.

A distinctive Catholic culture emerged at a variety of levels. Its growth was represented in the increase at all levels of Catholic education. For instance, according to one influential commentator on Catholic higher education, a "Catholic life of the Mind" existed in which a Catholic professor's academic life of teaching and research had a "sense of totality" and a "sense of tradition" that made Catholic higher education distinctive.[4]

Catholic culture was evident also in the area of religious vocations. Catholic seminaries and convents enjoyed an upsurge in numbers of applicants. It was not uncommon for religious communities of men or women to accept more than fifty applicants a year. The establishment and growth of Catholic organizations gave further evidence of a distinctive Catholic way of life. Previously Catholics had banded together in organizations such as the Knights of Columbus to extend the practice of their faith and were encouraged by their church leaders to join labor unions to secure their rights. As Catholics became more educated they began to join professional organizations. Edward Pace helped to organize the American Catholic Philosophical Association in 1926. Similar organizations included the Catholic Hospital Association (1915), the American Catholic Historical Association (1919), and the Catholic Anthropological Conference (1926). Catholic organizations were founded for biblical scholars (1936), sociologists (1938), canon lawyers (1939), economists (1941), and theologians (1946). In 1949, through the leadership of Fr. William Bier, S.J., the American Catholic Psychological Association was established.

The growth of Catholic institutions allowed the Catholic moral voice to be heard in American society, especially regarding the rise of secularism. According to Gleason, secularism meant "the practical exclusion of

God from human thinking and living" and involved "the process whereby traditional religion had been displaced by science in the sphere of knowledge, and the church had been displaced by the state as the most important shaper of social life."[5] Through its institutions and leaders, American Catholicism fought a battle against such secularistic tendencies. As Gleason further notes, shortly after the war the American Catholic bishops issued several statements indicating their concern about the development of faith within American society: "The Christian in Action" (1947), "The Christian Family" (1949), and "The Child: Citizen of Two Worlds" (1950).[6]

The American Catholic Church's quarrels with secularism were evident in its opposition to certain forms of psychological thought, especially psychoanalysis. During the period between 1945 and 1962 the professions of American psychology and psychiatry enjoyed immense growth. In psychology it was a time when the neobehaviorism of B. F. Skinner (1904–91) and Clark Hull (1884–1952) with its deterministic systems of conditioned learning was particularly influential. The behaviorist school was seen as antithetical to Judeo-Christian views of freedom. By this time, however, psychology as a profession had become so diversified that behaviorist positions did not warrant the Catholic Church's public opposition.

The Thomistic revival initiated by Pope Leo XIII in 1879 continued in the United States during the years following World War II. Patrick Carey estimates that in the years following the war more than 50 percent of the philosophy professors at Catholic higher educational institutions identified themselves as neo-Thomists, which helps explain how Catholic college degrees were identified with Thomistic thought.[7] This influence was reflected in the popularity of such Catholic journals as *The Modern Schoolman, Thought,* and *The Thomist.* While Thomistic thought flourished, however, efforts to synthesize Thomistic philosophy with academic psychology to form a "neo-Thomistic psychology" began to wane.

In his *History of American Psychology* (1952) A. A. Roback devoted a chapter to neoscholastic psychology and critically appraised its values. He named two primary reasons why most psychologists neglected neoscholastic psychology. First, most psychologists eschewed the Thomistic emphasis on finding a place for the soul in psychology. For them the "soul" is a construct that cannot be quantifiably proven. Second, many psychologists, like other scientists, were still rankled by the church's dogmatic silencing of predecessors such as Galileo and Copernicus and by its burning at the stake Giordano Bruno and other scientific thinkers. Any science related to the Catholic Church was viewed with suspicion by most scientists.[8]

Roback attempts to give neoscholastic psychology a fair hearing by providing an overview of the psychology of Thomas Aquinas and citing the work of Pace and Moore, but he finds such psychology quite limited. He says that dissertations produced at Catholic University under Moore and others had both adequate and inadequate standards. They demonstrate "a broad survey of the literature and elaborate statistical treatment of the somewhat meager results, on the one hand, and a profuse citation of the literature, on the other hand, in lieu of delving into the core of the problem at issue."[9]

Roback's critical analysis perhaps sounded the death knell for neoscholastic psychology. Signs of its demise could be seen in the movement toward mainstream psychology by the psychology department at the Catholic University, which coincided with Moore's retirement from the department in 1947.[10] But neoscholastic psychology was not the only expression of Thomistic thought to fall under suspicion. By the mid-1950s Catholic philosophers and theologians were questioning some underlying assumptions and principles of neoscholastic thought, and the seeds of their efforts bore fruit in the aftermath of the Second Vatican Council.

From an intellectual standpoint the period between the Second World War and the Second Vatican Council may be divided into two phases, which reflect the ways in which academic and clinical psychology were perceived and how they contributed to the growth of Catholic involvement in the disciplines and the professions of psychology. In the first phase, American Catholic intellectuals, continuing the neoscholastic revival, were conservative because of the threat of encroaching communism and cautious as a result of Pope Pius XII's encyclical *Humani Generis*.[11] Moreover, Catholic intellectuals in philosophy and theology were largely dependent on the scholarship of European schools. If a young Catholic man or (infrequently) a young Catholic woman was thought to have the potential for such scholarship he or she was generally sent to a European university such as Louvain or the Gregorian. Only on rare occasions were Catholic priests, sisters, and brothers interested in philosophy or theology permitted to attend the great secular universities of the United States.[12]

A second phase of Catholic intellectual life developed during the decade leading up to the Council when intellectuals, Catholic and non-Catholic alike, cited a paucity of intellectual accomplishments among American Catholics and challenged Catholic leaders and institutions to revise their standards. Fr. John Cavanaugh, a former president of Notre Dame, stated that American Catholics were not "producing anywhere near their proportion of leaders."[13] Sr. Annette Walters, speaking before the National Catholic Educational Association in 1956, cited "a complete absence of an intellectual tradition in our American Catholic population."[14] But the scholar who most significantly sparked controversy over the dearth of Catholic scholarship was a history professor at Catholic University, Fr. John Tracy Ellis.[15]

In an address before the Catholic Commission on Intellectual and Cultural Affairs in 1955, Ellis made critical observations about the state of Catholic intellectual life in America. He cited studies which revealed that very few American Catholic scholars were in *Who's Who in America, American Men of Science,* or even the Pontifical Academy of Sciences. Moreover, while several Catholic women's colleges were included among the best women's colleges, not one Catholic university was listed among the top fifty universities of the United States.[16]

Ellis found a primary reason for the dearth of American Catholic scholarship in the deep anti-Catholic prejudice that for decades had existed in the United States, especially during the nineteenth century. He noted that many American Catholics were either immigrants themselves or were within two generations of having immigrated. Archbishop Cushing was cited by Ellis:

> In all the American hierarchy, resident in the United States, there is not known to me one Bishop, Archbishop or Cardinal whose father or mother was a college graduate. Every one of our Bishops and Archbishops is the son of a working man and a working man's wife.[17]

Ellis then listed four internal reasons for the paucity of Catholic scholarship in America. First was the betrayal of the church's tradition of humanities and the liberal arts. Catholic universities established graduate schools of engineering, business, and nursing, which depleted their resources for the humanities and scholastic philosophy. Ellis believed that such schools were inferior imitations of programs at secular institutions.

A second reason was the stiff competition among Catholic graduate schools, which exhausted their limited resources and condemned them to mediocrity. Ellis thought it wiser to allocate the resources into several rather than many institutions and to offer quality humanities programs like those at the University of Chicago, the University of Virginia, and Princeton University.[18]

Ellis further blamed the limited quality of Catholic scholarship on a piety that stressed otherworldliness, which he believed tends to an intellectual pride. And as the fourth internal reason, Ellis pointed to the overemphasis in Catholic education on moral development to the neglect of intellectual development.[19]

Ellis concluded his manifesto by asserting that among American Catholics there had existed a "pervading spirit of separatism" and that they "have suffered from the timidity that characterizes minority groups, from the effects of a ghetto they have fostered, and, too, from a sense of inferiority induced by their consciousness of the inadequacy of Catholic scholarship."[20]

Ellis's speculative arguments were subsequently followed by a socio-logical analysis, *American Catholic Dilemma* (1958), by Thomas O'Dea of Fordham. O'Dea tended to support Ellis and found five major concerns hindering the advance of intellectual life among American Catholics: intellectual formalism, authoritarianism, clericalism, moralism, and defensiveness.[21]

For O'Dea there were two types of formalism in the Catholic milieu. First, he cited an intellectual formalism in which "demonstration replaces research, abstractions replace experience, formulae replace content, and rationalistic elaboration replaces genuine ontological insight." O'Dea saw a second type of formalism in the way in which Catholic intellectuals viewed the world as "finished" and drew the conclusion that all things are obvious in their essence and meaning.

O'Dea described authoritarianism as the way in which ecclesiastical leaders, misinterpreting their roles as many Catholic leaders did, tended to impose solutions on complex problems simply through formal statements, thus closing debate once a problem was placed in its proper category.

The third concern listed by O'Dea, clericalism, involved the maximizing of the ecclesiastical perspective so that the worldview of the Catholic prelate was given priority over anything secular. Moralism, the fourth concern, was described as a neo-Jansenistic tendency in which all aspects of creation are interpreted in terms of morality and all activities evaluated as possible near occasions of sin. Finally, O'Dea attributed a defensive rigidity among Catholics to the fact that many American immigrants came from a long tradition as a minority prejudiced against or even persecuted.

The efforts of Ellis, O'Dea, and others who worked on the Catholic Commission of Intellectual and Cultural Affairs challenged the Catholic academic community toward greater competence and excellence. Their challenges served as harbinger of drastic changes at the Second Vatican Council and throughout the 1960s. The paucity of Catholic scholarship that Ellis and O'Dea described was symptomatic of the dependency of American Catholic philosophers and theologians on European scholarship.

European scholarship tended to view psychology and psychoanalysis differently from many American Catholic critics. French Catholic psychoanalyst Roland Dalbiez, for example, in *Psychoanalytical Method and the Doctrine of Freud,* clearly distinguished psychoanalytic method from psychoanalytic philosophy and from the personality of Freud. In his critical evaluation of Freud's work, Dalbiez argued persuasively for the contribution the Freudian psychoanalytic method could make to the understanding of human nature, though he recognized that "psychoanalysis leaves the fundamental problems of the human soul where it found them."[22] Before its translation into English, Dalbiez's work circulated through Catholic intellectual circles in Europe and influenced the noted French Thomistic scholar Jacques Maritain, who took up some of Dalbiez's arguments in an essay entitled "Freudianism and Psychoanalysis." Maritain popularized Dalbiez's distinction among the psychoanalytic method, Freudian psychology, and Freudian philosophy.[23] Such a distinction had wide appeal among American Catholic thinkers.

In addition to Dalbiez, other Europeans whose writings led to a more positive attitude toward psychoanalytic thought among American Catholics were the Italian Franciscan priest Agostino Gemelli and the Louvain professor Joseph Nuttin. Gemelli's *Psychoanalysis Today* (1955) was favorably received in America, as was Nuttin's *Psychoanalysis and Personality* (1953).[24] The latter book was one of the first works by a Catholic author to recognize the changes going on in psychoanalytic theory. In "Second Thoughts on Freud," Joseph Donceel found the Freudian paradigm replete with "errors, exaggerations and distortions," and as a consequence he rejected the Freudian system of psychoanalysis in its pure form.[25] Assisted by the interpretive work of Dalbiez, Karen Horney, and others, Donceel found that psychoanalysis "becomes gradually more acceptable":

> Lifted out of their materialistic context, pruned of their exaggerations, quite a number of Freudian discoveries can be reinterpreted in a sense which fits them neatly into a Christian conception of man, not only as confirmations of what was known before, but also as new and deeper insights into some aspects of man's nature.[26]

An essay by the French Catholic writer André Godin represented a significant development for American Catholic intellectual life. In "Psychotherapy: A New Humanism" (1952), Godin critically reviewed five works that he believed typified the emerging influence of psychology on American values and that he considered to signal the birth of a new humanism.[27] Godin said that the works of Bruno Bettleheim (*Love Is Not Enough,* 1950), Carl Rogers (*Client-Centered Therapy,* 1950), and Karen Horney (*Neurosis and Human Growth,* 1950) contain important although morally truncated psychological insights about human freedom.[28] He found them to be contributions to a psychologically informed "art of living," which he saw as the new humanism. Godin then considered two other psychological works which he believed recognized the moral and religious dimensions that the previous works lacked. The inclusion of *Counseling in Catholic Life and Education* (1952) by the Catholic psychologist Rev. Charles A. Curran and *Pastoral Counseling* (1951) by the Methodist pastoral counselor Rev. Carroll A. Wise alongside writings by better-known psychotherapists suggests that psychotherapy had begun to be translated into the pastoral realm.[29] In contrast to articles on psychology published in the *Ecclesiastical Review* and the *Homiletic and Pastoral Review* reported in the previous chapter, American Catholic scholars and priests were beginning to find broader and deeper resources through which to assimilate psychological insights. For Godin, Curran's book fulfilled a need long felt by Catholic priests and educators to adapt psychological insights to pastoral needs. Godin's favorable review of Wise's work started a trend in which psychological works by Protestants were recognized and recommended for Catholic pastoral use.

In addition to the works of Curran and Wise there appeared during the period between the Second World War and the Second Vatican Council other texts by European and American Catholics that interpreted the insights of psychology, psychiatry, and psychoanalysis for pastoral use. One of the first was *Psychiatry and Catholicism* (1952) by the Franciscan psychologist and ethicist Fr. James VanderVeldt and the psychiatrist Robert P. Odenwald, a convert from Judaism.[30] VanderVeldt, born in the Netherlands, was a psychology and philosophy professor at Catholic University. Odenwald became Moore's successor as director of the Child Guidance Center at Catholic University. According to Archbishop Patrick O'Boyle of Washington, writing in the foreword, their work "satisfies an urgent need" as they "present a safe and scientific synthesis of modern psychiatry and Christian ethics."[31]

Gregory Zilboorg

Perhaps no other psychoanalyst opened the Catholic mind to psychoanalytic thought and technique as forcefully and with as much controversy as Gregory Zilboorg. Born on Christmas Day, 1890, in Russia of Jewish Orthodox parents, Zilboorg for the last twenty years of his life persistently struggled to make Freud palatable to religious appetites, especially Christian. Beginning in 1939 with an article entitled "The Fundamental Conflict with Psychoanalysis," published in the *International Journal of Psychoanalysis,* Zilboorg worked out a systematic interpretation of Freud's work that minimized the influence of Freud's atheism on psychoanalytic theory and led religious scholars, especially Catholics, to be more willing to converse with other writers on psychoanalytic theory and technique. Then in *Freud and Religion* (1958) Zilboorg responded to Ernest Jones's three-volume biography of Freud by arguing against Jones's position that atheism was essential to psychoanalysis. Zilboorg asserted "that Freud utilized the premises of the psychoanalysis which he founded in order to justify his atheism, which seems to have presented for him a greater inner problem than one might at first suspect."[32]

In a series of essays collected and edited by his wife in the posthumous work *Freud and Religion,* Zilboorg elaborated detailed methods by which scholars, among them Catholic writers, could develop better and more nuanced understandings of Freud and psychoanalysis. Zilboorg's world was not confined to psychoanalysis; he was acquainted with the work of Thomistic scholars such as the Dominicans Noel Mailloux in Canada, Albert Plé in France, and A. Leonard in Belgium. He also influenced a generation of Jesuit scholars, since for several years during the 1950s he presented courses at Woodstock College in Maryland, where he befriended Jesuit theologians John Courtney Murray and Gustave Weigel, who were major American Catholic figures during the Second Vatican Council. His *History of Medical Psychology* (1941)[33] and numerous articles on various aspects of psychoanalysis made Zilboorg's subsequent conversion to Catholicism appear to represent not only a psychoanalyst's acceptance of Catholicism but Catholicism's acceptance of Freudian psychoanalysis, at least as presented by Zilboorg.

During the 1940s Zilboorg befriended Thomas Verner Moore, and it was Moore who, shortly before his retirement from Catholic University in 1947, proposed that Zilboorg be considered as his successor as the chair of Catholic University's department of psychology and psychiatry. However, this was before Zilboorg divorced his first wife and subsequently married his research assistant. Because of these actions such a sensitive position at Catholic University was not offered to him. At the time Zilboorg was a Quaker. It was not until 1954 that Zilboorg, lured by Catholicism's long tradition of scholarship and having obtained an annulment of his first marriage, entered the Catholic Church.[34] The same year, having established himself as one of the leading writers on psychoanalysis of his day, Zilboorg was invited to participate at the first summer seminars of the St. John's Institute.

St. John's Summer Institute

In 1953, the year of the pope's remarks to the International Congress of Catholic Psychotherapists, Joseph Quinlan, a chaplain at Hastings State Hospital in Minnesota, and two Benedictine monks, Fr. Walter Reger and Fr. Alexius Portz, proposed to Abbot Baldwin Dworschak of St. John's the idea of "getting some people together to talk about mental health problems."[35] The idea was enthusiastically accepted by the abbot and the St. John's University Board of Regents. In October 1953 plans were made to open the Institute in the summer of 1954. According to Fr. Portz, the Institute's first director, the purpose of the Institute was

> to assist clergymen to become better acquainted with emotional problems, more sensitive to their proper role and relationship to people

mentally disturbed, more capable of dealing with individual problems, and more qualified to give assistance and make referrals in the
prevention of mental illness.[36]

The Institute received the approval of the local ordinary, Bishop Peter
Bartholome of St. Cloud, and generous financial support from the Hamm
Foundation of St. Paul, Minnesota. A unique attribute of the enterprise
was that from the start the Institute sought to become ecumenical in scope
during an era when religious denominations often defined themselves in
terms of their differences rather than their commonalities. The Institute
had an ecumenical board that included two Catholic psychiatrists, a teaching sister with a doctorate in psychology, an Episcopalian and a Jewish
psychiatrist, and a Lutheran psychologist. The interfaith board set for
themselves the goal of having at least 25 percent of the Institute's participants drawn from non-Catholic denominations. According to Schwiebert's
report to the Hamm Foundation during the first summer 13 percent of the
participants were non-Catholic, but by 1959 the Institute reached its goal
of 25 percent and by 1962 had an all time high of 40 percent non-Catholic
participants. Over the years the Protestant participants came chiefly from
the Lutheran, Episcopal, Methodist, and Presbyterian denominations and
mostly from the Midwestern states. Throughout the Institute's life only a
handful of Jewish clergy attended, and women were not invited to attend
until 1971.[37]

The fact that the Institute was at St. John's meant that it was situated
in the farm heartland and hence distant from Catholic urban controversies.
The Benedictines of St. John's Abbey had established themselves as leaders
of Catholic liturgical reform. Led by Fr. Virgil Michel, Godfrey Diekmann,
and other monks, the university's community became a progressive source
for liturgical change, advocating innovations in the celebration of the Mass
long before the Second Vatican Council permitted the practice.

The Institute attracted an assortment of outstanding psychiatrists of the
era, Catholic and non-Catholic. Between 1954 and 1958, of the Institute's
forty-two faculty, six were past presidents of the American Psychiatric Association and one was past president of the American Orthopsychiatric
Association. During the three decades of its existence the Institute's faculty
included such illustrious members as Nathan Ackerman, M.D., Leo Bartemeier, M.D., Francis Braceland, M.D., Dana Farnsworth, M.D., Francis
Gerty, M.D., Rev. James Gill, S.J., M.D., Hyman Lippman, M.D., Noel
Mailloux, O.P., Ph.D., Elvin Semrad, M.D., Karl Stern, M.D., Sr. Annette
Walters, Ph.D., and Gregory Zilboorg, M.D. Given such a faculty, it was
easy to attract participants; between 1954 and 1973 more than twenty-five
hundred clergy had participated in the workshops.[38]

The Institute consisted of three consecutive week-long workshops involving lectures and seminars. Each session would convene some hundred participants on Monday, who would depart on the following Friday for their weekend services. The general theme for most of the workshops was "Psychotherapy and Pastoral Care." Beginning in 1963, advanced programs were instituted that were organized around specific topics such as marriage and the family.

The Institute's staff was instructed to cover those areas of mental health that were most relevant to pastoral care. They were expected to avoid issues that were too theoretical, especially ideas that might stir philosophical or theological controversies. According to Richard Sipe, who served as the Institute's director from 1965 to 1969, the orientation of most of the presentations tended to be Freudian or neo-Freudian.[39] This should not be surprising, since throughout the period of the Institute's life the psychoanalytic approach was predominant in most clinical training programs.

Boyd et al. reported that for participants some of the Institute's major benefits were the following:

They learn to recognize the outstanding characteristics of the different kinds of emotional illness.

They come to appreciate the value of listening attentively to their disturbed parishioners.

They learn how to refer patients who require psychiatric care.

They learn how to deal with the hostility of their sick parishioners.

They learn how to become better counselors through an understanding of ego therapy, especially methods of support and clarification.

They learn about the work of social agencies.

They learn the principles of personality development and of the genetic factors that produce family problems, disorganization, and delinquency.

They learn how unconscious factors influence the capacity of individuals to give and receive affection, relate themselves to others, and to enjoy the work they do.

They come to recognize the unconscious components in parents that force them to keep their children in a state of neurotic dependency or acting out in delinquency.

They learn that often, as a result of psychotherapy, the parishioner is able for the first time to accept religion and prayer, having been rid of an unconscious need to suffer and not be forgiven.

More than anything else, they learn that the workshop is not designed to make them fellow therapists and that to diagnose and treat emotionally sick people requires many years of intensive training.[40]

The program drew rave reviews and was featured at an American Psychiatric Association conference. In 1958 Boyd et al. published an article in the *American Journal of Psychiatry* describing the Institute and its programs. In addition, Farnsworth and Braceland edited a book entitled *Psychiatry, the Clergy and Pastoral Counseling* (1969),[41] which contained a number of the Institute's presentations. The book was used extensively in many Catholic colleges and seminaries and led to a further assimilation of psychological attitudes by clergy. As discussed elsewhere in this text, Thomas Merton, the Trappist monk and writer, attended one of the Institute's sessions in the summer of 1956.[42]

According to Schwiebert, the Institute made several major contributions to the dialogue between religion and mental health. First, the Institute's interdenominational character foreshadowed and facilitated future cooperative efforts that became commonplace after the Second Vatican Council. Second, the Institute pioneered a new approach to mental health education. In this respect the Institute addressed the misconceptions of many that, with a little knowledge, a pastor could be an expert in mental health. It also developed a forum that fostered a greater understanding and trust between religious leaders and psychotherapists. Third, the Institute enabled its pastoral participants to see more clearly the possibilities and limits of their role in dealing with the mental heath problems of parishioners. While developing the skills necessary to address certain needs, they were able to see the limits of their help. They learned when they could be of assistance in the early stages of emotional illness and when they should refer at the more advanced stages. Finally and for Schwiebert most importantly, the Institute provided a means for collaboration between clergy and psychiatrists that continued long after the workshops.[43]

The Menninger Clinic

Besides the St. John's Institute, collaboration between clergy and mental health professionals took place on a much smaller scale at the Menninger Clinic in Topeka, Kansas. Beginning in the late 1940s Karl Menninger invited a small group of clergy to receive basic training for an eleven-month period. Like the Institute, the Menninger Clinic brought clergy of different faiths together but, unlike the Institute's program, the Menninger Clinic provided a more intensive form of training to move the participants beyond the introductory level of pastoral counseling skills. Under the guidance of such figures as Karl Menninger and Paul Pruyser, the Menninger Clinic developed an outstanding reputation for providing a forum where mutual concerns of religion and mental health found common ground and collaboration on a variety of issues.[44] The Menninger Clinic still enjoys such a reputation today.

The programs at the Menninger Clinic and at the St. John's Institute of Mental Health went a long way toward augmenting understanding and collaboration between religious and mental health leaders. Sipe noted that at the Menninger Clinic conversation between the two groups took place in a psychiatric setting, while at St. John's it was in a monastic environment.[45] The contrasting environments demonstrated that the gap between the fields had narrowed and the suspicion and hostility had been reduced considerably. As a consequence, efforts at bridge-building between religion and the various fields of psychology increased. One major manifestation of the success of such efforts was a symposium on religion and mental health held at the American Psychological Association's annual convention in 1957. The symposium proceedings, published in the *American Psychologist* two years later, indicated the growing influence of such Protestant pastoral leaders as Anton Boisen, Paul Johnson, and O. Hobart Mowrer.[46] The symposium also was a further boost to the efforts of Catholics such as Fr. William Bier and the organization that he helped to establish, the American Catholic Psychological Association.

Rev. Edward C. Pace, Ph.D. Archives of the Catholic University of America, General Photographic Collection. Used with permission.

Rev. Thomas Verner Moore, M.D. Archives of the Catholic University of America, General Photographic Collection. Used with permission.

Leo Bartemeier, M.D.
Used with permission.

Francis Braceland, M.D. Fabian Bachrach Photographers.
Used with permission.

Sr. Annette Walters, Ph.D.
1966. Archives of the Sisters
of St. Joseph, St. Paul, Minn.
Used with permission.

Sr. Annette Walters, Ph.D.
1978. Archives of the Sisters
of St. Joseph, St. Paul, Minn.
Used with permission.

Rev. William Bier. Edward Tarr Photographers, New York. Used with permission.

Magda Arnold, Ph.D.
Courtesy of Joan Arnold.
Used with permission.

Eugene Kennedy, Ph.D.
Loyola University Chicago
Archives: Photograph Collection.
Used with permission.

Rev. Adrian van Kaam, Ph.D.
Photo by Jonas. Copyright 1995.
All Rights Reserved.
Jonas Photography, Pittsburgh.
Used with permission.

The Jesuit Spiritual Center in Wernersville, Pa.
Courtesy of Rev. Mark Scalese, S.J. Used with permission.

Chapter 7

Paradigm Shifts

Catholicism and Psychology

Vatican II and Its Pastoral Psychological Consequences

On January 25, 1959, Pope John XXIII proclaimed his intention to convoke the church's Twenty-First Ecumenical Council. Little did he or anyone know when the Council convened on October 11, 1962, that such an initiative would lead to transformations not only within the Roman Catholic Church but in its relations with other religious bodies and with the rest of the world. Indeed, the initial plans drawn up by some of the church's conservative prelates were immediately changed and new ones developed. Moreover, progressive theologians such as Yves Congar, John Courtney Murray, and Karl Rahner, each of whom had formerly been held suspect by the Vatican curia, became some of the Council's *periti*, or theological advisors. When the Council's fourth and last session concluded on December 8, 1965, the bishops at the Council sensed that the Catholic Church had redefined its relations with the world. During its four sessions the Council issued four constitutions, nine decrees, and three declarations. The content of the sixteen documents and the process by which they were discussed by some twenty-five hundred Catholic bishops and dozens of observers from other faith traditions created a cataclysmic change that continues to reverberate through the church's institutions and structures. As the theologian Karl Rahner later stated: "It seems appropriate and justified to regard Vatican II as the first great official event in which the church came to be realized as *world*-church.... Something like a qualitative leap took place."[1]

The church's "qualitative leap" had implications for its local and global institutions as well as for those world structures with which it was involved. Perhaps nowhere was this more evident than in the United States, where the Council's decrees had a significant impact on the way in which the Catholic Church perceived itself and was perceived. In light of the Council's significance, then, it would be well to consider briefly some of the decrees.

Probably the most representative of all the documents of the Second Vatican Council was the Pastoral Constitution on the Church in the Mod-

ern World (*Gaudium et Spes*), in which the Council sought to establish a
new understanding of the church's role in the modern world. Promulgated
on December 7, 1965, the document describes the intimate relations between the church and humanity and calls for a mutual dialogue between
the church and the world. The Council addressed its message not only to
Catholics but to all human beings. Sensing the emergence of a new *Zeitgeist,* the Council presented in some detail its perception of the "signs of
the times" facing the church and the modern world. As noted in chapter 3,
the church previously saw itself as a bastion of Christ's truth against the
world. This was evident in the discordant spirit that emanated from the
First Vatican Council and in the *Syllabus of Errors* of Pope Pius IX. The
bishops who assembled at the Second Vatican Council, however, and the
two popes who presided over it, Pope John XXIII and Pope Paul VI, went
out of their way to proclaim a new relationship by updating the church's
thought and structures to encounter the modern world. The term *aggiornamento,* meaning "updating," summarized this encounter and became the
guiding principle of the Council.[2] Among other concerns such a conversation included a recognition of advances made by psychology and the social
sciences in helping human beings confront recent changes. As the Council
stated: "Advances in biology, psychology, and the social sciences not only
bring men hope of improved self-knowledge. In conjunction with techni-
cal methods, they are also helping men to exert direct influence on the life
of social groups."[3]

Such assertions are a long way from the suspicion toward psychology
and social sciences held earlier in the century. *Gaudium et Spes* addressed
the role and responsibilities of the Catholic Church and described ways
in which the church gives and receives help from the modern world.[4] The
document established a new vision for Catholics in their relations with the
world, which broke down the siege mentality that had existed since the
Reformation. The church even took into account the influence of the developmental and evolutionary theories of Marx, Darwin, and Freud when
it asserted: "Recent psychological research explains human activity more
profoundly. Historical studies make a signal contribution to bringing men
to see things in their changeable and evolutionary aspects."[5]

As part of the dialogue in which the church sought to engage the modern world, the Council set forth some of the shared concerns between itself
and the culture at large. Of special relevance was the insistence that the
church strive to harmonize culture with Christian teaching not only by
means of theology and philosophy but also through the arts and sciences.
For example, in its concern for a new approach to pastoral care, the document asserted: "Appropriate use must be made not only of theological
principles, but also of the findings of the secular sciences, *especially of psy-*

chology and sociology. Thus the faithful can be brought to live the faith in a more thorough and mature way [emphasis mine]."[6]

Gaudium et Spes had a significant impact on the Catholic understanding of the sacrament of marriage. It saw marriage as an "intimate partnership" rooted "in the conjugal covenant of irrevocable personal consent" and an act "whereby spouses mutually bestow and accept each other."[7] Furthermore, the document redefined the primary purpose of marriage. No longer was it only for the procreation and nurturance of children: "Marriage to be sure is not instituted solely for procreation. Rather, its very nature as an unbreakable compact between persons, and the welfare of the children, both demand that the mutual love of the spouses, too, be embodied in a rightly ordered manner, that it grow and ripen."[8]

A couple's "intimate partnership" in marriage was put on an equal footing with the procreation of children. One of the implications of this emphasis on a couple's "intimate partnership" was that the church's canon law accepted a psychological category in its juridical considerations. In 1983 the church issued a new code of canon law and made explicit this redefinition of marriage and its emphasis on the couple's "intimate partnership": "The matrimonial covenant, by which a man and a woman establish between themselves a partnership of the whole of life, is by its nature ordered toward the good of the spouses and the procreation and education of offspring."[9]

This insertion of the psychological category of "partnership" into the church's canon law had significant ramifications for the Catholic Church's marriage tribunals. This increased emphasis on the psychological served to redefine the rationale for granting annulments, for example, when there never existed the psychological conditions necessary for a life of committed "intimate partnership." With the emergence of this psychological principle more annulments were issued by tribunals throughout the world, most especially in the United States.[10]

In an address before the Roman Rota Pope John Paul II expressed a concern about the psychological principle taking precedence in determining whether or not a marriage should be annulled. While recognizing the importance of assessing the psychic processes surrounding a marriage, the pope also stated that the psychological perspective, nevertheless, offers only a partial vision of the human. He asserted that the psychological experts and the church's judges must share a common "horizon of anthropology":

> It must be recognized that the discoveries and achievements purely in
> the fields of psychology and psychiatry are not capable of offering a
> truly complete vision of the person. They are not capable of resolving
> on their own the fundamental questions concerning the meaning of

life and the human vocation. . . . It appears that dialogue and constructive communication between the judge and the psychiatrist are easier if the starting point for both is located within the horizon of a common anthropology, in such a way that the vision of one remains open to that of the other, yet within their difference of method, interest and purpose.[11]

The pope went on to caution the Rota on relying upon psychological theories that are either so "pessimistic" or so "optimistic" about human nature that they are closed to essential Christian values that surround marriage.

The church's concern for entering into dialogue with the modern world is evident in other documents promulgated by the Council. Of special importance was its landmark call for the renewal of religious life in its Decree on the Appropriate Renewal of the Religious Life (*Perfectae Caritatis*). The issuance of this decree on October 28, 1965, led to major transformations in religious life, from the changes in religious dress to further encouragement for women religious to study for advanced degrees.[12] Such educational opportunities had a profound impact on the identity of American women religious and led many to pursue advanced degrees in a variety of psychological fields.

In a separate document the Council recommended changes in the pastoral formation of priests. Its Decree on Priestly Formation (*Optatam Totius*) recommend the use of psychology in priestly formation.[13] The Council envisioned new apostolic roles for the laity in its Decree on the Apostolate of the Laity (*Apostolicam Actuositatem*) and cited the necessity of involving more lay women in the apostolate.[14] This decree prompted a renewal of a sense of vocation among all Catholics, not just the clergy and religious, who were often seen as the only ones who "had a vocation." With the new understanding of religious vocation introduced by *Optatam Totius* and *Perfectae Caritatis,* many Catholics, young and old, priests and nuns, lay women and men, began to question what it meant to be a Roman Catholic in the modern world. Such questioning sent a series of shock waves throughout the Catholic world, prompting many not only to leave their habits but also their convents, monasteries, and rectories. The institutions and organizations of Roman Catholicism would never be the same after the Council.

The theologies of such theologians as Karl Rahner and Edward Schillebeeckx popularized by the Council placed an emphasis on categories of "experience." According to Sr. Kathleen Gallivan, S.N.D., who was formed as a religious during this period and who subsequently served as a formation superior for her order, this emphasis has led to the study and application of liberation and feminist theologies among women religious.[15] The emphasis on "experience" may have been a factor in the increasing enthusiasm for courses in psychology in seminaries. Fr. John Grimes, who was a seminarian during the conciliar period, found this to be true. He further noted that in his own experience as a priest-psychologist there has been since the 1970s a movement toward more formal training designed to improve ministerial competence in fields such as pastoral counseling. Such training has not been limited to priests and religious, however, as more ministerial responsibilities have been assumed by Catholic laity.[16]

Finally, of special importance for the American context was the Declaration on Religious Freedom (*Dignitatis Humanae*). Based on the careful work of the Jesuit theologian John Courtney Murray, it brought forth a new understanding of the relations between the church and state. The declaration promoted a greater spirit of harmony between church and state and reversed the spirit of Pope Pius IX's *Syllabus of Errors*. According to one commentator, on September 21, 1965, the day that the decree was voted upon, "a very ancient order of things—at least in principle—passed away. In principle, the era of Constantine—sixteen hundred years of it—passed away."[17]

The decree asserted general principles of religious freedom in light of revelation and reformulated the church's position regarding the state. In the words of one of its chief framers, John Courtney Murray:

> Taken in conjunction with the Pastoral Constitution on the Church in the Modern World, the Declaration opens a new era in the relations between the People of God and the People Temporal. A long-standing ambiguity has finally been cleared up. The Church does not deal with the secular order in terms of a double standard—freedom for the Church when Catholics are a minority, privilege for the Church and intolerance for others when Catholics are a majority. The Declaration has opened the way toward new confidence in ecumenical relationships, and a new straightforwardness in relationships between the Church and the world.[18]

The spirit of hope and reform created by the document was infectious throughout the Catholic world in particular and the religious world in general. A new era of understanding was initiated within and beyond the church. According to Walter Burghardt one of the impacts of the Council was to create in the minds of Catholics a shift from classicism to historical consciousness. He aptly summarized three major changes that ensued as a result of this shift: "Vatican II is of fundamental significance for Roman Catholics because the Council inserted the Catholic Church into history and into Christendom. A third fundamental significance of Vatican II for

Catholics is that the Council inserted the Catholic Church into the world, into the modern world."[19]

Only a few years after the Council, however, such a spirit was diminished with the promulgation of an encyclical whose contents, though they had been seriously debated for a decade within the church, had been avoided by the Council because of their controversial ramifications. The issue was contraception, and the encyclical was entitled "On the Regulation of Birth" (*Humanae Vitae*).

Humanae Vitae and Its Consequences

The encyclical *Humanae Vitae* had a major impact on the Roman Catholic Church, especially in the United States, but an exhaustive review is beyond the limits of this presentation. The following brief overview of the American Catholic response describes the divisive and tragic credibility gap that emerged between the church's hierarchy and American Catholics following the encyclical.

Intended as the Catholic Church's response to the increasing use of contraceptive methods, especially the recently developed antiovulant pills, the encyclical was actually a more progressive statement than the more severe encyclical *Casti Connubi,* promulgated by Pope Pius XI in 1930. What was contentious, however, was Pope Paul VI's forbidding the use of contraceptive devices. Besides the fact that mainstream Christian churches had earlier permitted such practices, what made the pope's encyclical so controversial was that the majority of the pope's own commission had recommended that, within certain guidelines, contraceptives could be permitted.[20]

The vigorous opposition of American Catholics, clergy and lay alike, was widespread. A corresponding occurrence during this period and possibly a consequence of such opposition was the considerable decline in the number of American Catholics going to confession. Rather than confessing an action that church authorities believed to be sinful, but they did not, many chose not to go to confession at all. Instead, they chose to see a counselor or a therapist.

Among the voices questioning the encyclical was the American Catholic Psychological Association. Only a few weeks after the promulgation of the encyclical the ACPA, at its annual convention in September 1968, issued a statement that conveyed some dissatisfaction with the encyclical:

> As psychologists concerned with human problems, we recognize our responsibility to speak out on the issues which affect the human person. As Catholic psychologists we are sensitive to our responsibility to assist the Church as teacher. We share in the Church's process of

continued reflection on the nature of human personality and human relationships. In light of these obligations it is important to examine the statements on man which the Church issues and to offer positive assistance whenever possible. It is in recognition of these responsibilities that the members of the American Catholic Psychological Association meeting in San Francisco raise these questions about the recent encyclical *Humanae Vitae*.[21]

A list of fifteen questions expressed the organization's concern, among them:

Does the encyclical reflect a consistent view of the human person?

Does it at times employ a faculty psychology which is no longer accepted as fully adequate?

Does the encyclical give evidence of an understanding of the complex of conscious and unconscious psychological factors operative in the total experience of marriage?

Does the history of the encyclical's development and promulgation conflict with the Church's teaching that responsible human beings must develop a mature conscience?[22]

The ACPA's statement reflected the widespread public dissent and for many the private disobedience toward the encyclical's birth-control ban, which would become rampant among Catholics across the world. A critical consciousness toward the church and its authority soon emerged. News conferences were held and petitions circulated opposing the encyclical. The most famous case occurred in the Archdiocese of Washington, where Cardinal Patrick O'Boyle removed the faculties of fifty-one of his priests for signing a petition against the encyclical.[23] Given the widespread enthusiasm that greeted the Council's Declaration on Religious Freedom, *Dignitatis Humanae,* the encyclical's assertions and the disciplines imposed upon those who opposed them created not only disappointment but disillusionment. The priest-sociologist Andrew Greeley later remarked that the church's view of sex was not the only issue; what became even more prominent was the primacy of the individual's conscience.[24] In describing such disillusionment and the way *Humanae Vitae* shattered the optimism and euphoria that the Council had created, Greeley noted:

Humanae Vitae canceled out the positive results of Vatican II and sent the church into a sudden and dramatic decline: priests refused to endorse the teaching in the confessional; Sunday church attendance dropped off sharply; church collections diminished; resignations from the priesthood increased, while those who remained diminished their efforts to recruit young men for the vocation, and family support for religious vocations eroded. Acceptance of papal authority declined dramatically.[25]

While America's sexual revolution, the Vietnam War, and distrust of political authority contributed to an oppositional attitude among many American Catholics, especially in sexual matters, the promulgation and in certain cases the rigid enforcement of *Humanae Vitae* created a large credibility gap. Among Catholics and non-Catholics the authority of the Catholic Church in the American context was doubted and distrusted. Ironically, during a decade when the Catholic Church was on the way toward removing the last vestiges of hostility toward psychiatry, clinical psychology, and psychoanalysis, it was perceived by many Catholics as making stern judgments on the psychological expression of conscience and sexual intimacy.

Paradigm Shifts in Psychology

Beginning in the 1960s there occurred changes in the approach, method, and content of psychology. As in theology, the fields of psychology underwent what the philosopher of science Thomas Kuhn called a "paradigm shift."[26] Numerous scholars, psychologists and theologians among them, utilized Kuhn's construct of paradigm. According to Sigmund Koch, psychology moved from an "Age of Theory" with its behavioristic, neo-behavioristic, and Freudian models to an "Age of the Paradigm" with the emergence of new models. In this respect, for Koch, the promotion of paradigms became a form of psychological commerce.[27]

Such paradigm promotion, with a decidedly less deterministic emphasis, coalesced into what was termed humanistic psychology or psychology's "third force." The latter term was meant to distinguish the new paradigm from the previously dominant paradigms of psychology, namely, behaviorism and psychoanalysis. According to Schultz and Schultz four essential characteristics distinguish humanistic psychology:

1. an emphasis on conscious experience;

2. a belief in the wholeness of human nature and conduct;

3. a focus on free will, spontaneity, and the creative power of the individual;

4. the study of everything that is relevant to the human condition.[28]

These characteristics led many American Catholics to gravitate toward humanistic psychology. The writings of Abraham Maslow and Carl Rogers, the movement's leading proponents, began to be read and taught in Catholic seminaries.[29] Maslow, who was initially trained in the methods of behaviorism, eventually found its focus and methods too narrow and largely irrelevant to the critical concerns of human beings. Serving on the faculty of Brandeis University from 1951 until his death in 1969, Maslow developed a series of holistic constructs pertaining to the human personality. Many in the popular culture, Catholics included, appropriated Maslow's insights. As a result such Maslowian constructs as "self-actualization," "peak experiences," and the "hierarchy of needs" became common parlance.

A similar development occurred with Rogerian psychology. Carl Rogers, who had retreated from his religious training as a minister into clinical psychology, rejected Freud's determinism and emphasis on the unconscious early in his clinical training. Instead Rogers developed what he termed a "client-centered" approach to therapy that highlighted empathy and "unconditional positive regard" as pathways to understanding and healing. Rogers's methods were applicable not only to individual therapy but also to group therapy and group dynamics. As a result, while religious life was going through its renewal and reforms, some religious superiors were led to appropriate Rogerian strategies as a way of renewing their community formation structures. Some attended workshops conducted by Rogers and his associates.[30]

The holistic and positive approaches to the human personality of Maslow and Rogers struck a cord in the American optimistic spirit during the postwar period. Rogers's approach contrasted with more pessimistic understandings of the human personality developed by Freudians and the neobehaviorists. Although the work of Maslow and Rogers had been known in psychological circles for some time, it was not until the 1960s that their approach began to take shape as a movement. In 1961 the *Journal of Humanistic Psychology* was founded, and in the following year the American Association of Humanistic Psychology was established. In 1972 the American Psychological Association institutionalized the movement by creating the Division of Humanistic Psychology.

Many American Catholic psychologists sympathetically read and studied the works of Maslow, Rogers, and other humanistic psychologists. As discussed elsewhere in this book, Rogers's approach was popularized among Catholics in the writings of his former student Fr. Charles A. Curran. For three decades, principally at Loyola University of Chicago, Curran trained hundreds of psychologists and counselors in the methods of Rogers's client-centered therapy.

Jung and Catholicism

Throughout his life Carl Jung had a fascination with Catholicism. Perhaps it began with an emotional encounter with a "dangerous" Jesuit in a cassock whom he had seen as an impressionable child.[31] This episode, combined with watching his father struggle with his ministry as a Swiss Reformed pastor, led Jung to an approach-avoidance relationship with religion in general and Catholicism in particular. On a number of occasions Jung wrote in both complementary and critical ways about Catholicism. He even expressed in a short essay why he chose not to become a Catholic[32] and presented a series of lectures on the Spiritual Exercises of St. Ignatius.[33] In the essay he described Catholicism as essentially antiscientific, and, according to one Jesuit Jungian therapist, in the lectures Jung stated that the ways the Spiritual Exercises were presented to young men who aspired to be Jesuits could be manipulative.[34] On the other hand, Jung found wisdom in asking an exercitant to pray by using all five senses to enhance the imagination. For Jung this method of Ignatius allowed for the "fullest possible 'realization' of the object of contemplation."[35]

It should come as no surprise that Catholic theologians and spiritual writers would also have an approach-avoidance attitude toward Jung and his analytical concepts and principles. Victor White, a British Dominican and an early commentator on Jung's writings, carried on a friendly correspondence with Jung. As one of the first Catholic theologians to study Jung's approach to religion, White wrote eloquently and during the 1940 and 1950s popularized Jungian approaches to a Catholic audience, particularly in two works: *God and the Unconscious* (1953) and *Soul and Psyche* (1960).[36] White even had Jung write the foreword to *God and the Unconscious,* in which Jung stated: "Surely it would be valuable for the theologian to know what is happening to the psyche of the adult; and it must be gradually dawning on any responsible doctor what any incredibly important role the spiritual atmosphere plays in the psychic economy."[37]

Raymond Hostie, a Jesuit on the faculty of Louvain in 1957, also published an overview of Jung's psychology.[38] Hostie's complementary and at times critical presentation of Jung became an influential work in Catholic circles. Catholic theologians and thinkers began to explore Jung's thought with fewer reservations than they had with Freud. It was not until after the Council, however, that some American Catholic scholars began to apply Jung's insights to religious beliefs. Such appropriation began in Catholic retreat houses and spiritual centers. One reason for the sudden keen interest in Jungian thought was, no doubt, the *Zeitgeist* of the 1960s when many scholars and students were looking for psychological and spiritual bridges between East and West. Many found a bridge in Jungian psychology with its constructs of archetypes and the collective unconscious. Within the American Catholic context the enthusiasm for Eastern thought, best exemplified in the influential writings of the Cistercian monk Thomas Merton, was coupled with conciliar reforms that triggered new ways of approaching the spiritual life.

The appropriation of Jungian thought by American Catholic spirituality was evident in the *Review for Religious,* the most popular of Catholic spiritual periodicals, which during the 1970s began publishing articles on Jungian typology. Articles included "Jungian Typology and Christian Spirituality," "Staging, Typing, and Spiritual Direction," and "The Spiritual Direction of 'Thinking' Types."[39] This Jungian influence on Catholic spirituality was further demonstrated in the popularity of weekend programs at Catholic spiritual centers that introduced Jungian thought to wider audiences. Moreover, to enhance their members' understanding of one another many religious communities of men and women began to use the Myers-Briggs Type Indicator, a psychological inventory based on Jung's eight-factor typology of extrovert-introvert, sensate-intuitive, thinker-feeler, and judger-perceiver. Its widespread use further demonstrated how far American Catholic attitudes had come in appropriating psychology. Whereas previously there was a general reluctance by religious superiors to use psychological tests, and whereas Moore, Bier, and others had had to persuade church authorities of the value of such tests for religious candidates, now entire communities of vowed religious were using psychological tests like Myers-Briggs to improve their community through a psychological understanding of one another.[40] As we shall see in chapter 10, Jung's insights influenced the way Catholic spiritual directors would conduct retreats.

Object Relations Theory and Religion

The considerable influence that psychoanalytic thought had in America became more diffused during the 1960s. While still Freudian in their basic orientations, ego psychology, object relations theory, and self psychology moved away from the determinism of classical psychoanalysis. With a greater emphasis on intrapsychic freedom of the "self" in interpersonal relations, these neopsychoanalytic approaches tended to reduce the hostility that Catholics once had toward psychoanalysis. For example, the British object relations theory of D. W. Winnicott became a means for finding theoretical bridges between psychoanalytic thought and religion. The use of Winnicott's theoretical insights applied to religious matters was evident in Ana-Maria Rizzuto's landmark work *The Birth of the Living God* (1979). Rizzuto utilized insights drawn from Winnicott to describe the origin, development, and use of God images or representations.[41] William Meissner in his *Psychoanalysis and Religious Experience* (1984) developed Rizzuto's work to argue that religious belief need not be seen by psychoanalysts as an infantile fantasy or as an escape from reality.[42] In *The Attachment Cycle* (1988) Michael Garanzini, S.J., used insights of object relations theorists throughout his work to describe a cycle of attachment, separation, loss, and reattachment, and then applied such a cycle to pastoral counseling.[43] A further example of a Catholic scholar's use of object relations theory may be seen in Michael St. Clair's *Human Relationships and the Experience of God* (1994). St. Clair, a former Jesuit, describes the development of a person's image of God throughout early childhood interactions and goes on to give evidence of this development in the lives of St. Augustine and St. Thérèse of Lisieux.[44]

Object relations theory has been used in theological circles as well. For example, Catherine Mowry LaCugna, in speaking of "persons in communion," a notion that helped her describe the relations among the "persons" of the Holy Trinity, drew upon the work of John MacMurray, which she found closely affiliated with the object relations theories of W. R. D. Fairbairn, D. W. Winnicott, and John McDargh.[45]

Psychological Influences on Moral Theology

In the decade prior to the Council, there were signs that psychology was beginning to have a significant impact on American Catholicism. As noted in the previous chapter, psychiatrists, psychologists, and even psychoanalysts helped to train American Catholic clergy and religious to address pastoral concerns through special symposiums such as the Collegeville Institute and the Fordham lecture series. Except for an occasional treatise about alcoholism,[46] however, American Catholic moral theologians tended to shy away from psychological constructs, especially with regard to sexuality.

Since Augustine, Catholic moral theology had been the fruit of an integration of faith and reason. Largely in reaction against the Protestant emphasis on Scripture alone, Catholic moral theologians had for the most part avoided extensive biblical research and had placed their emphasis on articulating morality through reason and natural law. The long and rich tradition of natural law in classical Catholic moral theology was congenial to the categories of Thomistic rational psychology. In contrast, the concepts and findings of empirical and clinical psychology were not to be trusted.

In the decades before the Council a paradigm shift had begun to take place in Catholic theology, at least in Europe. Catholic French theologians led by Marie Dominique Chenu, Yves Congar, and Henri de Lubac in their *nouvelle théologie* had begun incorporating the findings of biblical research into their own work. Prompted by such a movement and supported by

Pope Pius XII's encyclical *Divino Afflante Spiritu,* Catholic moral theology "set out to 'Christianize' morality by rooting it more deeply in scripture and the mysteries of faith."[47] Catholic theological anthropology became more personalist as constructs such as covenant, conversion, responsibility, and vocation entered theology in a more thematic way during the post-war period. As noted in the previous chapter, Catholic progressive thought was at times suspect, as evidenced in Pope Pius XII's encyclical *Humani Generis.*[48] There nevertheless occurred progressive developments in Catholic theology, such as personalism and the French *nouvelle théologie.* American theologians, for the most part, refrained from teaching theology thought suspect by the Vatican, so that the only exposure that American seminarians could have had to such new movements in theology was if they had studied in Europe, principally at Louvain.[49]

Reports that emanated from the Council and the subsequent decrees sent shock waves through the rock-hard conservatism of American Catholicism and altered the way in which American Catholic theologians approached moral norms. The progressive spirit of the European theologians finally began to have its influence in America. Pastoral issues such as divorce, annulments, remarriage, and above all contraception were more commonly discussed in prestigious Catholic journals and debated among lay Catholics. Moreover, for an increasing number of better-educated laity, the seemingly straightforward answers of moral theology or pastoral dictates in the confessional no longer sufficed. This attitude was particularly evident in the widespread antipathy to *Humanae Vitae.*

Meanwhile, in response to the Council's documents and their call for clarification and reform, a paradigm shift occurred in all branches of theology. The theologian Avery Dulles, building upon Thomas Kuhn's theory of paradigms, eloquently described the shift in ecclesiology in his influential work *Models of the Church.*[50] In moral theology signs of a paradigm shift away from the church's rationalistic approach were evident in the ways in which some Catholic moral theologians began to incorporate the empirical and clinical findings of psychology.

Before the Council, Catholic moral theology was seen primarily as a discipline to prepare priests to hear confessions.[51] With the pastoral concerns raised by *Humane Vitae,* moral theology no longer was confined to the confessional or to seminary classrooms. Instead, for many American Catholics raised in strict and authoritarian church structures, the various social forces that coalesced in the 1960s, combined with the structural and symbolic changes promoted by the Council, led them seriously to question their faith and morals. Moral theology, consequently, came to the forefront of common conversations among American Catholics. Moreover, moral issues and debates made good copy for the secular and Catholic press as well.[52] The Catholic confessional, meanwhile, began to be replaced by the counseling couch as Catholics looked not so much to their parish priests as to therapists for wisdom and guidance. Catholic moral theology went through a process of reappraisal. The sacrament of penance became the sacrament of reconciliation; the long lines of Catholics waiting to see a confessor in a dark booth were replaced by short lines waiting to see a priest face to face. The new understanding of sin led the Protestant psychiatrist Karl Menninger, who worked with many priests at the Menninger Clinic, to entitle a work *Whatever Became of Sin?*

As Richard McCormick notes, the Council said very little about moral theology.[53] Still, in speaking of the church's relations with society in *Gaudium et Spes,* the Council recognized the need to engage in greater dialogue with modern science:

> May the faithful, therefore, live in very close union with the men of their time. Let them strive to understand perfectly their way of thinking and feeling, as expressed in their culture. Let them blend modern science and its theories and the understanding of the most recent discoveries with Christian morality and doctrine. Thus their religious practice and morality can keep pace with their scientific knowledge and with an ever-advancing technology.[54]

The statement was a harbinger of the controversies that exploded into the Catholic world with the issuance of *Humane Vitae.* Prior to the Council, Catholic moral theology was seen as "too often canon law-related, sin-centered and seminary-controlled."[55] Even before the Council, however, there were signs from Europe that changes in moral theology were under way. One sign, which was to become especially relevant for psychology's impact on moral theology, was the construct known as the "fundamental option."

"Fundamental option" or basic freedom emerged from the theological anthropology of Karl Rahner as he sought to recover for the Catholic tradition a greater sense of the depth of the moral act.[56] Rahner spoke of a transcendental freedom or basic freedom and distinguished it from mere categorical freedom. Categorical freedom is demonstrated in the decisions involved in our concrete actions. Basic or transcendental freedom, on the other hand, has as its object God, the "original, transcendental experience." For Rahner, every act of freedom involves at the categorical level a definite object and a specific person. Within such acts, however, there is always present an unthematic basic or transcendent freedom. As Rahner wrote:

> Since in every act in freedom which is concerned on the categorical level with a quite definite object, a quite definite person, there is

always present, as the condition for the possibility for such an act, transcendence towards the absolute term and source of all our intellectual and spiritual acts, and hence towards God, there can and must be present in every such act an unthematic "yes" or "no" to this God or original, transcendental experience.[57]

Rahner's theological anthropology focuses on the self-communication of God as the original, transcendent experience, and he considers freedom to be the human capacity to accept or reject the original transcendental experience as grace. As McCormick points out, Rahner emphasizes that a human being's "yes" or "no" toward God is not a self-disposition, a categorical or empirically observable experience. Instead, it may be seen as an unthematic mystery that is basic and allows for a human being's experience of freedom.[58]

Rahner's notion of basic or transcendental freedom revolutionized Catholic moral theology. Using Rahner's notion, a fellow Jesuit theologian, Joseph Fuchs, was one of the first to speak of a "fundamental option" as a reality more basic than the mere psychological freedom of choice:

Basic freedom...denotes a still more fundamental, deeper-rooted freedom, not immediately accessible to psychological investigation. This is the freedom that enables us not only to decide freely on particular acts and aims but also, by means of these, to determine ourselves totally as persons and not merely in any particular area of behavior. It is clear that man's freedom of choice and his basic freedom are not simply two different psychological freedoms. As a person, man is free. But this freedom can, of course, be considered under different aspects. A man can, in one and the same act, choose the object of his choice (freedom of choice) and by so doing determine himself as a person (basic freedom).[59]

For Fuchs then the goodness or wickedness of human actions should be seen not so much in terms simply of individual acts but as a whole ordering of actions. It was an effort to further explain Fuchs's concept of "basic freedom" as well as to concretize Rahner's notion of transcendental freedom that led Bernard Häring to turn to psychology. Häring, a German Redemptorist, had already established himself as a major moral theologian through a three-volume work entitled *The Law of Christ*, in which he presented a personalist approach to morality. Twenty-five years later, in 1978, influenced by the spirit of the Council and by developments in humanistic psychology, Häring furthered his personalist approach to morality in another three-volume work entitled *Free and Faithful in Christ*. This was widely used in Catholic seminaries and theology classes, as it offered one of the first comprehensive approaches to understanding moral issues from not only a theological perspective but a psychological one as well. It represented a paradigm shift in Catholic morality, especially in the manner in which Catholics regarded sin. In his introduction Häring aptly described this shift:

> Moral theology, as I understand it, is not concerned first with decision-making or with discrete acts. Its basic task and purpose is to gain the right vision, to assess the main perspectives, and to present those truths and values which should bear upon decisions to be made before God.[60]

Like those of Rahner and Fuchs, Häring's approach to moral actions was deep and broad; he did not focus on the value of discrete actions as did generations of Catholic moralists. Moral life had begun to be understood not as a series of discrete actions judged to be right or wrong, but as a lifelong growth process. Confessors were encouraged to help Catholics receive the sacrament of reconciliation not by reciting a "laundry list" of sins, but by reflecting on a pattern of sinfulness and the ways they desired to grow in faith.

In his consideration of the "fundamental option," Häring drew from a variety of resources that he considered psychological. From the existentialist writings of Søren Kierkegaard he used the notion of "stages on life's way." Häring also turned to the character types developed by Edward Spranger, Abraham Maslow's notion of "peak experience," Viktor Frankl's logotherapy, and the life-cycle proposed by Erik Erikson. It was in Erikson's writings that Häring found evidence for substantiating a moral "fundamental option."

Häring presented Erikson's eight stages of life and found special relevance in Erikson's principle that at "various critical moments in life, achievements are won or failures occur in a way that the future is either better or worse for it."[61] Such critical moments are for Erikson developmental crises that tend to be normative. Häring, however, viewed such crises as calling for the making or the deepening of a fundamental option. He saw morality as developmental, like Erikson's emotional-relational stage theory of development. Especially pertinent to Häring's moral theory was Erikson's fifth stage, namely, "Identity versus Identity Confusion." For Erikson this stage dominates development during adolescence although its influence permeates one's entire life. Just as for Erikson identity does not arise all at once but develops in a series of developmental steps, so for Häring one's fundamental option arises developmentally insofar as one chooses to remain faithful to one's identity:

It becomes clear how near Erikson's concept of identity is to what theologians call fundamental option. It does not arise all at once. The groundwork is laid, however, when it comes to the self-commitment of a person in the very discovery of identity. And this, in turn, is dependent on fidelity which itself entails courage and trust expressed in self-commitment.[62]

According to Häring, Erikson's three adult stages invoked "fundamental choices" between intimacy and isolation, generativity and stagnation, and ego-integrity and despair.[63] For Erikson each stage challenges the adult to make choices for growth; for Häring each stage requires that the adult Christian remain "free and faithful in Christ." Häring recognized certain limitations in applying Erikson's developmental theory to moral theology, but on the whole he found it a useful framework to explain the moral theological principle of the "fundamental option":

> Erikson does not provide us with a readily made definition of funda-
> mental option, but he offers a framework and many lively insights for
> better understanding the underlying dynamics that we might call the
> fundamental option. We cannot simply equate our notion of funda-
> mental option with Erikson's vision of identity, but they have much
> in common. It is identity that gives the ego strength so necessary
> for a total commitment. It is, again, identity that allows the develop-
> ment of generativity and integrity. The description given by Erikson
> allows us to recognize in them what we call basic dispositions and
> attitudes insofar as they draw their direction and strength from the
> fundamental option.[64]

Häring's use of the works of Erikson and other psychologists was a major breakthrough in Catholic moral theology. After the Council other moralists began to incorporate psychology into their approaches. The American Jesuits Robert Springer and Giles Milhaven had earlier made cases for using scientific findings in moral theology, although not without criticism.[65] Ironically, for Catholic theologians perhaps the most balanced and most influential statement regarding the use of empirical sciences in moral theology came from the United Church of Christ theologian James Gustafson, who was widely read in Catholic circles. In 1971, Gustafson presented an address entitled "The Relationship of Empirical Science to Moral Thought" before the Catholic Theological Society of America. He encouraged moralists to use data from the empirical sciences when it enhanced their understanding of the human person. He nevertheless raised the following three questions that he thought should continually be addressed by moralists when using such data:

1. What data and concepts are relevant to the moral issues under discussion?...In many instances the empirical studies used in moral theology and social ethics were not designed to help the moralist answer his questions; the studies were not done to resolve moral questions.

2. What interpretation of a field should be accepted? And on what grounds?...If the moralist accepts an interpretation on its "scientific" adequacy, he has the burden of making his case for his choice on scientific grounds....The moralist clearly needs to be in communication with scholars in the areas from which he borrows in order to avoid horrendous mistakes of judgment, but he has to accept responsibility for making choices within the best of his knowledge.

3. How does the moralist deal with the value biases of the studies that he uses?...His preferences for certain values is likely to have a considerable measure of effect on how he defines his research problem, what he is looking for, and what he consequently sees.[66]

The significance of these questions later became evident when moral theologians had to adjust their positions because developmental psychologists were forced to adjust their own, particularly because of limitations found in the developmental psychology of Lawrence Kohlberg. In the early 1970s Kohlberg, influenced by the stage theories of Erikson and Jean Piaget, published a series of works dealing with the stages of moral development, especially applied to education. Kohlberg's theory of moral development involved three levels and six stages and became widely accepted in educational psychology. His theory, however, came under sharp criticism in the early 1980s when the educational psychologist Carol Gilligan demonstrated that Kohlberg's developmental markers, based primarily on studies done with males, did not apply to women.[67] The critique of Gilligan and others led moralists to revise their use of Kohlberg and reinforced Gustafson's cautions about using empirical studies.

In recent moral theology, empirical findings have continued to be used to support and substantiate moral arguments. Recently Mark Poorman, seeking theoretical support in his discussion of the significance of discernment in morality, turned to the interactional psychology of Norma Hann and Elarine Aerts.[68] Their approach goes beyond Kohlberg and builds upon Gilligan's critique. Hann and Aerts conceive of moral development in terms of the ability to interact with others in moral matters. In his pastoral approach to moral discernment, Poorman incorporated Hann and Aerts's psychological model. Poorman's use of psychology along with philosophy and theology demonstrated psychology's continued usefulness for Catholic moralists.

Catholic moralists continue to heed the caution of Gustafson and others concerning the use of empirical studies and have been careful not to allow psychological findings to serve as the basis for their moral arguments. On the whole, however, most American Catholic moralists have come to place a greater emphasis on inductive rather than deductive methods. Perhaps Richard Gula best captured this shift in emphasis on the role of psychology and other social sciences today:

> The historically conscious worldview of modern moral theology supports a method that is empirical and inductive. This is not to say that deductive reasoning has no place in modern moral theology. It still does. But moral theology today is more likely to begin with historical particulars, the concrete and the changing. It is reluctant to draw conclusions independently of a consideration of the human person and the complexities of human existence. This requires a greater concern for the *developmental, personalist* and *social structural* dimensions of lived experiences. In order to gain access to this experience, the *social sciences* must form an integral part of the reflection on complex moral dilemmas [emphasis mine].[69]

Since the Council, Catholic moral theology has become more global and more ecumenical. The influence of theologians from Latin America, Asia, and Africa has begun to influence the shape of theological thinking. Catholic moral theology continues to seek to integrate faith and reason, revelation and science, grace and nature. For Gula psychological data and theory influence moral theology through reason, science, and nature. As Gula suggests, however, too much emphasis on any of these avenues may lead to too much secularization. On the other hand, overemphasis on the side of faith, revelation, or grace may lead to sectarianism.[70] This tension will require theologians to be both creative and consistent. For Gula, the future development of Catholic moral theology will require more attention to progress in psychology. Under the conditions set forth by Gustafson and with the caution against secularization offered by Gula, psychological thought can play an important role in Catholic moral theology.

Chapter 8

Grace Still Builds on Nature

Bridge Builders between Psychology and Catholicism

While less contentious than psychoanalysis and clinical psychology, the profession of psychiatry was also held suspect by many in the Catholic Church. Certainly, the work and witness of Don Thomas Verner Moore demonstrated that compatibility between Catholicism and psychiatry was possible. Still suspicion toward psychiatry was not uncommon. However, following World War II the growing number of Catholic psychiatrists, many of them practicing according to a biological model developed by such luminaries as Adolf Meyer at Johns Hopkins, served to quell the qualms of many Catholics. The increase led to the formation of the National Guild of Catholic Psychiatrists, whose meetings and periodical went a long way toward dispelling concerns. Moreover, the work and witness of three Catholic psychiatrists in particular made psychiatry more acceptable to Catholic clergy and the laity at large. In their own way Leo Bartemeier, Francis Braceland, and John Cavanagh promoted new understanding of the way psychiatry can inform their Catholic faith.

Leo Bartemeier, M.D. (1895–1982)

Leo Bartemeier was born in Iowa in 1895 and attended the Catholic University of America, where he served for a time as secretary to Thomas Verner Moore. Bartemeier received his B.A. in 1914 and his M.A. in 1916, following the acceptance of his research thesis on animal psychology. He went on to attend medical school at Georgetown, from which he obtained his degree in 1920. After interning at the Henry Ford Hospital in Detroit, Bartemeier received psychiatric training at the Phipps Psychiatric Clinic of the Johns Hopkins Medical School in Baltimore. One of his mentors was Adolf Meyer, the leading American psychiatrist of his day. In 1926 Bartemeier returned to Detroit, where he developed his practice. At the same time he began training as a psychoanalyst at the Chicago Institute of Psychoanalysis, which at the time was directed by one of Freud's pupils, Franz Alexander. In 1931 Bartemeier was elected vice president of the Chicago Psychoanalytic Society, but it was not until 1938 that he completed his work and became the first American Catholic psychoanalyst.

Besides having a private practice in Detroit, Bartemeier served from 1942 to 1954 as the director of the professional staff at the Haven Sanitarium in Rochester, Minnesota, and from 1944 to 1954 he was an associate professor of psychiatry at the Wayne State University Medical Center. In 1954 Bartemeier returned to Baltimore and became the medical director of the Seton Psychiatric Institute as well as a clinical professor at Georgetown. In 1971 he retired from full-time practice and teaching, but he remained associated with Seton until shortly before his death in 1982.

Bartemeier's sphere of influence included his leading a commission of psychiatrists to Europe in 1945 to advise the Army on war neurosis. Shortly afterwards he worked with Karl and Roy Menninger at the Menninger Clinic and served on the clinic's board. Bartemeier's professional positions included his serving as president of the International Psychoanalytic Association (1949–50), of the American Psychiatric Association (1951–52), and of the American College of Psychiatrists (1951–52). In addition, Bartemeier was the chairman of the Council on Mental Health of the American Medical Association from 1952 to 1956.

In these positions Bartemeier showed that it was possible for a believing Catholic to be a professional psychiatrist and psychoanalyst. To prevent any misunderstanding, before allowing his name to be considered for president of the International Psychoanalytic Association, Bartemeier had a private audience with Pope Pius XII. He later recounted that their meeting was a very affirming one:

> When I met him and acquainted him with my problem I told him that my religion was far more important to me than the possible high honor to which I might be elected, so I had to ask him his views on psychoanalysis. Quite immediately he said that Freud had discovered more about human nature than anyone preceding him for thousands of years.[1]

When Bartemeier asked the pope his views on psychoanalytic therapy, the pope replied that "this depended upon the character of the physician." As Bartemeier's meeting with the pope came to a close he was advised, "If you are elected to the presidency, my son, accept it and do honor to the Church."[2]

Several years later Bartemeier invited Pope Pius XII to address the International Congress of Psychotherapy and Clinical Psychology when the organization met in Rome in 1954. It was at this convention that the pope blessed those professional therapists and psychoanalysts who assisted the church's quest "for the knowledge of the soul"—a blessing that went a long way toward reducing the controversy surrounding Catholic attitudes toward psychology, psychiatry, and psychoanalysis.

Francis Braceland, M.D. (1900–1985)

Francis Braceland was a Catholic who also rose to prominence in the American psychiatric profession during the mid-twentieth century. Raised in the poor Philadelphia neighborhood known as "Brewerytown" and educated in Catholic parochial schools, Braceland was twenty-six years of age before he was able to scrape together enough money to complete his college education. Graduating from the Christian Brothers' La Salle College, in 1926 Braceland went on to attend Jefferson Medical College, where he came under the tutelage of Dr. Edward Strecker, a prominent Philadelphia psychiatrist. Strecker opened to Braceland the doors of the Philadelphia psychiatric establishment, which at the time included very few Catholics. So impressed was Strecker with Braceland's abilities that he recommended him for the prestigious Rockefeller Fellowship. Braceland was awarded the fellowship and spent the mid-1930s developing his psychiatric abilities at Switzerland's renowned Anstalt Burghölzi in Zurich. Braceland also used his time in Zurich to sit at the feet of Carl Jung and became one of the first American Catholic psychiatrists to receive training in analytical psychology. Braceland took advantage of the international ambiance of Zurich to meet various intellectual luminaries, among them the German expatriate Thomas Mann. Later in his career Braceland became known for his ability to turn a phrase, and his reputation as a writer and speaker may well have been shaped by his acquaintances during this period of his life. Braceland's fellowship also allowed him to undertake neurological training at the National Hospital in London, where he was exposed to British approaches to psychiatry. On the basis of his experiences in pre–World War II Europe, he was transformed from a parochial Philadelphia physician into a first-rate psychiatrist with cosmopolitan connections.

Returning home, Braceland received numerous offers from Philadelphia's leading universities and psychiatric institutions. He accepted many, including instructor in psychiatry and assistant professor at the University of Pennsylvania, associate professor at the Women's Medical College, and visiting lecturer in abnormal psychology at Swarthmore College and Villanova College. Braceland served on the staff of seven hospitals in the Philadelphia area. Then in 1941 he accepted the position of dean of Loyola University Medical School. He was there for only a year; with the entrance of the United States into the World War II Braceland enlisted in the Navy, where he was quickly assigned to a leadership position in Washington as a commander. His abilities were noticed by his superiors, and he was recommended to serve as one of President Roosevelt's personal physicians.

Following the war Braceland returned to the Midwest and began working at the Mayo Clinic. He became part of the esteemed hospital's new Section of Neurology and Psychiatry. Braceland's reputation as a clinician, researcher, and instructor continued to grow. Moreover, because of his abilities as a speaker he was widely sought out by lay and professional audiences. He also collaborated with Minnesota's government in the establishment of ten clinical training programs for physicians throughout the state. Because of his standing in governmental and professional circles Braceland became one of the most renowned psychiatrists in America. By the end of his career it was reported that he had served as an advisor to close to two hundred organizations.[3]

In 1951 Braceland, his wife, Hope, and their two children, Mary Faith and John Michael, returned east, where he assumed the position of psychiatrist-in-chief at Hartford's Institute for Living. While at the Institute from 1951 to 1965 Braceland once again became an important figure in governmental circles, serving as a consultant to several Connecticut governors and congressional representatives. He also was invited to give lectures at Yale, Harvard, and other prestigious institutions. In 1965 Braceland assumed the position of editor of the *American Journal of Psychiatry* and during his thirteen years of leadership was credited with enabling the journal to keep pace with the era's vast accumulation of information. He directed the journal and also supervised the movement of its operations to Washington, D.C., while he worked in Hartford. His editorial leadership even from a distance evoked praise, as two of his colleagues later noted:

> Even though he was (as he frequently called himself) an "absentee landlord," attending to his editorial duties through twice-monthly visits from Hartford and frequent telephone calls, he established a style of leadership that profoundly affected everyone on the editorial staff. His warmth, his wonderful twinkling sense of humor, his gracious manner, his deep respect for others, his sensitivity to the needs and feelings of authors (especially those whose papers he was forced to reject)—all played a vital part in setting the tone of the journal he edited.[4]

Braceland's competence and the high esteem in which he was held in the medical profession helped him to contribute significantly to opening American Catholic leaders and institutions to psychiatry. He was one of the first Catholic psychiatrists to draw attention to the work of Alcoholics Anonymous. In an article in the *Ecclesiastical Review,* "Psychiatric Aspects of Chronic Alcoholism," Braceland encouraged priests to appreciate how the then fledgling AA organization could serve as a referral resource for alcoholic Catholics.[5] Braceland's enthusiasm for AA, however, was challenged in the *Review*'s subsequent issue by Fr. Paul O'Connor from the Jesuit Theologate an St. Mary's, Kansas. O'Connor raised a cautionary concern since AA was founded by Protestants and thus could threaten the faith life of parishioners. O'Connor's suspicion typified the way American Catholicism perceived organizations such as AA and the YMCA (Young Men's Christian Association) during this period. In the same issue of the *Review* Braceland respectfully responded to O'Connor, stating that "I have watched them [AA groups] for a period of about five years, and I do not know of anyone who lost his faith because of his work with them."[6]

Braceland's impact on American Catholic attitudes toward psychiatry was considerable and is exemplified by three important books he wrote or edited. In 1955 Braceland edited *Faith, Reason and Modern Psychiatry: Sources for a Synthesis.* He saw the book as demonstrating how psychiatrists and priests could work together to "confront the cosmos" and "interpenetrate" their respective fields. In the book's opening chapter Braceland's skill in asserting areas of mutuality is demonstrated:

> In these essays in integration it becomes readily apparent that sound psychiatric thought, far from being prejudicial or inimical to the life of the spirit, rather liberates the mind of the afflicted one so that he can realize more fruitfully his religious and spiritual ideals—even to mastering the art of suffering more intelligently and efficaciously. In turn, theology is shown to uphold the age-old notion of the unity of man which psychiatry is presently rediscovering and laboriously bringing to the attention of its sister medical specialties; and to this notion it adds important corollaries on the operation of grace in the human spirit.[7]

In 1963 Braceland collaborated with Fr. Michael Stock, O.P., to publish *Modern Psychiatry: A Handbook for Believers.* Written for clergy and laity alike, the book offered a comprehensive overview of the advances at the time. In response to the critical views held by some Catholic leaders toward Freud, Braceland and Stock presented an entire chapter analyzing Freud and psychoanalysis. While critical of some aspects of Freud's thought the authors noted:

> Freud was a dedicated, hard-working, good-living, honest man. Religious belief was not one of his attributes, however, and no amount of wishful thinking can attribute it to him. Yet religion was much more of a problem for Freud than even he knew.[8]

Braceland was also a major force in the success of the St. John's Summer Institute. His participation in the Institute and service on its board for many years contributed immensely to the Institute's outstanding success. In 1969 Braceland coedited with Harvard psychiatrist Dana Farnsworth *Psychiatry, the Clergy, and Pastoral Counseling,* which contained twenty-six chapters written by participants at the Institute. Once again, the book indicated Braceland's efforts to create an atmosphere of cooperation between psychiatry and religion; he believed that the Institute made a significant contribution to this relationship. Braceland and Farnsworth state:

> The time has come to leave the old arguments about conflicts between psychiatry and religion to those who may need such diversion to avoid coming to grips with the vast number of emotional and spiritual problems faced by people everywhere. For the rest of us in psychiatry and religious endeavor, collaboration such as we have described, emphasizing our opportunities shared in common, can be one of the most important elements in meeting the emotional needs of large numbers of our people.[9]

Throughout his long career Braceland was a loyal citizen, attaining the rank of rear admiral in the Navy; he was also a faithful Catholic and an influential advisor to clergy and laity alike. For many years he was active in the National Guild of Catholic Psychiatrists. In 1951 Pope Pius XII awarded him Knighthood of St. Gregory, and in 1963 Pope Paul VI made him Knight Commander, two of the highest ecclesiastical positions that a lay person can attain. After a long life of service as a clinician, consultant, editor, speaker, and teacher, Braceland died on February 23, 1985, and was laid to rest in Arlington National Cemetery.

John Cavanagh, M.D. (1904–82)

Born in Brooklyn in 1904, John Cavanagh received his B.S. from Georgetown University in 1928 and his M.D. from there in 1930. He did his internship at Providence Hospital, where he no doubt became acquainted with Thomas Verner Moore. In 1935 he joined the faculty of Georgetown's Medical School and then in 1939 became a lecturer in pastoral psychiatry at Catholic University. Cavanagh's interest in psychiatry during a time when Catholicism was highly skeptical of the field was not without its obstacles. Indeed, the dean of Georgetown University's Medical School dissuaded Catholics from specializing in psychiatry as to do so might result in the loss of their souls.

This antagonistic atmosphere toward psychiatry resulted in a dearth of information among Catholic clergy concerning psychopathology and psychology in general. In response, Cavanagh wrote up his lectures to the seminarians at Catholic University and published them as a series of articles in the *American Ecclesiastical Review,* at the time one of the leading periodicals for clergy. The articles helped clergy to gain a good grasp of psychiatric problems as they affected their pastoral work. Among the pastoral principles that Cavanagh presented through these articles were criteria by which priests could distinguish between neurosis and psychosis. Years later, no less a figure than the moralist Charles A. Curran cited Cavanagh's article as having helped his pastoral understanding as well as that of a whole generation of priests. Curran cited as one of Cavanagh's important principles: "The priest must keep in mind that the moral responsibility of the neurotic is diminished in about a direct ratio to the severity of their symptoms."[10]

During the Second World War Cavanagh served as a commander in the U.S. Navy and later returned to resume his teaching at Catholic University. After the war Cavanagh was instrumental in the growth of the National Guild of Catholic Psychiatrists. From 1950 to 1969 he served as editor of the organization's *Bulletin,* and in 1954 he was elected its president.

Cavanagh was a prolific writer who authored more than a hundred articles. He also wrote several books including: *Fundamental Psychiatry* (1953, with the Jesuit philosopher James McGoldrick), *Fundamental Marriage Counseling* (1958), *Fundamental Pastoral Counseling* (1962), *The Popes, the Pill, and the People* (1965), *Counseling the Invert* (1965), and *Counseling the Homosexual* (1977).[11] His book on marriage was perhaps his most successful. The depth and range of his writings helped him become one of the more influential psychiatrists among his professional peers and bishops alike.

Perhaps Cavanagh's most controversial work came when he was a member of the Papal Commission on Birth Control between 1964 and 1966. As an ardent Catholic he initially supported the church's teaching against artificial birth control. Based upon the findings of a survey that he conducted among Catholic women, however, he came to the conclusion that the rhythm method could have harmful psychological effects and so reversed his position. As a result, Cavanagh disagreed with the position of Pope Paul VI concerning contraception and was one of twenty professors at Catholic University to sign a petition of protest in response to the encyclical.

Despite his disagreement with *Humanae Vitae* Cavanagh was the recipient of three papal medals. Through his teaching and writing Cavanagh was a builder of bridges between psychiatry and Catholicism; he saw these bridges as representing a modern means of connecting faith and reason. After Cavanagh's death, Curran aptly summarized the Catholic psychiatrist's life and work: "no one else on the Catholic scene in the United States wrote more on bringing together psychiatry and religion, moral theology and counseling."[12]

Charles A. Curran, Ph.D. (1913–78)

As noted earlier in chapter 4, Curran introduced the therapeutic constructs of Carl Rogers to the American Catholic world. Through his four decades of teaching Curran had an enormous impact on priests and religious. His writings reflect a conscious attempt to articulate psychological understanding and to do so in a Catholic framework, which throughout most of his life was held together through the Thomistic synthesis. Curran's style of integrating psychology into a Catholic theological framework is demonstrated in three of his books: *Counseling in Catholic Life and Education, Religious Values in Counseling and Psychotherapy,* and *The Word Becomes Flesh.*

In *Counseling in Catholic Life and Education* (1952), Curran shows that counseling from a client-centered perspective is consonant with the Thomistic model. Perhaps to defuse the suspicion with which the Catholic Church viewed psychology, Curran not only had his local bishop, Michael J. Ready, write a foreword, but he also had Italian Cardinal Eugene Tisserant write a preface. Both were complimentary of the work. The cardinal explains what he sees as essential to Curran's work: "Combining a thorough and accurate knowledge of modern psychological science with a sound integration of Thomistic philosophy and theology, it offers ready at hand for the work of Catholic Action a fund of very practical information and skill."[13] Endorsements from Tisserant and Ready enhanced the book's popularity in the Catholic world; it was translated into four languages.

Throughout the book Curran demonstrates a sound knowledge of counseling theory and technique and Thomistic insights into human virtue. He pays special attention to the virtue of prudence, which he believes can be particularly enhanced through counseling. Curran's alacrity in moving his reader between Rogerian psychology and Thomistic philosophy made the book a landmark work for its time, establishing him as a psychologist to whom many bishops, clergy, religious, and lay people turned.

It was shortly after the publication of this book that Curran left St. Charles Seminary in Columbus, Ohio, and joined the faculty of Loyola in Chicago. His classes dealing with pastoral counseling soon overflowed with clergy and religious. In one survey of the pastoral counseling classes Curran taught between 1961 and 1963 he was given high praise for his theory, technique, and training. As one student remarked, "Fr. Curran's theory is honest and self-consistent, and I consider him practically unmatched as a practicing counselor. His emphasis on ideational content (as opposed to mere feeling) puts him a notch above even Rogers."[14]

Because he was able to incorporate psychology into a Catholic system of thought, Curran was in high demand by the Catholic hierarchy during the Second Vatican Council (1962–65). He was named a *peritus* (or expert advisor) to American bishops at the Council and received a papal medal for his work.

Influenced by the dialogue that he witnessed and the documents that were produced by the Council, Curran's own theory underwent a noticeable shift. He believed the Council gave birth to a "new Christian self-concept," one that emphasized "the need for a genuine effort to understand, respect, and love one another, other Christians, and the world."[15] Curran's subsequent writings resonated with the changes in Catholic theology and pastoral practices brought on by the Council. For instance, *Religious Values in Counseling and Psychotherapy* (1969) shows a clear contrast with his earlier work, *Counseling in Catholic Life and Education,* with a shift in emphasis from virtue to value. Now Curran borrows fewer categories from Thomism and instead uses such post-Council catchwords as "encounter," "engagement," and "experience."[16] "Religion and the religious encounter have not yet profited from this modern psychological development to the degree that they could and should."[17] Finding that the dynamics of psychology and the concepts of theology often run parallel, Curran attempts a new approach at integrating the two fields.

Referring to counseling as an "incarnate-redemptive process," he compares the Christian mystery of God's bridging the distance between divinity and humanity through the incarnation of Christ with the ways in which the counselor-client relationship is made closer through the incarnational presence of the counselor for the sake of the client. Just as Christ's incarnation relieved the alienation of humanity from God, so too does the counselor and the counseling process relieve a client's alienation from self and others. Such analogies indicate that Curran achieved sophisticated levels of integration as he sought to "demonstrate that certain awarenesses adapted from counseling therapeutic knowledge and applied to the religious situation can be significant and effective aids to religion."[18]

Curran also carries the incarnational theme into his approach to homiletics, on which he wrote several volumes. He takes a "psychodynamic approach" to homiletics, articulated in *The Word Becomes Flesh* (1973). The task of the homilist, he says, is to "humanize the word" by incorporating the psychodynamic process:

> A profound psychodynamic process is essential if we are to preserve and deepen our fundamental value system—a value system that has much of its origin in the Old and New Testament. This would be the core and central purpose behind humanizing the Word.[19]

This requires that the homilist be in touch with themes of anxiety, conflict, courage, weakness, and forgiveness, which are part and parcel of the human condition. By listening the homilist becomes more attuned to his listeners and, like the therapist, offers to others "a warm and rich sharing of the incarnate redemptive process of being a man beloved of God."[20]

The life and work of Charles Curran had a significant impact on the American Catholic Church during critical periods before, during, and after the Second Vatican Council. Curran's teachings and writings enabled his many American Catholic followers as well as others to engage psychological issues and still remain consistent with their identities as Catholics.

Adrian van Kaam, Ph.D. (b. 1921)

One needs only to view Pittsburgh's three-river vista from the vantage point of its Mount Washington to understand why the panorama has often been compared to a European setting. With a plethora of bridges crossing the Allegheny, the Monongahela, and the Ohio, the city resembles cities along the Danube or the Rhine. In the nineteenth century waves of immigrants arrived from Eastern and Western Europe, many attracted to work in the steel mills nestled along Pittsburgh's rivers. To educate and pastorally serve these immigrants was a mission of the Congregation of the Holy Ghost (later known as the Spiritans). Members of this missionary and educational order first arrived in Pittsburgh in 1874. In 1879, at the request of the Pittsburgh Catholic ordinary, Bishop Michael Domenec, the order founded the Pittsburgh College of the Holy Ghost. Located on a bluff overlooking Pittsburgh's three rivers, the college would eventually become Duquesne University, the city's first and only Catholic university.

Like most Catholic institutions of higher education during the first half of the twentieth century, Duquesne's academic reputation was known chiefly within its metropolitan area. Shortly after World War II, the institution's philosophy department began importing from European academia some of the new continental approaches to philosophy, psychology, and theology, namely, existentialist philosophy and phenomenology. Drawing from their Belgian, Dutch, German, and French roots, the Holy Ghost Fathers established a singular identity in American academia not only through the university's faculty, but also through its university press. During the 1950s and 1960s Duquesne University Press was a leading conduit of existential and phenomenological writings, publishing such Catholic thinkers as Henry Koren, Remigius Kwant, and Wilhelmus Luijpen. During this period of Duquesne's academic emergence, there arrived a Holy Ghost Father by the name of Adrian van Kaam.

Van Kaam was born in The Hague in the Netherlands and was ordained a Holy Ghost Father in 1946. His formation as a seminarian was
greatly enhanced by his friendship with his "soul friend," Marinus ("Rinus") Scholtes, whom he first met in 1935.[21] They shared an enthusiasm
for spiritual conversation and a desire to improve the spiritual lives of
Dutch laity. Van Kaam and others at the seminary were impressed by the
holiness and wholesomeness they witnessed in Rinus. However, as he was
approaching the profession of his final vows, Rinus developed a serious
illness and died in 1941 at the age of twenty-two. The impact that his
friendship with Rinus had on van Kaam's spiritual life and future ministry
was indelible. This lasting admiration for Rinus's spirituality and ministerial vision was demonstrated more than fifty years after his friend's death
when van Kaam edited and published Rinus's diary as *Become Jesus: The
Diary of a Soul Touched by God.*[22]

Another formative experience of van Kaam's seminary life occurred
during World War II when he lived through the German occupation of
Holland. In the summer of 1944 the occupation became especially oppressive after the Allies lost the battle of Arnhem. This defeat meant a
prolonging of the German occupation of substantial parts of the Netherlands until the war's end. Basic supplies and foodstuffs diminished as the
occupation army enforced its desperate plans to save Hitler's Third Re-
ich. Increasingly Jews and suspected leaders were sent to concentration
camps, while many others were deported to work in German factories. Van
Kaam along with other seminarians and many university students went into
hiding.

A small attic above a stable on a country farm served as his hiding place.
With others who were also in hiding, many of whom were not Catholic,
van Kaam spent much time conversing about issues that he would spend
the rest of his life working out in a systematic way. "We talked about the
characters of collaborators with the enemy, or profit mongers, and of the
uncommitted and indifferent who did not help us."[23] Existential questions
of life and spiritual issues about God were discussed with people of different faiths. Van Kaam found the spiritual insights he gained from his
friendship with Rinus as well as his Thomistic training put to ready use.

Throughout his course of studies van Kaam greatly admired Thomas
Aquinas's speculative system of philosophy and the way it integrated
other disciplines. He recognized, however, that the thirteenth-century philosopher did not have knowledge of present-day empirical science. Van
Kaam believed that a more complementary "empirical-experiential" system of thought was necessary, one that would connect peoples of different
faiths and backgrounds like those with whom he shared his life in hiding.
Reflecting on those experiences he later wrote:

I soon concluded that I could foster spiritual ties among the people hiding with me by appealing to their empirical-experiential mind-set. I decided that it was time to complement the pretheological study of philosophy with pretheological studies in experiential life formation. My approach should be critical toward, yet appreciative of, empirical-experiential thinkers. It would parallel in some ways Aquinas's approach to the philosophical thinkers of his time.[24]

During that terrible ordeal of the 1944–45 "hunger winter," there deepened in van Kaam his original desire to develop and communicate a systematic science of formative spirituality. This ideal was to become his life project of integrating philosophical anthropology, the human sciences, and spirituality.

Van Kaam's first systematic attempts at this intellectual integration came following the war and shortly after his ordination in 1946. Besides teaching philosophy at his seminary, he served as a consultant and a teacher for a Dutch program for young adults known as "The Life Schools." Conducted in corporations and factories, the program was highly successful. Van Kaam's participation in the program drew the attention of the Vatican secretary of state, Monsignor Giovanni Baptista Montini, who two decades later became Pope Paul VI. Montini, through the papal nuncio in Holland, requested that van Kaam's superiors allow him to receive the training necessary to develop a theory of formation based on his experience in the Dutch Life Schools. With ecclesiastical approval, therefore, van Kaam began in earnest to develop the science, anthropology, and theology of formation. Over the years his order would support his leadership in psychological and philosophical systems in such a way that Msgr. Montini's mandate and van Kaam's dream would come to fruition. Most of his adult training, teaching, and writing would take place in the United States, which would lead to a unique formulation incorporating anthropological psychology into American Catholic thought.

In 1954 van Kaam came to the United States to begin doctoral studies in psychology at Western Reserve University (now Case Western Reserve University). He received his doctorate in 1958 after writing a dissertation entitled "The Experience of Really Feeling Understood by a Person." The dissertation furthered van Kaam's interest in developing a distinct field of psychology as a human science. He did his postdoctoral training with Carl Rogers at the University of Chicago and later went to Brandeis University to work with Kurt Goldstein and Abraham Maslow. Van Kaam established a good rapport with his mentors. For instance, when Maslow went on sabbatical from Brandeis during the academic year 1958–59, it was van Kaam who taught his classes. For a Catholic priest to teach classes at Brandeis, a

Jewish university, in the late 1950s represented a significant breakthrough
in Catholicism's relations with psychology as well as in Catholic-Jewish
relations. Van Kaam had to have had the approval of Boston's cardinal archbishop, Richard Cushing. Moreover, Maslow's invitation indicated that
van Kaam had earned the respect of one of the leading psychologists of
the time.

After the 1958–59 academic year van Kaam assumed the position of
assistant professor of psychology at Duquesne, where he helped to build
its psychology department. He would spend the next several decades of
his life associated with Duquesne, integrating various streams of thought:
European and American; existential-phenomenological and theological;
psychological and spiritual. And for van Kaam each stream moved toward
a science of formative spirituality to which he had long ago committed his
ministry. Several phases of his thought may be traced.

In America van Kaam initially established a reputation in psychology.
His work with Rogers and Maslow enabled him to associate with leading figures in the field. Furthermore, his work in developing Duquesne's
program in psychology brought him into contact with other leading Catholic psychologists, like William Bier and Virginia Staudt Sexton, and with
psychologists interested in religion, like Rollo May.[25] During his psychological studies and training at some of America's finest universities and
training institutes, van Kaam sought to incorporate what he learned into
his earlier pastoral experiences and scholarship. At that time he found in the
existential-phenomenological thought flourishing in Europe a means for
developing an integrated system he called "anthropological psychology."
With his articulation of existential-phenomenological approaches to psychology van Kaam became a leader in professional psychology's focus
on distinctively human development. This approach had a close ally in
psychology's humanistic movement, or "third force." He brought this emphasis to Duquesne's psychology department and worked with faculty
members who shared the same phenomenological perspective. As noted
above, the existential-phenomenological perspective was also well represented by members of Duquesne's philosophy department and Duquesne
University's press. Before long van Kaam furthered Duquesne's reputation as the place to go for training in phenomenological approaches to
psychology as well as philosophy.

From 1961 to 1967 van Kaam served as the editor of the *Review of Existential Psychology and Psychiatry,* a quarterly journal that published articles
by leading American and European writers. It was just one of a series of
periodicals with which van Kaam would become closely involved.[26] In one
article he wrote for the *Review,* "The Impact of Existential Phenomenology on the Psychological Literature of Western Europe," he surveyed more

than 250 articles and books by continental authors on topics related to existential phenomenology. He cited the writings of such thinkers as Buber, Heidegger, Husserl, Jaspers, Kierkegaard, and Sartre and introduced to an American audience important but relatively unknown figures such as L. Binswanger, F. J. J. Buytendijk, A. De Waelhens, J. H. Vanden Berg, and J. Von Uexkull.[27]

Despite his phenomenological interests, van Kaam saw existential psychology as only a temporary movement that could challenge and help reconstruct scientific psychology, a view not held by all his colleagues at Duquesne and at the *Review*. Van Kaam eventually drifted away from editing, teaching, and writing about existential and psychological topics. He later said that psychology was never his first love or career choice; instead his intellectual interests centered on the project that he first envisioned during his seminary days: how best to address spiritual insights and wisdom to contemporary audiences. He saw his training in psychology with its rich understanding of the human being as making possible a dynamic approach to spirituality. It should be noted that he helped establish Duquesne's psychology department not based on his own initiative but as a response to the request of his superiors.

In 1963 van Kaam was given permission by Duquesne's administration to relinquish his academic responsibilities in the psychology department and establish "The Institute of Man." At the Institute, which offered a three-year master of arts degree, he no longer felt constrained to express insights using psychological categories alone. He recruited faculty colleagues and students to join him in his project of developing a systematic theory of foundational formative spirituality. This does not mean, however, that van Kaam completely abandoned formulating psychology from an existential-phenomenological perspective. In 1966 he published two significant works on existential psychology, *The Art of Existential Counseling: A New Perspective in Psychotherapy* and *Existential Foundations of Psychology*.

In *Existential Counseling* he incorporates into the therapeutic setting such existential themes as authenticity, encounter, existential will, and project. Rather than teaching the specifics of a therapeutic method, Van Kaam promotes attitudes with which a counselor or a therapist might learn to become open and recognize existential topics as they present themselves. For van Kaam such themes offer clients avenues for developing a greater sense of freedom and owning more responsibility for their lives.[28] In *Existential Foundations* Van Kaam offers a series of critiques of prevailing positivistic approaches to scientific psychology, which he considers invested with determinism. He elucidates a model of anthropological psychology that "integrates empirical, clinical, and theoretical psychologies within an open theory of personality that serves as a comprehensive frame of reference for all the significant theories and data in the field."[29] The two books represent van Kaam's most systematic attempt to integrate existential phenomenology and psychology. They would also serve as a foundation for his systematic approach to spirituality.

During the same period, van Kaam began to publish books that integrated themes related to psychology and spirituality. The titles themselves indicate his efforts at integration: *Religion and Personality* (1964), *Personality Fulfillment in the Spiritual Life* (1966), *Personality Fulfillment in Religious Life* (1967), and *The Vowed Life* (1968).[30] At the time, the audience for this literature consisted primarily of priests and religious. With the changes emanating from the Second Vatican Council and its call for the enhancement of lay spirituality, van Kaam sought a wider audience for his writings. This effort can be seen in titles such as *On Being Involved* (1970), *On Being Yourself* (1972), and *Envy and Originality* (1972).[31] It was also during this period that van Kaam began collaboration with Dr. Susan Muto, a lay woman and writer whose own spiritual writing embodied the themes van Kaam sought to address. Muto, along with another Dutch Holy Ghost Father, Bert van Croonenburg, assisted van Kaam in publishing two highly successful works, *The Emergent Self* (1968) and *The Participant Self* (1969).[32] Muto later served on the faculty of the Institute and became a leading spiritual writer in her own right.

In its first decade the Institute of Man flourished as it attracted priests, religious, and lay people from all over the world. Under van Kaam's editorial leadership the Institute also published *Humanitas* and *Envoy,* the latter an organ for publishing the Institute's papers. In 1978, to indicate a more inclusive orientation, the Institute changed its name to the Institute of Formative Spirituality.

During the 1970s, van Kaam began to publish works more focused on his developing science of spiritual formation. In *Studies in Formative Spirituality* he published a "provisional glossary" that explained key concepts. In his *In Search of Spiritual Identity* (1975) and *The Dynamics of Spiritual Self-Direction* (1976) he began to articulate a style of thought more intentionally spiritual and dealing with fewer topics of a psychological nature.[33] This style was also evidenced in works that he wrote with Muto, *Tell Me Who I Am* (1977), *Am I Living a Spiritual Life?* (1978), and *Practicing the Prayer of Presence* (1980).[34] Other works by van Kaam were directed toward biblical themes: *The Woman at the Well* (1976) and *Looking for Jesus* (1978).[35]

During the 1990s, following van Kaam's retirement and the appointment of Muto as executive director of the Epiphany Association, the number of students attending the Institute significantly decreased. By 1993 Duquesne's new administration determined that all smaller graduate programs were no longer financially viable and mandated their closing. Van Kaam, however, aided by the administrative leadership of his colleague Muto, continued the study of formation science and formation theology through the Epiphany Association, which they had founded in 1979.

Their common project came to greater maturation starting in 1983 when van Kaam published the first of a series of volumes on formative spirituality. The titles give some indication of its various dimensions: vol. 1: *Fundamental Formation* (1983); vol. 2: *Human Formation* (1985); vol. 3: *Formation of the Human Heart* (1986); vol. 4: *Scientific Formation* (1987); vol. 5: *Traditional Formation;* vol. 6: *Transcendent Formation* (1995); vol. 7: *Transcendence Therapy* (1995). The emphasis on "form" should not be construed as something neo-Platonic, for van Kaam views his theory as dynamic and embodied, as may be seen from the definition he gives to the term "Core Form of Life":

> The relatively enduring ground form of life formed during the period between birth and early adulthood. In later life, it is usually not changed fundamentally, but is continuously modulated by the succession of provisional current forms life assumes. In the Christian view, the core form, or heart, of life becomes the integrative responsible-sensible center of global formative affects, which tend to give a basic concrete form to the soul's image of Christ, under the guidance of the Holy Spirit.[36]

While van Kaam admits that his spiritual, scientific, anthropological, and theological writings remain within the framework of a Christian formation tradition, he believes that the pretheological science and anthropology of formation, which he elaborates in these volumes, are applicable to any tradition of spirituality. In this respect they resemble the writings of Aquinas; van Kaam's system is intended to hold true for Christians as well as non-Christians. In his foreword to *Contemplative Psychology*, by Han de Wit, van Kaam summarizes his project's purpose:

> The best way to facilitate genuine communication and understanding between different spiritual paths is not to restrict oneself to mere doctrinal, philosophical or theological expositions, no matter how crucial these may be for the development of other basic aspects of ecumenical and transecumenical dialogues. Without empathic insight into the paths of spiritual formation, our understanding of other traditions is neither complete nor experientially profound and trustworthy. A grasp of both their foundational doctrines and their experiential points of reference is necessary. They need to shed light on one another, for only in the understanding and communication of their

respective faith and formation traditions can they be fully appreciated for what they truly are.[37]

Van Kaam's complete written legacy totals more than thirty books and hundreds of articles. To assess his influence and the impact that his writings have had and will have in the future is virtually impossible at this point as he moves toward the completion of a multivolume dictionary on human and Christian character formation. Thus far, his most popular works appeared during the 1960s, when he was gleaning insights from existential phenomenology to relate psychology with spirituality. His later works on formation sciences seem esoteric to many readers. At the same time, these works reflect the life project he took upon himself during his seminary days and the mandate he was given by Msgr. Montini, the future Pope Paul VI. More recently, in the summer of 1996 when van Kaam celebrated his fiftieth anniversary in the priesthood, he met with Pope John Paul II, from whom he received a special commendation for his life-long labors. Since formation science is still in its infancy, time alone can determine its significance for contemporary thought. What can be concluded is that Adrian van Kaam has led a remarkable life as a philosopher, a psychologist, and a priest. His writings have been prolific and profound and have contributed to the shaping of new American Catholic attitudes toward psychology as well as spirituality.

William Meissner, M.D. (b. 1931)

During the postconciliar era the most significant American Catholic author in the field of psychoanalytic scholarship has been Fr. William Meissner, S.J. Author of numerous articles and more than a dozen books during four decades, in many of his writings Meissner has undertaken the task of building bridges of dialogue between psychoanalysis and religion. Having obtained a medical degree from Harvard University and performed a psychiatric residency, Meissner later went on for training in psychoanalysis. He then became a training analyst himself at the Boston Psychoanalytic Institute. Such extensive training in psychiatry and psychoanalysis, combined with his philosophical and theological formation as a Jesuit, well qualified Meissner to explore the relationships among these various fields.

Ironically, Meissner's early intention as a Jesuit was to concentrate his studies in biology. During his Jesuit scholastic studies, however, his superiors suggested that he move toward a ministry in medicine, especially psychiatry. Under the mentorship of the Jesuit theologian John Courtney Murray, Meissner set about the task of integrating issues surrounding psychological and spiritual identity, personally, pastorally, and professionally.

From his earliest writings one detects a movement from a focus on integrating psychology and theology to one of relating psychoanalysis and spirituality. This is evident in his comprehensive *Annotated Bibliography in Religion and Psychology,* published in 1961.[38] Meissner's bibliography is exhaustive: it reviews more than twenty-nine hundred articles written between 1900 and 1960 in more than three hundred journals in English and French. Meissner organizes his bibliography into more than forty topics relevant to the relationship between psychology and religion. The bibliography not only provides the reader with the most comprehensive review of the literature of psychology and religion up to that time, but also leaves the impression that Meissner had prepared himself well for a lifetime of exploration of the shared interests of psychology and religion.

In 1964 Meissner published an article entitled "Prolegomena to a Psychology of Grace," in which he raises a question to which he would return during the next several decades, namely, is it possible to relate psychological identity with spiritual identity? Meissner indicates that his formulation of a psychology of grace is "preliminary" and "tentative." Using the Thomistic axiom *gratia perfecta natura* (grace builds on nature), Meissner sees his formulation as grounded in "a major presumption of a theological order, namely, that the order of grace is perfective in the order of nature."[39] Implicit in this presumption is Meissner's conviction that there is a "basic correlation and interaction between a variety of elements in which the growth of each is dependent on and integral to the growth of the others."[40] Using the stage development theory of Erik Erikson, Meissner proposes psychological correlates of grace and explores how grace works in and through the resources of ego, thus showing how psychological identity relates to spiritual identity. Later in an edited work, *Foundations for a Psychology of Grace,* he states that understanding how the two identities are integral to one another is one of the vital tasks facing the Christian psychologist:

> The great challenge to the Christian psychologists ... is to shape a theory of man's psychological functioning which incorporates the data and insights of modern psychological understanding, and which is also fully consonant with the penetrating insights of the Christian tradition.[41]

Twenty years later in his work *Life and Faith,* Meissner's extensive psychoanalytic training as well as change in psychoanalytic theory enabled him to articulate more fully what he had expressed in his earlier writings. Besides using Erikson's stage theory of development, Meissner also turned to the psychoanalytic object relations theories of Otto Kernberg, Margaret Mahler, Ann Marie Rizzuto, and Donald Winnicott to further refine his psychology of grace. Their approach to psychoanalysis, combined with Karl Rahner's theological insights about grace as divine self-communication, enabled Meissner to articulate a psychology of grace rooted in relationality. He uses three principles to express this relationality. First is the principle of *reciprocal influence,* by which Meissner means that for grace to be operative in the ego, it depends upon the functioning of the ego to produce a desired effect. This represents a contemporary understanding of how grace perfects human nature. Meissner asserts that spiritual identity builds upon psychological identity:

> The perfecting of nature is reflected on the psychological level in the parallel development of the ego in autonomy, control, freedom, and maturity of function, together with the emergence of a sense of spiritual identity.[42]

As a second principle for his psychology of grace Meissner discusses *compensatory activation,* whereby the actions of grace energize ego-functions. This energizing serves a sanative function through which any healing takes place. However, Meissner reiterates that grace cannot force healing upon a person; it cannot violate the functions of the ego.

Meissner's third principle, *epigenesis,* refers to the ways in which psychological and spiritual identity are related. He concurs with Erikson that ego strengths are developed especially through crisis and shows how each of Erikson's eight stages of psychosocial crises has a psychospiritual correlate of virtue.

In his recent writings Meissner has attempted to articulate how psychoanalysis and religion can enter into a more fruitful dialogue. In his most important work on the subject, *Psychoanalysis and Religious Experience* (1984), for which he won the prestigious Oscar Pfister award, Meissner works out a rapprochement between psychoanalysis and religion.[43] One of the ways he attempts to improve the often antagonistic relations between the two fields has been in his discussion of the work of the object relations theorists Donald Winnicott and Ann Marie Rizzuto. Winnicott, a British psychoanalyst, developed the notion of "transitional phenomena," which refers to the way both children and adults grow by means of certain kinds of illusions. Winnicott broke from the Freudian view that illusions are necessarily pathological in adults. Rather, for Winnicott, illusions are the source of creativity and play. Later in her landmark work, *The Birth of the Living God* (1979), Rizzuto applied Winnicott's notions of transitional phenomena to show how representations of God are developed as a means of facing reality.[44]

Meissner uses the views of Winnicott and Rizzuto to state the case against Freud's position that religious belief is illusory and an avoiding of reality. He argues that what Freud saw as a pathological in religion can really be healthy and helpful. Meissner's reinterpretation of one of the central tenets of Freud's psychoanalytic critique of religion establishes a bridge between psychoanalysis and religion. In recent years Meissner has continued not only to write on psychoanalysis but also to explore religious personalities and topics from a psychoanalytic perspective. Four works in particular demonstrate this: *Ignatius of Loyola: The Psychology of a Saint* (1990); *Thy Kingdom Come: Psychoanalytic Perspectives on the Messiah and the Millennium* (1995); *To the Greater Glory: A Psychological Study of Ignatian Spirituality* (1999); *The Cultic Origins of Christianity: The Dynamics of Religious Development* (2000).

Meissner's psychohistorical work on St. Ignatius Loyola richly portrays the psychodynamics of Ignatius's life. For example, in speaking of the psychodynamics of Ignatius's mysticism, Meissner brings together both the psychological and theological:

> I would submit that in his periods of prayer and mystical ecstasy Ignatius entered...a realm of transitional experience. His mystical experiences were forms of illusion, in Winnicott's sense, that were expressions of his inner subjective psychic life, with its complex needs and determinants—infantile, narcissistic, libidinal, and otherwise—as they intersected with an external reality that can be described in theological terms as divine presence, grace, infused contemplation, and other transcendental manifestations.[45]

In *Thy Kingdom Come*, Meissner asserts the view that psychoanalysis has entered a new and more respectful phase in its attitude toward religious experience. Recognizing the rise of millenarianism, Meissner uses his psychoanalytic methods to respectfully explore the motivations and fantasies of people who hold extreme apocalyptic and eschatological beliefs.[46]

Meissner again took up an investigation of Jesuit psychology in *To The Greater Glory: A Psychological Study of Ignatian Spirituality*. Here he looks at the foundational works of a Jesuit's psychological and spiritual identity, namely, the Spiritual Exercises, the Constitutions of the Society of Jesus, and St. Ignatius's autobiography.[47] Here again Meissner brings a psychoanalytic perspective to his study of religious topics, seeking to bridge the gap between psychoanalysis and religion and to integrate psychological and spiritual identity. The leitmotif of Meissner's decades of research in the area, namely, the relation between the divine and the human, was central to the founder of his beloved order:

Although it remains more or less a background consideration in the book, it is matter consistently indicated by Ignatius himself. . . . I refer to the question of the interaction between the influence of divine grace and human motivation. There is resident in Ignatian formulations and understandings the components of such a psychology, but it remains implicit and assumed in his thinking. . . . My assumption throughout is that, to the extent that grace operates in human nature and has effects on that nature, its influence does not do violence to man's psychic capabilities, but works in and through those potentialities to effect whatever psychic change might be in question. Grace does not work its effects exclusively from or in contradiction to the inherent potentialities of the human mind and heart. The pervasive question, then, concerns how Ignatius envisions those effects and what psychological perspectives can we draw on to illumine that understanding of the interplay of grace and nature that lies at the heart of his method.[48]

In *The Cultic Origins of Christianity: The Dynamics of Religious Development,* Meissner examines the formation of cults as they emerge through a paranoid process of introjection and projection and are maintained and reinforced through paranoid construction. Using these psychoanalytic concepts as hermeneutical tools, Meissner goes on to show how the early Christian community may be seen as a cult. As such, it exhibited such psychoanalytical processes as it emerged as a marginalized social movement in its encounters with other cultic movements, for example, Apocalypticism and Gnosticism.[49]

A hermeneutical key to understanding Meissner's own psychological and spiritual identity is that for fifty years he has been a member of the order founded by Ignatius of Loyola, who formulated his own understanding of "the influence of divine grace and human motivation." Long before Meissner's writings, so many of which reveal ways of integrating psychology and spirituality through a contemporary understanding of grace and nature, Ignatius of Loyola struggled with the Christian problematic of how divine grace perfects human nature. The mind of William Meissner, Jesuit priest, psychiatrist, and psychoanalyst, is very much in line with that of the founder of his Jesuit order.

Conclusion

The witness and work of Leo Bartemeier, Francis Braceland, John Cavanaugh, Charles A. Curran, Adrian van Kaam, and William Meissner demonstrate how the dialogue between American Catholicism and professional psychology has evolved through the untiring efforts of individual clinicians and academicians. In each case we have seen how a trained clinician waded the currents that streamed from modern psychology and met the sometimes turbulent waters of Catholic culture both before and after the Second Vatican Council. Such endeavors have inspired others to see psychology as a conduit for one to enter the contemporary confluence of Catholicism and culture where the perennial questions of faith and reason meet and where one learns how grace continues to build on nature.

Chapter 9

Monk and Psychologist

Thomas Merton and Henri Nouwen

Thomas Merton:
A Monk Who Encountered a Psychoanalyst

Of all the American Catholic authors of the twentieth century no other quite matches the spiritual breadth and depth of Thomas Merton. His first book, a spiritual autobiography titled *The Seven Storey Mountain*, was a national bestseller in 1948. But Merton did not write for a popular audience. His thirty years of publications, including some seventy books and a host of articles, attracted an audience bent on grappling with the serious issues facing faith in the modern world. In Merton's writings readers from all sorts of backgrounds, believers and unbelievers alike, sought meaning amid the vast deserts of the secular world. It was natural, therefore, that Merton read the major psychologists of his day and critically evaluated what they had to offer.

As a young man Merton sought solace in psychology before finding it in spirituality. In fact, he later said that his brief foray into psychology almost led him astray from authenticity. While a student at Cambridge, Merton embarked on a spiritual search in which he "began to get all the books of Freud and Jung and Adler" and studied them "with all the patience and application which my hangovers allowed me."[1] Merton discovered such readings to be unrewarding:

> Day after day I read Freud, thinking myself to be very enlightened and scientific, when as a matter of fact I was about as scientific as an old woman secretly pouring over books about occultism, trying to tell her own fortune, and learning how to dope out the future from the lines in the palm of her hand. I don't know if I ever got very close to needing a padded cell: but if I had ever gone crazy, I think psychoanalysis would have been the one thing chiefly responsible for it.[2]

As he recounts in his autobiography Merton waded through the currents of contemporary psychology toward a classical monastic spirituality that, among other things, calmed some of the psychological tensions of his life. Still, while he did not find his identity through psychology, Merton did come to appreciate its value and incorporated some of its insights into his life and work. He borrowed theories from psychology especially when he served as master of scholastics at Gethsemani between 1951 and 1955 and master of novices between 1955 and 1965. It appeared that he did a lot of learning on the job, and as one incident suggests Merton may have gone too far in his appropriation of psychology. It occurred during the summer of 1956 when he met psychoanalyst Gregory Zilboorg.

Merton and Zilboorg

Merton met Zilboorg while both were at the St. John's Summer Institute in Collegeville, Minnesota. As noted in chapter 6 Zilboorg was a major figure in Roman Catholic psychological circles. Before their meeting at Collegeville, Merton and Zilboorg had heard of one another. Merton made the first contact when he sent Zilboorg a draft of an article he was considering publishing entitled "Neurosis in the Monastic Life." Zilboorg, in turn, was interested in meeting the famous monk and through a mutual friend invited Merton to visit him in New York. This proved unacceptable to Merton's abbot, Dom James Fox, but on learning that Zilboorg would be giving lectures at the St. John's Institute that summer, Fox permitted Merton to attend.

Fox accompanied Merton to Collegeville as did another monk, John Eudes Bamberger. Bamberger, who had entered Gethsemani in 1951 with a medical degree, later received permission to receive psychiatric training at Catholic University. As we shall see later, this was the same monk-psychiatrist who figured prominently in the life of Henri Nouwen.

At the time he met Zilboorg, Merton had been going through a difficult discernment with regard to his role in his Trappist community. For several years he had expressed to his superiors a desire to live as a hermit within the community's spacious Kentucky acreage. On the other hand, having successfully served as the community's master of scholastics, Merton had assumed the position of master of novices. In these respective roles of formation Merton had begun to explore ways in which he could incorporate psychological theories and techniques into the spiritual formation of his men. With an entirely different motivation than that of his earlier days at Cambridge, Merton plunged into the psychological literature and read the works of Karen Horney and Otto Rank. The essay that he submitted to Zilboorg, "Neurosis in the Monastic Life," was an attempt to show how some of the principles of psychoanalysis could be applied to religious formation.[3]

Merton's tenure as spiritual master occurred during the heyday of religious vocations. While embracing one of the strictest standards of any Catholic religious order, the Trappists still drew a good number of applicants. Merton's reputation put Gethsemani on the map, and it became a Mecca for pilgrims and applicants alike. However, Merton soon learned that not every novice or scholastic was psychologically capable of enduring the rigors of Trappist asceticism. Some form of a psychological screening process was necessary, and so with Bamberger's help, Merton's community was one of the first to make use of psychological tests. Merton even took it upon himself to learn how to give the Rorschach Test.[4]

During his two weeks at St. John's Merton attended Zilboorg's lectures and found them informative and stimulating. Zilboorg's thick accent, stocky physique, bushy mustache, and thick hair—Russian caricature—cast a spell on his listeners. The mystique was not lost on Merton, who thought Zilboorg resembled Joseph Stalin. The classes and the meetings Merton had with the Russian psychoanalyst gave Merton a wealth of insight and helped him appreciate what his personal psychological quests and his psychodynamic enthusiasms could and could not accomplish. According to Mott the conversations between Merton and Zilboorg were some of the most pivotal of Merton's life.[5]

Commenting on the article Merton sent him, Zilboorg accused him of verging on quackery. In Merton's words, Zilboorg criticized the article as "utterly inadequate, hastily written, will do harm, should not even be revised, should be left on the shelf while I read—not Rank, or any other analyst—but Freud. And especially (this astonishes me) Freud's works *against* religion. This is very interesting—they were the last thing I would have bothered with."[6]

Merton had two meetings with Zilboorg at Collegeville, one private and the other with Abbot Fox. After the first meeting Merton recorded in his journal that Zilboorg had challenged his desire to be a hermit, suggesting that it was narcissistically motivated. Merton recalled Zilboorg telling him, "You like to be famous, you want to be a big shot, you keep pushing your way out—into publicity—megalomania and narcissism are your big trends."[7] From this first meeting Merton seemed to have accepted Zilboorg's challenges without too much difficulty. What was difficult for Merton to accept was Zilboorg's critical comments when they met in Abbot Fox's presence. Once again, Zilboorg challenged Merton about the hermitage request: "You want a hermitage in Times Square with a large sign over it saying, 'HERMIT.'"[8] This time Zilboorg's challenges were too much for Merton, especially since they were made in his superior's presence. Merton responded with anger and tears and even exclaimed, "Stalin, Stalin."[9]

Merton's ascetical humility, however, allowed him to remain open to Zilboorg's criticisms. There was at one time a possibility that Merton might go to New York to be analyzed by Zilboorg. The idea, however, was discouraged by Zilboorg himself. Six months later Zilboorg visited Merton at Gethsemani; on this occasion they met in private and so the meetings were less threatening.

"The Neurotic Personality in Monastic Life"

In 1991 "The Neurotic Personality in Monastic Life" was published posthumously by *Merton Studies,* and it reveals Merton to be a very keen psychological writer. One presumes, of course, that Merton made changes in response to Zilboorg's criticisms. It is unfortunate that Merton did not submit it for publication before his death in 1968, for its subject matter and Merton's approach would have made a significant contribution to monastic formation and religious formation in general. Some of its themes remain relevant to this day

The article makes clear that as one responsible for the formation of novices and scholastics Merton knew all too well that "many of the problems that most deeply affect souls in the cloister are psychological rather than ascetic."[10] His twelve years of directing the formation of monks led him to recognize the importance of addressing psychological concerns in the monastic setting; when this is done effectively and compassionately, then "a great work will be done for God."[11]

Merton distinguishes between psychiatry and asceticism, noting that the disciplines "aim at the maturing and perfection of the human soul," but "do so in different ways and indeed in different spheres."[12] Merton sees the value of psychiatry for the ascetic, noting that psychiatry teaches the soul to solve the ordinary emotional problems of life on a mature rather than on an infantile level.[13] He then thematically considers anxiety, self-will, and transference in the monastic context.

Believing mental health to be more than an adjustment to society, Merton considers anxiety to be universal and indeed necessary: "The anxiety that springs from maladjustment to an unbalanced world can therefore be a means of spiritual progress."[14] He uses the insights of Eric Fromm, Gabriel Marcel, and Karen Horney to explicate anxiety. Merton also distinguishes between existential anxiety (a universal) and neurotic anxiety (produced by an "idealized image of an immature mind").[15]

Incorporating the psychology of Otto Rank into his essay, Merton asserts that the problem of the neurotic is not a strong will, but a weak one. That is to say, the neurotic's will is infantile and not mature:

The truth is that the neurotic is one who wants to will without willing, because he wants to remain an infant and have everything done and willed for him. Like the infant, he wants to continue to substitute emotion for will and desire for judgement. The function of others is to do the willing and provide the necessary satisfactions for his desires.[16]

Finally Merton speaks of transference as a phenomenon all too common in the monastery, especially with regard to superiors. Just as a patient transfers subconscious feelings onto the therapist, so too are the subconscious fears and feelings of community members transferred onto their religious superiors.

All in all, Merton presents a worthwhile overview of the psychodynamics operative in the monastic setting. It is indeed unfortunate that this was his only foray into psychology. This is not to say that Merton did not keep abreast of some of the currents in psychology as they affected American culture and the subculture of the monastery. One of the ways he did this was in conversations with visitors to Gethsemani, including one whom Merton referred to as "Nau," that is, Henri Nouwen.

Henri Nouwen:
The Psychologist Who Encountered the Monk

The influence of psychological training on spirituality is probably most evident in the writings of Henri Nouwen, arguably the most popular Catholic spiritual writer of the last quarter-century. Nouwen is a unique figure in post–Vatican II American Catholicism. A prolific writer and inspiring lecturer, Nouwen authored more than forty books and dozens of articles. Several books were bestsellers, with sales of more than a hundred thousand copies each (e.g., *Out of Solitude, The Return of the Prodigal Son*).[17]

While Nouwen never seriously harbored any ambitions for a career in psychology, his spiritual writings are replete with psychological themes and insights. For him psychology was a tool for deepening his understanding of people and thus enhancing his ministry as a priest. Early in his priesthood Nouwen recognized the significance of psychology for theology and counseling for spirituality.

Born in Nijerk, Holland, on January 24, 1932, Henri Nouwen was the first child in a family of two other sons and a daughter. Both his parents were well educated. His father was a distinguished lawyer, while his mother was a linguist especially adept in translating Italian. Years later Nouwen related that he had internalized two parental voices. The one, his father's, said, "You, my son, are gifted. You can accomplish very much. I believe that you can do better than you think." The other, his mother's, said, "You are wonderful, beloved, no matter what you do."[18]

Like every family in Holland Henri's family felt the oppression of the Nazi occupation during World War II. He experienced the anxiety of hiding his father from German patrols in search of able-bodied Dutch men. After the war Nouwen received his secondary education at the Jesuit-run Aloysius College in The Hague. He then entered the seminary to fulfill his childhood dream of becoming a priest.

Nouwen spent a year at a minor seminary and six years at the major seminary at Rijensber for the Archdiocese of Utrecht. His seminary training required two years of philosophy and four years of theological studies. At the time of his seminary education Catholic institutions in Holland were flooded with existential and phenomenological literature that placed great emphasis on ways of describing and understanding faith in light of one's experience. This approach contrasted with the more apodictic categories of scholasticism. It was in this environment that theologians like Romano Guardini and Karl Rahner were read, and Dutch theologians such as Bernard Häring and Edward Schillebeeckx had been bred. These theologians would later influence the theology that permeated the spirit of the Second Vatican Council. This atmosphere no doubt played a role in shaping Nouwen's eloquent descriptions of his personal experiences and pastoral struggles.

Nouwen was ordained a priest in 1957, and although his superior, Archbishop Bernard Alfrink, intended that he study more theology at the Gregorian University in Rome, Nouwen requested and received permission to study for a doctorate in psychology at Nijmegen. He believed that psychology would afford him the means of developing pastoral insights and understanding that would speak to the post–World War II world. From the very beginning of his studies his quest was not a career as a priest-psychologist, but to become a psychologically informed pastoral minister. His first apostolates enabled him to use his training in both psychology and theology as a chaplain and clinical psychologist for the Dutch army; he also did pastoral work among coal miners and factory workers.

In 1962 Nouwen obtained a position as a chaplain for the Holland-America line and used the opportunity to visit the United States. He went to Boston where, through an introductory letter from Richard Cardinal Cushing, Nouwen was able to meet with the noted Harvard psychologist of religion Gordon Allport. In response to Nouwen's inquiry about the best means for integrating psychology and pastoral theology, Allport advised Nouwen to complete his psychology studies at Nijmegen and then apply to the Menninger Clinic in Topeka, Kansas. Nouwen followed Allport's advice and returned to Holland, where he fulfilled the course requirements for a doctoral degree in psychology. Objecting to the quantitative methods of the field, Nouwen never completed a dissertation. His return to Europe during this time was also fortuitous in that it allowed him to attend the opening ceremonies of the Second Vatican Council in October of 1962 and to follow the momentous changes issuing from its proceedings.

Nouwen returned to the United States in 1964 and entered the pastoral psychology program at Menninger. There he met and collaborated with some of the leaders of the clinical pastoral movement, all of them Protestants. They included renowned psychiatrist Karl Menninger, pastoral theologian Seward Hiltner, and Nouwen's compatriot pastoral psychologist Paul Pruyser. Nouwen had a special fondness for Hiltner, who was a leader in incorporating psychological practices and theory into pastoral settings.

At Menninger Nouwen was exposed to the case study method developed by Anton Boisen, the father of Clinical Pastoral Education (CPE). Earlier during his studies in Holland Nouwen had become familiar with the life and work of Anton Boisen and admired the transformative journey of this "wounded healer." As Boisen recounts in his book *The Exploration of the Inner World: A Study of Mental Disorder and Religious Experience* (1936), he had had a mental breakdown from panic attacks that required institutionalization.[19] Boisen's recovery and reflections on his experiences led him to see the need for clinically astute chaplains who would minister in the clinical setting. This training would require that chaplains develop a case study method not dissimilar from that of physicians. Together with Dr. Richard Cabot, Boisen began a movement in which seminarians, at that time mostly in Protestant institutions, were instructed in pastoral care and clinical practices for hospitals and other medical institutions.

In 1964 Nouwen visited Boisen, who in his later years was once again institutionalized. Nouwen later recorded that he was taken a back by the encounter, for he found Boisen alone and despondent. There was a sense of desolation in the man's life expressed in Boisen's question to Nouwen concerning the presence of God. Nevertheless, Nouwen's admiration for Boisen's pastoral theology, the case study method he developed, and the clinical pastoral education movement that he initiated led Nouwen to publish an article entitled "Boisen and the Case Method."[20] In the article Nouwen highlighted Boisen's role in CPE and the importance of the case study method for the training of chaplains. This publication was one of the few places in which Nouwen directly demonstrated his abilities as a clinician. One wonders if Nouwen's own life story as a "wounded healer" did not in some ways parallel Boisen's.

At Menninger, Nouwen met John Santos, who in 1965 had established a department of psychology at the University of Notre Dame. Santos offered Nouwen an appointment as a visiting professor of psychology. Nouwen accepted and taught courses in abnormal psychology and personality theory. His charismatic teaching style and pastoral insights soon made him a popular campus figure. He also began to write essays for campus publications, which drew the attention of the fledgling Catholic periodical, the *National Catholic Reporter* (*NCR*). The *NCR* invited Nouwen to write some articles about contemporary pastoral concerns. His success with these articles led to Nouwen's first book, *Intimacy: Pastoral Psychological Essays* (1969).

In this work Nouwen tackles such sensitive subjects as depression, homosexuality, and religious growth, themes that were beginning to draw increasing attention in the ambiance of the post–Vatican II church. In this initial work Nouwen borrows categories and insights from psychology, thereby opening up to his readers ways in which pastoral ministry could integrate psychology and theology. This was a relatively new approach for Nouwen's mostly Catholic readership. In discussing religious growth, for example, Nouwen incorporates Erik Erikson's eight stages of human development, and in describing depression among seminarians, he considers psychological problems related to personal and vocational identity. In a chapter entitled "Homosexuality: Prejudice or Mental Illness?" Nouwen discusses homosexuality from the perspectives of psychiatry, phenomenology, and pastoral theology. Indeed, *Intimacy* was one of the first Catholic publications to treat the issue of homosexuality from a pastoral perspective.[21] The work set a tone for Nouwen's subsequent writings, in which he addressed contemporary psychological and spiritual struggles with brilliant insight and sensitivity. The popular response to his psychospiritual style launched Nouwen's career as a writer.

Nouwen followed *Intimacy* with a work entitled *Creative Ministry: Beyond Professionalism in Teaching, Preaching, Counseling, Organizing and Celebrating* (1971).[22] The title suggested that by then Nouwen had claimed his own ministerial identity apart from the professionalism of clinical or academic psychology. He dedicated the work to the Hiltner family on the loss of their son and brother, a gesture expressing the friendship that he had developed with his Protestant mentor. In the work Nouwen echoed Hiltner's concern about the professionalism that was beginning to take over ministry. Like Hiltner, Nouwen felt that psychology, while important for pastoral training, could take the priest and minister only so far:

> I do not want to underestimate the tremendous importance of the great help the social sciences can offer the pastor. One of the main reasons for great hope in the field of pastoral care is precisely the

still developing dialogue between pastors, sociologists, social workers, psychologists, and psychiatrists. But I also feel that there is a
unique dimension to pastoral care that goes beyond the expertise of
the behavioral sciences and even beyond professionalism.[23]

Nouwen reiterated this theme in a subsequent work, *Reaching Out: The
Three Movements of the Spiritual Life* (1975). In a thematic consideration of
hospitality Nouwen suggested the trappings associated with the growing
professionalization of psychology:

> During the last decades psychology has made great contributions to
> a new understanding of interpersonal relationships. Not only psychi-
> atrists and clinical psychologist, but also social workers, occupational
> therapists, ministers, priests and many others working in the help-
> ing professions have made grateful use of these new insights in their
> work. But maybe some of us have become so impressed by these
> new findings that we have lost sight of the great wealth contained
> and preserved in such ancient concepts as hospitality.[24]

In the same work Nouwen further voiced his concern about the distance
between caregiver and receiver augmented by increasing professionalization: "How many return from their consultations with psychiatrists,
psychologist, social workers or counselors, increasingly irritated by the
noncommittal attitude and professional distance they encounter?"[25]

A few years later in an interview for *The Critic* Nouwen more sharply
stated his reservations about psychology. For Nouwen, if one stayed in
the psychological world, only psychological questions would be raised and
only psychological answers would be given. He wanted more:

> That's one of the struggles I am having in my writing and teach-
> ing. We are children of a psychological age. We are very familiar with
> words such as conscious and unconscious; depression and regres-
> sion; frustration and defense mechanisms. These words are used more
> frequently by students than words such as atonement, resurrection,
> sin, forgiveness and grace. These words are much less existentially
> powerful than the psychological terminology. I, however, feel that
> if you simply remain in the psychological world, if you raise only
> psychological questions, you will get only psychological answers.[26]

Nouwen integrated psychology into his pastoral ministry as an instrument, but one that did not take precedence over the spiritual. For him the
spiritual had been overshadowed by the psychological: "It is very important for us to know psychological dynamics and know what depression and

aggression and all of those things mean. But I would like to say that spiritual dynamics cannot be reduced to or identified with these psychological dynamics."[27]

As a professor at Yale Nouwen said that his task was not "to deny the validity of the question that is shaped by the psychological perspective, but to say that there is a new level of questioning which opens up new perspectives and basically puts the question in a wholly different context, the context of God's reconciliation of the world in Jesus Christ."[28]

Nouwen's journey as a pastoral minister trained in psychology was evident in the major geographical and psychological displacements in his life. In 1968 Nouwen returned to Holland, where he taught psychology and spirituality at the University of Utrecht. During the same period he did doctoral studies in theology at the University of Nijmegen and earned a "doctorondus," the American equivalent of an "ABD" (all but dissertation). Then, in 1972, based on the success of his books, Nouwen was invited by the dean of the Yale Divinity School to an appointment as a faculty member. So in 1973 Nouwen returned to the United States and resumed his American academic career, which would lead him to two of the nation's most prestigious universities. Nouwen's appointment at Yale lasted for six years (1973–79) and was followed by another six years at Harvard's Divinity School (1979–85).

In the middle of his tenure at Yale, Nouwen spent a sabbatical at the Genesee Abbey in upstate New York. As described in *Genesee Diary,* Nouwen spent six months under the guidance of the Genesee abbot Fr. John Eudes Bamberger. Thus began one of most important relationships of Nouwen's spiritual life. Bamberger, a psychiatrist who had received his novitiate training at Gethsemani under Thomas Merton, encouraged Nouwen to deepen his psychospiritual integration. His meetings with Bamberger deepened Nouwen's spirituality, and he would come to see the monk as one of the most important spiritual mentors of his life. Nouwen's appropriation of spirituality may be seen in one of his journal entries at Genesee:

> Ever since my studies for the priesthood I have felt especially attracted to what was then called, "Ascetical and Mystical Theology," and all my other studies in psychology, sociology, and similar fields never seemed fruitful for me unless they led me to a deeper understanding of the questions of the spiritual life.
>
> I have always moved from the psychological to the theological level and from clinical considerations to spiritual concerns. A sequence of courses—personality theory, clinical psychology, psychology of religion, pastoral psychology, ministry and spirituality, the history of

Christian spirituality, prayer and the spiritual life—seems to illustrate the movement of which I have always been part.[29]

Nouwen's classes at Yale Divinity School and then at Harvard Divinity School were usually filled to capacity and drew rave reviews. All the while Nouwen kept publishing. His books were more and more oriented toward the pastoral and the spiritual. While at Harvard Nouwen took a six-month sabbatical between October 1981 and March 1982 to live in a more radical pastoral setting in the Third World. He had become acquainted with the Maryknoll community and through them had the opportunity of participating in one of their apostolic missions in Peru. As he relates in his book *Gracias!* Nouwen saw this engagement as a means of responding to the question he had harbored for several years, namely, "Does God call me to Latin America?"[30] He prepared by going to Bolivia in 1981 for a three-month intensive course in Spanish at the Maryknoll center in Cochabamba. The following year he moved to Peru, where he worked in the barrios of Lima. It was while he was in Peru that he saw first hand the oppressive conditions from which emerged liberation theology and the writings of Gustavo Gutiérrez. Nouwen became a proponent of this theology as he experienced it in Peru and later in his visits to Mexico and Nicaragua. Having to endure the realities of the Peruvian poor enabled Nouwen to broaden his pastoral psychological perspective. Living in a culture quite unlike the American academic communities with which he had become accustomed, much less the culture of his native Holland, brought forth new psychological perspectives within him. As he adapted to the Peruvian poor he observed within himself "the re-emergence of long-forgotten conflicts." In *Gracias!* Nouwen recorded his feelings about the ways that he was challenged by Peruvian culture. One sees how Nouwen relied upon his training in psychology and his own experiences in psychotherapy to deepen his awareness of his experiences:

> In displacing ourselves into a new and unfamiliar milieu, old, unresolved conflicts often start asking for attention. When our traditional defense systems no longer are available and we are not able to control our own world, we often find ourselves experiencing the feelings of childhood.... This return to childhood emotions and behavior could be a real opportunity for mental and spiritual growth. Most of the psychotherapies I have been exposed to were attempts to help me relive those times when immature ways of coping with stress found their origin.... Going to a different culture, in which I find myself again like a child, can become a true psychotherapeutic opportunity.[31]

Nouwen returned to the United States after his Latin American sabbatical and resumed his teaching at Harvard. The Latin American experience made a deep impression on him and his approach to pastoral ministry. He returned to Latin America in 1983, visiting Mexico and Nicaragua, but his interests eventually led him in an entirely different direction. In 1985 through the encouragement Jean Vanier, Nouwen visited one of Vanier's communities for the mentally handicapped known as L'Arche. His visit there left such an impression that Nouwen resigned his position at Harvard and in September 1986 moved to the L'Arche community called Daybreak, near Toronto. It was in this community that Nouwen underwent the most significant psychological and spiritual challenges of his life, challenges that would deepen his psychological and spiritual well-being. As he later recounted, he faced a "second loneliness," one that eventually resulted in an emotional breakdown. So, instead of being the therapist, between December 1987 and June 1988 Nouwen was a patient. Like Boisen before him, Nouwen faced the burden of entering into the emotional depths of his life, and like Boisen he survived to tell the tale. *The Inner Voice of Love: A Journey through Anguish to Freedom* is the journal of his recovery. In sixty-three "spiritual imperatives" Nouwen, the patient, brings the reader into his work where psychology meets spirituality, showing how a patient encounters his God in and through his self-understanding. For example:

> It is not easy to stay with your loneliness. The temptation is to nurse your pain or to escape into fantasies about people who will take it away. But when you can acknowledge your loneliness in a safe, contained place, you make your pain available for God's healing.[32]

With the encouragement of his friends and therapists, Nouwen edited his journal ten years later for publication. It was finally published on September 20, 1996, the day before Nouwen died of a heart attack.

What might we say of the influence of Henri Nouwen on American psychology? Perhaps there is not too much to say about his academic or professional influence. On the other hand Nouwen's pastoral and professional journey as a priest-psychologist is an example of a contemporary figure who successfully incorporated psychology's insights and techniques so as to broaden and deepen his ministry. Through his writing and teaching Nouwen vigorously demonstrated psychology's potential for modern spirituality, but he also saw and asserted the limits of psychology for ministry. Like Merton, Nouwen was profoundly sensitive to the cultural currents of his age and through his writing struggled to provide spiritual responses to them. His remarkable life and voluminous writings embody an integration of professional training and pastoral vocation that will be one of his lasting legacies.

Chapter 10

Psychology and Spirituality
The New World

Settled amid the rolling hills of Pennsylvania's Berks County and not far from the region's famous Amish country lies the quaint town of Wernersville. Living along one of the nation's mainline railroads, the town's residents for decades have been besieged by the piercing whistles and vibrating rumbles of freight trains. It seemed rather odd, therefore, that it was at Wernersville that Nicholas and Genevieve Brady chose to build a Jesuit seminary. Their choice was even more remarkable since the edifice overlooked a region well established by Congregationalists, Mennonites, and Lutherans. The prospect of building a bastion of American Catholicism in an area inhabited by few Catholics troubled Nicholas, but not his wife, Genevieve. Nicholas, a Catholic convert and a New York tycoon, had made millions with New York Edison. Many years later, a relative and a namesake would serve as the treasurer of the United States. Together with his devoted but childless wife, Nicholas Brady became one of the most important benefactors to American Catholic institutions. A friend to bishops and cardinals on both sides of the Atlantic, Genevieve, with her cultured tastes, challenged the stereotypical impressions that America's elite had of Catholics. Her special fondness for the Society of Jesus led her to persuade her husband to buy 250 rolling acres in Wernersville. There, during the pre-Depression years of the 1920s they committed themselves to building a massive Jesuit novitiate and juniorate. They chose a hill that overlooked the town, a hill that for two centuries had been occupied by Hain's Congregational Church. A cemetery dating back to the Revolutionary War spread across its grounds. In the preecumenical era such construction may have been viewed as provocative, but for the Bradys and the Jesuits it represented the often risky challenge of mission.

On June 2, 1930, two dozen scholastics of the Maryland Province left the New York Province's novitiate of St. Andrew's, located on the Hudson River, and entered the just completed Novitiate of St. Isaac Jogues. These young men were stalwart witnesses to American Catholicism's confident and assertive faith. Had not an Irish American Catholic, Al Smith, just run

148

for president of the United States? The young cohort of Jesuit novices saw themselves as instruments to bring the Catholic Church toward new horizons both in the United States and beyond. The seminary structure that greeted them served to reinforce this special sense of mission. From the Romanesque chapel that in a year's time would be adorned by a Hildreth Meiere mosaic of Christ's passion to the cloister gardens Genevieve's refined taste could be seen.[1] In every one of the edifice's more than two hundred rooms one could see the dedication and love that the Brady couple had for the Society of Jesus.

Nicholas died on March 27, 1930, shortly before the opening of the novitiate, and was buried underneath the main altar. Genevieve, meanwhile, bought a house on the novitiate grounds and used it for occasional visits when she would add meticulous and refined touches to the building and its spacious grounds. She also used her influence to invite a noteworthy ecclesiastical friend to visit, Eugenio Pacelli, the Vatican secretary of state. In the fall of 1936, several years before he became Pope Pius XII, Pacelli made an American tour that on October 19 included Wernersville. He spent several days enjoying the magnificent ambiance that the generous Genevieve and her deceased husband had bestowed on the American Catholic Church. On November 24, 1938, Genevieve Brady, the mother figure of the "mother province" of the American Jesuit Assistancy,[2] died while visiting Rome and was buried beside her husband below the novitiate's main altar.

Forty years later, with the significant decline of Jesuit vocations, the novitiate, like dozens of other Catholic seminaries, faced a crisis. In its heyday the novitiate-juniorate housed more than one hundred men in formation and several dozen priests and brothers. In one year alone (1959), sixty men entered the novitiate. The cataclysmic changes of the 1960s, however, took their toll so that by 1970 the juniorate has closed and only six novices entered that year. The great Catholic bastion of Nicholas and Genevieve Brady was on the verge of becoming a white elephant.

Faced with this institutional crisis Jesuit leaders had to discern and decide quickly. Fr. James Connor, S.J., the provincial of the Maryland Province, was faced with the question of whether the novitiate and its acreage should be sold. He and his assistants gave the possibility serious consideration. Together they recognized, however, that the building and the land that the Bradys provided for the Jesuits contained a myriad of memories and meanings. Indeed they knew that many Jesuits saw Wernersville as the province's symbolic center, "the womb of the province," and so a plan was commissioned to transform the building's west wing, consisting of some ninety rooms, into a spiritual center. Fr. George Schemel, S.J., who had been serving as one of Fr. Connor's assistants, volunteered to begin the project.

Not only did Schemel embark on the task of transforming a seminary wing into a spiritual center, but he also entered into a movement that introduced an entirely new approach to Ignatian retreats, namely, the one-to-one directed retreat. By placing greater emphasis on an individual's experience of prayer, this approach opened new pathways for psychological insights and methods to be incorporated into one of Catholicism's great spiritual traditions. The Spiritual Exercises themselves are filled with psychological insights. Through more than three hundred annotations and principles, Ignatius proposes ways of deepening one's intimacy with God in the person of Jesus Christ. For centuries the standard way of presenting the Spiritual Exercises of St. Ignatius and its four "weeks," or phases, had been by presenting a sequence of meditations to a group of retreatants.[3] While appealing to the imagination, this approach also tended to focus primarily on faith as understood conceptually and intellectually. As such it tended toward a dualistic spirituality in which one's faith was informed primarily by reason and creedal statement to the neglect of affectivity and intuition. Such a spirituality was congruent with Jesuit educational endeavors designed to shape the beliefs and minds of students.

In the decade before the Second Vatican Council, several Jesuits in Europe (notably Ignacio Iparraguirre in Spain and Jean Laplace in France) who were researching the history of the Spiritual Exercises had rediscovered the directed retreat.[4] They began to call for a return to Ignatius's original method in giving his Exercises, namely, in a one-to-one directed format. They recognized that Ignatius himself never gave a preached retreat. In the 1960s Paul Kennedy, a British tertian master at St. Beuno's in Wales, introduced the individual directed retreat to his Jesuit tertians and suggested ways that it could be used in giving Ignatian retreats. This retreat modality, with its focus on the director's listening to the individual's reporting of the spiritual movements of prayer, readily became an important means for psychological insights and processes to be incorporated into spirituality. Having spent nearly an entire year under Kennedy's tutelage, many tertians would later introduce the directed retreat to their respective apostolates.[5] In 1971, faced with the project of transforming a wing of a seminary into a spiritual center, Schemel saw the opportunity for bringing to fruition the ideas of his tertian director. Moreover, he not only introduced in systematic fashion the individually directed retreat, but he did so in ways that appropriated and applied a great deal of psychology, notably that of Carl Jung.

The new undertaking was ably assisted by Dominic Maruca, commissioned by Connors in 1969 to set up programs for Jesuits to learn how to present the Exercises using the one-to-one rather than the preached approach. Maruca, who from 1964 to 1968 had served as the novice director for the Maryland Province and who had a doctorate in Spiritual Theology and considerable training in psychology, had also experienced the directed retreat while visiting Ireland in 1961. In 1969–70 Maruca trained more than fifty Jesuits to give the directed retreat. He and other Jesuits went on to advise numerous religious communities throughout the country so that it was not long before one-to-one retreats had become one of the great landmarks for the renewal of religious life.

The Jesuit Center for Spiritual Growth was opened on October 4, 1971. Besides Schemel two other Jesuits were assigned to the project, artist Fr. George Krieger and missionary Fr. Henry Haske. The three used their respective talents to establish a spiritual center that was to become known for its creativity and innovations. Schemel led the way in shaping a vision for the center, a holistic spirituality rooted in the Spiritual Exercises, but incorporating the insights and techniques of Jungian psychology. Initially seen as a risk, the center soon became quite a success story and gained an international reputation. Schemel brought to the center a threefold matrix: the Spiritual Exercises with the new experiential ways that its spiritual richness was being mined through the directed retreat; a theology informed by the spirit (*aggiornamento*) and the documents of the Second Vatican Council; and the analytic psychology of Carl Jung.

Schemel did his theological studies at Woodstock, Maryland, where he met and befriended faculty members such as John Courtney Murray and Gustave Weigel, both of whom played significant roles at the Second Vatican Council. Shortly after his ordination in 1964 Schemel went to Rome to study mystical theology at the Gregorian University. While there Schemel was able to attend some of the Council's sessions, and he carried the impressions they made with him into his pastoral ministry. He also studied extensively the writings of St. John of the Cross and St. Teresa of Avila and found in them insights into the human psyche. Schemel's research into spirituality led him to the theological principle that grace is mediated in and through human experience, which he incorporated into his approach to the Spiritual Exercises.

Schemel found that Jung's psychological insights complemented both his theology and the Spiritual Exercises. Just as the Second Vatican Council opened Catholic consciousness to more experiential forms of spirituality, so too did Jung's concepts take on an added vitality for Catholic spiritual directors. Among important Jungian concepts were the active imagination, the anima/animus archetype, dreams, symbols, and the shadow. In addition, Jung's theory of temperaments as it was incorporated into the Myers-Briggs Type Indicator (MBTI) was an important resource. Developed into a psychometric instrument by Katharine C. Briggs and her daughter Isabel Myers, this indicator was a most significant adaptation of

Jung's theory for psychologists and spiritual directors alike. Originally published in 1962 the MBTI attracted wide attention among spiritual directors "because it gave a psychological matrix that was compatible with classic spirituality."[6]

Schemel and his Wernersville staff became one of the first retreat teams to apply Jung's concepts and make ample use of Myers-Briggs. In 1974 he and his assistant Sr. Judith Roemer were certified by the Center for the Application of Psychological Types to use the Myers-Briggs instrument. They saw it as helpful for staff development as well as for individuals and groups. In theological terms it could help one see how God's grace was mediated through one's psychological type.

During the 1970s the center staff grew as Schemel was joined by Jesuit Fathers Francis Miles and James Borberly. William Sneck, a Jesuit clinical psychologist who specialized in Jungian psychology, joined the staff in 1980 and helped develop the center's psychological matrix. His psychological training enabled the staff to offer a variety of workshops integrating Jungian concepts into spirituality. Besides presenting the theory of psychological type the workshops treated such topics as archetype, anima/animus, and the shadow. Meanwhile, Borberly coauthored with Schemel *Facing Your Type,* a booklet for using the Myers-Briggs Indicator. For more than a decade Schemel and his colleagues promoted the adaptation of Ignatian methods of prayer and principles of discernment for individuals as well as groups. In addition to a host of individual religious attending eight-day or thirty-day retreats offered by the center, a good number of religious attended weekend workshops on topics pertaining to communal discernment and decision making. During an era when every religious community was given the mandate of renewal, an understanding of Ignatian principles of discernment and decision making was highly prized, and individual superiors as well as their staff attended programs sponsored by the center. By instructing these leaders on principles of Ignatian decision making, Schemel and his staff had a profound impact on the renewal of religious communities.

Schemel directed the center until 1983, when he moved to Scranton, Pennsylvania. There with Roemer he continued his Ignatian program and established the Institute for Contemporary Spirituality at the University of Scranton. It became a center for providing spiritual direction as well as workshops on various Ignatian and Jungian themes. Before his death on June 18, 2000, Schemel enunciated his ideas on individual and corporate spirituality in several publications, videos, and most especially in *Beyond Individuation to Discipleship.* Written in collaboration with Roemer, the book was published posthumously and represents Schemel's and Roemer's psychospiritual insights into the giving of the Spiritual Exercises.[7]

Schemel's apostolic work was marked with bold creativity as he imagined ways to expand the applications of the Spiritual Exercises. His study of Jung was one of the chief instruments for relating the spiritual with the psychological. In addition to the center that he established at Wernersville, Schemel's legacy may be witnessed in his contribution to the popularization of the individually directed retreat. He was one of the first to combine the Spiritual Exercises and Jungian psychology in the postconciliar church.

The Emergence of American Catholic Psychospirituality

As noted above, the 1960s brought forth a whole series of changes in human awareness of self, others, and God, as evidenced in the documents as well as the spirit of the Second Vatican Council. It was also seen in the cultural shifts in the United States and elsewhere, many of which had to do with greater awareness and subjective consciousness.

The enthusiasm for individually directed retreats reflected a turn toward the experiential and assessing one's experience of God. Jesuit theologian Bernard Lonergan described how theological method had begun to shift from the objective to interiority and intersubjectivity. Spiritual writers began to call for an examination of one's "consciousness" instead of one's "conscience." In one of the most widely read religious essays of the period, George Aschenbrenner, who from 1968 to 1975 served as a director of Jesuit novices, suggested that the Ignatian spiritual practice of "the examen" needed to move toward an awareness of one's affective experience and away from a simple assessment of one's virtues.[8] Aschenbrenner emphasized that the examen and prayer in general serve as a means for developing intimacy with Christ. For Aschenbrenner intimacy implied affectivty. Like Schemel, Aschenbrenner addressed spiritual development by borrowing psychological principles and strategies.

A more complete demonstration of the impact of psychology on American Catholic spirituality became evident in *The Practice of Spiritual Direction*. Published in 1982 by the Jesuits William A. Barry and William J. Connolly, the work has been translated into six languages and has drawn a wide readership among spiritual directors. Barry, who in 1968 received a doctorate in clinical psychology from the University of Michigan, and Connolly, a theologian, helped to found in 1972 the Center for Religious Development in Cambridge, Massachusetts. For more than three decades the center has been a leading training institution for spiritual directors. Drawing on their experiences at the center, Barry and Connolly describe basic principles for developing a more intimate relationship with God. The authors note that their approach represents a shift, resembling the scientific paradigm shift described by Thomas Kuhn in his seminal text,

The Structure of Scientific Revolution. Rather than the traditional stress on
self-renunciation and the practice of virtue as one strives toward spiritual
perfection, their approach attended to a person's life of prayer as it reflected
an ongoing relationship with God. Integrating the emphasis given to experience by theologians such as Lonergan and Rahner with nondirective
strategies for listening enunciated by Carl Rogers and others, Barry and
Connolly focused on one's religious experience:

> We define Christian spiritual direction, then, as help given by one
> Christian to another which enables the person to pay attention to
> God's personal communication to him or her, to respond to this per-
> sonally communicating God, to grow in intimacy with this God, and
> to live out the consequences of the relationship. The *focus* of this
> type of spiritual direction is on experience, not ideas, and specifically
> on religious experience, i.e., any experience of the mysterious Other
> whom we call God.[9]

In their description of the tasks of a spiritual director, the authors
appropriate the nondirective strategies of Rogerian therapy:

> In any carefully drawn list some place will be given to (1) empa-
> thetic listening, (2) paying attention, (3) affirming, (4) assisting
> in clarification, (5) raising questions when the directee wants them
> and (6) helping the directee to recognize the affective attitudes that
> influence his attitude to God.[10]

While they are careful to distinguish spiritual direction from counseling
and psychotherapy, the authors nevertheless freely borrow basic psychological principles and make reference to the works of such psychological
theorists as Ernest Becker, Ralph R. Greenson, Henri Ellenberger, Otto
Rank, and Carl Rogers. These theorists support their arguments that an
effective spiritual director should be sensitive to the dynamics of the
director-directee encounter. They stress the importance of "facilitating"
contemplation and developing a "working alliance" with the directee. Relying on *Basic Concepts of Psychoanalytic Psychiatry*, written by their Jesuit
companion William W. Meissner and Elizabeth Zetzel,[11] Barry and Connolly describe the roles that transference and countertransference play in
spiritual direction. They argue that the spiritual director should not be naive
to the transferential dynamics involved in the director-directee encounter.

The books's popularity over two decades suggests that other spiritual directors have incorporated such psychological and psychoanalytic principles
into spiritual direction. Meanwhile, the Center for Religious Development
that Barry and Connolly helped to establish has for three decades continued
to flourish as a training center for spiritual directors. Barry later described

the center as being a place where "Freud and religion had really kissed and made up."[12] A poignant account of the center's methodology for training spiritual directors is presented by Connolly and his colleague Madeline Birmingham in *Witnessing to the Fire*.[13] Barry, meanwhile, went on to author or coauthor a dozen books and numerous articles on spirituality, publications that have borne witness to his creative ways of integrating his spiritual training as a Jesuit priest with his clinical training as a psychologist.

Besides the spiritual centers at Wernersville, Guelph, and Cambridge, other institutions initiated training programs for spiritual directors. In master's degree programs at universities such as Creighton and Fordham, at religious institutions such as the Mercy Center in Burlingame, California, and at ecumenically staffed programs such as Shalem in Rockville, Maryland, more and more people sought a greater understanding of spirituality and training in the dynamics of spiritual directors. By the 1980s a new profession, no longer restricted to Catholic priests and religious, had emerged. This movement toward professionalization led to the creation of Spiritual Directors International, an international and ecumenical organization that supports the development of the profession through regional meetings, workshops, and a quarterly journal, *Presence*.

The blending of spirituality with psychology may also be seen in the popularity of other Catholic writers whose approach to spirituality has been informed by training in psychology, for example, Joyce Rupp, Robert Wicks, Evelyn and James Whitehead, Elizabeth Liebert, Joann Wolski Conn, and Benedict Groeschel.

Joyce Rupp, one of the most widely read American Catholic writers of spirituality today, has integrated such influences as Thomas Merton, Teilhard de Chardin, and Matthew Fox with her training in transpersonal psychology at the Institute of Transpersonal Psychology in Palo Alto. A Servite sister, Rupp, beginning in 1985 with the publication of *Fresh Bread . . . and Other Gifts,* has published a series of books that has spoken to a variety of psychospiritual themes: change and growth (*Fresh Bread* and *Dear Heart Come Home,* 1996), bereavement and loss (*Praying Our Goodbyes,* 1988, *Your Sorrow Is My Sorrow,* 1999), the rhythms and seasons of prayer (*May I Have This Dance?* 1992, *Little Pieces of Light,* 1995, and *The Cup of Our Life,* 1997), and sophia-feminine wisdom (*The Star in My Heart,* 1990, and *Prayers to Sophia,* 2000).[14] Her popularity has demonstrated her success at combining spiritual content with transpersonal techniques such as guided meditations and journal keeping.

During the past two decades the most prolific psychospiritual American Catholic author has been Robert J. Wicks. The author or editor of more than thirty books, the chair of a leading program in pastoral counseling, and a popular public speaker both in the United States and abroad,

Wicks has consistently and creatively sought out various pathways for integrating psychology and spirituality, for example in *Clinical Handbook of Pastoral Counseling,* vols. 1 and 2 (1993, with Richard Parsons and Donald Capps), *A Handbook of Spirituality for Ministers,* vol. 1 (1995) and vol. 2 (2000).[15] Wicks has also served as an editor of "The Integration Series" for Paulist Press, a project designed to encourage collaboration between psychology and spirituality. Wicks's own psychospiritual writings include: *Availability: The Problem and the Gift* (1986), *Living Simply in an Anxious World* (1988), *Seeking Perspective: Weaving Spirituality in Search of Clarity* (1991), *Touching the Holy: Ordinariness, Self-Esteem and Friendship* (1992), *Seeds of Sensitivity* (1995), *After Fifty* (1997), *Living a Gentle, Passionate Life* (1998), and *Sharing Wisdom: The Practical Art of Giving and Receiving Mentoring* (2000).[16]

Wicks received his clinical training at Hahnemann University in Philadelphia, where he became interested in the treatment of stress and burnout. This training in turn led him to specialize in working with priests, religious, and laity engaged in stressful situations. For this work he received a papal medal from Pope John Paul II in 1996.

Other contemporary spiritual authors have incorporated the insights of developmental psychology into their writings. For instance, Evelyn and James Whitehead, in *Christian Life Patterns: The Psychological Challenges and Religious Invitations of Adult Life* (1979), used Erikson's eight-stage theory of development to describe the life patterns of a Christian.[17] In *Changing Life Patterns: Adult Development in Spiritual Direction* (1992), Elizabeth Liebert uses the ego developmental theory of Jane Loevinger and the evolving self theory of Robert Kegan. These structured developmental theories lead her to a consideration of how spiritual growth occurs through the course of a lifetime of psychological development.[18] Joann Wolski Conn in *Spirituality and Personal Maturity* (1989) compares the developmental theories of Carol Gilligan and Robert Kegan in arguing for a comprehensive theory of spiritual development.[19]

While known primarily as a spiritual advisor and television teacher, Fr. Benedict Groeschel, C.F.R., has had considerable impact on the consciousness and culture of American Catholicism. Having received a doctorate in educational psychology from Columbia University in 1971, Groeschel has for three decades used his psychology background to minister to emotionally disturbed youth at Children's Village in Dobbs Ferry, New York. At the same time Groeschel has gained a reputation as a spiritual advisor and mentor, serving as the director of the Archdiocese of New York's Office for Spiritual Development. At one time he was a spiritual director for the late Cardinal Terrence Cook, whose beatification cause he now supervises.

Groeschel's psychological training has enabled him to provide the psychological assessments for persons seeking admission into seminaries and religious communities. Moreover, in the tradition of Bishop Fulton J. Sheen, Groeschel has become well known as a national speaker and for his television series. Since 1982 he has had an arrangement with Mother Angelica, the producer of the Catholic television network ETWN, to give an annual series of lectures on spirituality.

Groeschel has published fifteen books, including *Spiritual Passages: The Psychology of Spiritual Development* (1983) and *Stumbling Blocks or Stepping Stones: Spiritual Answers to Psychological Questions* (1987).[20] His writings reveal that he is not afraid to be critical of psychological theories and strategies that appear to him hedonistic and "selfist."[21] A priest known for his orthodoxy, Groeschel has a considerable following among traditionally minded Catholics. While his focus is primarily spiritual, Groeschel's clinical training and work come through in some of the practical advice he offers. A no-nonsense man, he has at times challenged the practicality of psychological and spiritual integration.

The Psychospirituality of the Enneagram

In recent years a psychological system derived from Eastern philosophy has become popular in American Catholic circles. Known as the Enneagram, the system proposes a personality theory of nine types. Seen by many spiritual directors as a helpful heuristic typology, the Enneagram system is derived from Sufi philosophy and, according to Don Richard Riso, made its way into the Western world in the 1920s through the writings of Ivanovitch Gurdjieff (1877–1949) and the workshops of a Bolivian, Oscar Ichazo (b. 1931).[22] After presenting the system at institutes in Bolivia and in Chile, in 1971 Ichazo founded the Arica Institute in California and began teaching the method to a number of psychiatrists from the Esalen Institute, among them Claudio Naranjo. It was from Naranjo that Robert Ochs, a Jesuit, learned the psychological system and began using the Enneagram with his fellow religious. While seemingly simple, the system nevertheless is seen by its adherents as capable of profound interpretations. During the 1970s it proved quite useful in religious formation circles, especially those at the Jesuit theologates in Berkeley, Chicago, and Toronto. Classes and workshops were given in circles of Catholic religious communities, and a small movement began which produced several publications. One of the first was *The Enneagram: A Journey of Self-Discovery* (1984), which was published by three religious, Maria Beesing, O.P., Robert Nogosek, C.S.C., and Patrick O'Leary, S.J. Don Richard Riso, a former Jesuit, became familiar with the Enneagram during his theological studies in Toronto and began to popularize it in a series of lectures, essays, and books. Its popularity over the years has been enhanced through other Catholic spiritual writers, among them James Empereur, Richard Rohr, and Suzanne Zuercher.[23]

Unlike the Myers-Briggs instrument, however, the Enneagram has not caught on in the arenas of academic and professional psychology, and it has been subjected to very few empirical studies that would evaluate its validity and reliability. While Zuercher does mention that descriptive research of this oral tradition is progressing,[24] it remains to be seen whether the Enneagram can make the leap from its origins in the "oral tradition" into the more rigorous refinements of empirical study.[25]

Conclusion

The literature of contemporary Catholic psychospiritual writers has seen a dramatic increase in recent years. At the same time, there has been criticism of the way spiritual writers have uncritically accepted and assimilated the concepts of psychology. Has it gone too far? This criticism was hinted at in Philip Rieff's seminal work, *The Triumph of the Therapeutic: Uses of Faith after Freud*.[26] First published in 1966, it presented a critical synopsis of how Western culture had supplanted religious norms with psychological ones. A decade later, Rieff's work was echoed by Christopher Lasch's *The Culture of Narcissism: American Life in an Age of Diminishing Expectations* (1978) and Paul Vitz's *Psychology as Religion: The Cult of Self-Worship* (1977).[27] In conservative Catholic circles this criticism of psychology's influence on religion and spirituality is found in Mitch Pacwa's *Catholics and the New Age: How Good People Are Being Drawn into Jungian Psychology, the Enneagram, and the Age of Aquarius* (1992).[28] Conservative Christian periodicals like *First Things* have at times taken Catholicism to task for accommodating too much to certain forms of psychospirituality.

Nonetheless, it appears that the incorporation of psychological concepts, insights, and methods into Catholic spirituality is here to stay. Whether in retreat houses or in classrooms, the close cooperation between psychology and spirituality continues. Indeed it may be seen as a contemporary demonstration of the medieval Thomistic principle that grace builds upon nature.

Epilogue

Current and Future Issues

Controversy and Collaboration

The present volume has offered an overview of individuals, institutions, and issues that have influenced the relationship between psychology and Catholicism in America. This final chapter will serve as a review of some of the issues that have shaped the dialogue between psychology and American Catholicism and a preview of the future.

Contemporary Catholic *Cura Animarum:* Confession or Therapy?

The appropriation of psychology into the Catholic approach to the *cura animarum* is a significant dimension of the dialogue between psychology and Catholicism. Over the last two thousand years, Christians have developed some sophisticated ways of caring for the soul. Within the Roman Catholic tradition these have been institutionalized through the seven sacraments. The sacrament of penance in particular has been a characteristic Catholic approach to caring for the soul. The emphasis on individual confession, in which the penitent seeks God's forgiveness through the sacramental mediation of a priest, has been a defining feature of Catholicism; indeed it is one of the church's precepts that every Catholic should receive the sacrament at least once a year.

Catholic moralists have had a significant impact on changing the church's approach to the *cura animarum* by means of psychology. As discussed earlier, moralists such as Bernard Häring incorporated the insights of Erik Erikson into a new understanding of sin and its relationship to human development. Although Häring's writings were not popularly disseminated in the United States until after the Council, they soon contributed to a new understanding of the sacrament of penance.

When the "new psychology" broke away from its metaphysical and religious roots and began to establish itself as a "science of the soul," it threatened the church's position. As we saw in the early criticisms of the new psychology by Hughes, there was a good deal of consternation and

159

suspicion toward the emerging discipline's usurpation of the "soul" for science. Only gradually and with some resolve for reconciliation on the part of psychologists and theologians did psychology begin to be seen as an ally rather than as an enemy. The work of American psychologists such as Pace, Moore, and Bier as well as of European psychologists such as Mercier and Gemelli had a considerable impact on this transformation. The writings of Charles Bruehl in the *Homiletic and Pastoral Review* dispelled some of the prejudices and suspicions of many Catholic clergy toward psychology. Bruehl's series of articles that brought the psychology and even the psychoanalysis of his day to bear on such topics as abnormality, personality, temperament, and the unconscious lent credibility to the insights of the emerging psychology.

The emphasis placed by psychoanalysis on the unconscious created controversy in Catholic pastoral circles, more accustomed to rational explanations of behavior. Bruehl's writings and later those of Curran, Kennedy, Sexton, Meissner, Nouwen, and others did much to dispel suspicion. In European Catholic circles, writings of Dalbiez and Godin lent clarity amid much confusion and paved the way for a more sophisticated Catholic understanding of psychoanalysis. In the pronouncements of Pope Pius XII, though with some reservations toward certain features of psychoanalysis, the church recognized the important contributions or psychoanalysis to understanding human nature and considered it a new means for attaining "a knowledge of the soul."

As we have seen, during the 1950s Catholics began to turn seriously to psychology to assist in the ministry of *cura animarum*. The conferences at Collegeville and Fordham, the emergence of the American Catholic Psychological Association and the National Guild of Catholic Psychiatrists, and the series of articles and books about psychology all contributed to the growing realization among American Catholics of psychology's significance for ministry. It was during this decade, when vocations to the religious life were at their zenith, that psychological testing of religious candidates became more appreciated and widespread. Bier and other psychologists introduced such testing, and although they initially met with some resistance, it was not long before taking a battery of psychological tests was a requirement for entrance into most religious communities and seminaries.

In terms of the *cura animarum,* however, is psychology enough? Have American Catholics abandoned confession for psychotherapy? Instead of seeking the counsel of priests in the sacrament of reconciliation are the Catholic faithful flocking to counselors? As noted earlier, since the 1960s fewer Catholics have been receiving the sacrament of reconciliation. While there are no studies demonstrating that they are going to counselors and psychotherapists instead, an extensive study by Princeton sociologist Robert Wuthnow does suggest that psychology has had an impact. In *After Heaven: Spirituality in America since the 1950s,* Wuthnow discusses the conclusions from detailed interviews of two hundred individuals representing a cross-section of middle Americans. Wuthnow finds that a paradigmatic shift has taken place among believing Americans: we have gone from a nation of spiritual "dwellers" (adhering to religious tradition expressed in regular attendance at a local church or synagogue) to a nation of spiritual seekers (with more mobile and individualistic styles of faith).[1] Wuthnow believes that the seekers are responding to the changes and demands of American secular society, and he includes some American Catholics in the category of seekers. Psychology, with its emphases upon individual behavior and experience, no doubt has played a role in the spirituality of the seekers.

On the basis of Wuthnow's study, one might surmise that, while Catholics with a "dwelling" spirituality would more likely continue the practice of confession, the Catholic "seekers" would more likely look for solace for their "innerself" through reading certain forms of psychological literature. For instance, in his description of the searching of one former Catholic, Wuthnow says that he found meaning in the works of psychologists such as Erich Fromm, Rollo May, and Viktor Frankl.[2] Given the phenomenon of "spiritual seeking," one wonders if confession and for that matter the church's traditional reliance on the sacraments is enough. In its *cura animarum,* how does the church in the twentieth-first century respond to such "spiritual seekers"?

Perhaps an understanding of *cura animarum* with a more inclusive view of spirituality is in order. As mentioned at the beginning of this study, a stream of spiritual literature has flowed into the marketplace, quenching the thirst of millions of Americans. Books such as *Care of the Soul* by Thomas Moore have restored the notion of soul to popular American consciousness, if not conscience. What Moore means by soul, however, is not precisely what Catholicism has traditionally meant. For Moore, a former Catholic monk, while connoting depth and spiritual substance, "soul" does not refer to religious belief or immortality.[3] He considers "soul" to be an expression of how one deals with oneself, with other persons, and with the rest of creation. Moore seems to be speaking to Wuthnow's "spiritual seekers" when he asserts that spirituality should be rooted not only in religious tradition but also in psychological insights.[4]

Within the academy and professional organizations of both psychologists and theologians, others have sought new understandings of spirituality. Discussing psychological and theological understandings of spirituality, Erik Mansager finds an interesting comparison between the presidential addresses of leaders in the two disciplines, Kenneth Pargament (Division 36 of the APA) and Sandra Schneiders (Society for the Study of Christian Spirituality).[5] According to Mansager, Pargament considers spirituality as a worthy construct for the psychology of religion if one understands spirituality to be a "search for the sacred." Pargament warns his fellow psychologists about the danger of seeing spirituality simply as an "individual" phenomenon and religion as an institution, often viewed pejoratively. Pargament asserts that spirituality, if it is to be competently studied by psychologists of religion, must be seen in a social context.

Mansager discusses Schneiders's concern that "the discourse on spirituality has become so widespread in our culture that it risks becoming a catch-all term for whatever anyone else takes seriously."[6] Schneiders's remark suggests a present and future danger in psychological and theological conversations pertaining to spirituality. It appears that contemporary writings on the soul and spirituality are undergoing what John Haught calls a "conflation," in which science and religion, in this case psychology and theology, are "woven into a single fabric where they fade into each other, almost to the point of becoming indistinguishable."[7] Contemporary programs in pastoral counseling and spirituality run the risk of promoting a similar conflation. While potentially a very positive phenomenon in American culture, the fascination with spirituality and the soul needs to be carefully nuanced by religious institutions, intellectuals, and professionals. Only through such a careful approach will future attempts to face the church's perennial challenge of *cura animarum* prove to be competent as well as compassionate.

Neuralgic Concerns: Sexual Abuse, Addiction, and Abortion

Of recent concern and a cause for collaboration between psychology and American Catholic institutions and leaders has been the issue of boundary violations. The trauma caused by religious perpetrators has resulted in considerable psychological damage to victims. In addition, public disclosure has done untold damage to the image of the church and its ministers; the trust that the faithful had in their religious leaders has been fractured. Ironically, it was the false accusation of sexual abuse leveled against Cardinal Joseph Bernadin that received the greatest attention.

In response to the crisis, American Catholic institutes and services have been established for victim and perpetrator alike. The Interfaith Sexual Trauma Institute at St. John's University, Minnesota, St. John Vianney in Downingtown, Pennsylvania, and St. Luke's in Silver Spring, Maryland, represent significant responses to the clergy and religious abuse. At the

Christian Institute for the Study of Human Sexuality, presently located in Chicago, Jesuit psychiatrist James Gill and his assistant, Linda Amadeo, have for a decade been instructing formation leaders on the intricacies of sexual issues in the context of celibate religious development.[8]

American Catholic institutions and leaders have found special value in twelve step recovery programs such as Alcoholics Anonymous almost since their inception in the 1930s. Programs for priests and women religious at "Guest House" in Michigan and Minnesota and such comprehensive treatment programs as those at the Hazelden Foundation in Center City, Minnesota, are major testimonies to the cooperation between American Catholicism and mental health movements and institutions.[9]

Issues surrounding abortion will continue to be controversial for Catholicism and psychology. Since psychological professionals for reasons of mental health support at times encourage a woman's choice for abortion, conflict will continue between values espoused by Catholic morality and those practiced by many in psychology. In addition, looming on the horizon will be controversies surrounding neuropsychology, especially when recent developments in genetic psychiatry are implemented. Neuropsychological manipulation of DNA structures is now a reality. Such advances have moral implications and will need to be addressed, even when this results in conflict between American Catholicism and its mental health allies.

Catholic Higher Education and American Psychology

The evolution of American Catholic attitudes toward psychology has involved changes in ideas and institutions. Catholic higher education has been one of the principal settings for such changes, for it has been on the Catholic university campus that the forces of religion and science, tradition and experiment, reason and revelation have come together.

Outstanding examples of American Catholic higher education's appropriation of psychology were the work and witness of Edward Pace and Thomas Verner Moore. Pace's establishment of the first psychology laboratory on a Catholic campus and one of the first on any American campus placed him and the Catholic University of America on the cutting edge of American psychology, at least for a short period. The laboratory was a profound achievement as well as a symbolic expression of the spirit of Pope Leo XIII's *Aeterni Patris,* namely, a will to become current with the sciences of the modern age. Ironically, the pope who helped to inspire Pace's experimental psychology venture was the same one whose papal pronouncement *Testem Benevolentiae* placed restrictions on Catholic University's progressive intellectual leadership. This papal pronouncement and its condemnation of Americanism stifled the spirit of dialogue with American culture that was beginning to emerge in Catholic higher educational institutions. It would be decades before such a spirit was allowed to return to the Catholic campus.

Despite American Catholic fears surrounding Americanism and later Modernism, Catholic scholarship in the area of psychology did continue to develop in a limited way. The remarkable life of Dom Thomas Verner Moore, most of it lived in the environment of Catholic University, represents the outstanding embodiment of American Catholicism's dialogue with psychology. From his dissertation and research days under Pace and later Wundt to his final days as a Carthusian monk, Moore witnessed some sixty years of psychology's penetration into American Catholicism's institutional, intellectual, and professional life. Perhaps more than any other American Catholic he was responsible for its appropriation by American Catholicism. Moore realized that a setting in Catholic higher education was necessary for the new psychology to be accepted by Catholicism. Moore displayed a creative and courageous spirit in establishing St. Anselm's Benedictine Priory near the campus of Catholic University, although he was able to attract only a handful of men who shared his vision of encountering Catholic University's intellectual world while rooted in the contemplative world of monasticism. Still, Moore's ministry as a child psychiatrist, as a scholar who published numerous articles and books, as a professor who taught psychology to several generations of students, as director of a clinic, and as chair of a department demonstrated unique ways of opening the minds of American Catholics to psychology. Moore's various accomplishments in such a variety of niches would not have been possible without the sustaining environment of the university.

The witness and work of one of Moore's students, William Bier, likewise required an academic setting. As a psychologist and as a professor and administrator at Fordham University, Bier was able to use an academic setting to distill psychological understandings for American Catholics. A less prolific scholar than Moore, Bier had influence through his considerable administrative skills. As we have seen, during his three decades of service to Fordham, Bier organized a series of pastoral psychology institutes. Perhaps Bier's greatest achievement, however, was his administrative leadership in organizing other Catholic academic and professional psychologists to form the American Catholic Psychological Association, which later became Division 36 of the American Psychological Association (Psychologists Interested in Religious Issues).

The engaging environment of the College of St. Catherine encouraged the energies and fostered the talents of Sr. Annette Walters. Her ability to share her psychological expertise in the classroom as well as in convent cloisters opened new vistas for women religious. Her considerable charisms led to her leadership in the Sisters Formation Movement, an organization that helped to transform American Catholic religious life. Walters's lifelong friendship with the behaviorist B. F. Skinner, despite their philosophical and religious differences, demonstrated how American psychology and American Catholicism could collaborate.

The Catholic academic environment was also crucial for the work of such innovative psychologists as Magda Arnold and Charles A. Curran at Loyola University of Chicago, Adrian Van Kaam at Duquesne University, and Virginia Staudt Sexton at Fordham University. Moreover, the establishment of psychology departments and institutes helped legitimate psychology in American Catholicism. More than any other vehicle, it was through the Catholic colleges and universities that ACPA's primary goal of "interpreting the meaning of modern psychology, and advancing its acceptance in Catholic circles" was achieved.

In recent years American Catholicism's conversations with psychology have become more complex and controversial, as demonstrated by the encyclical *Ex Corde Ecclesiae* issued by Pope John Paul II on August 15, 1990. The pontiff composed the encyclical in response to the concerns brought to him by American bishops about what they saw as Catholic higher education's tendency toward accommodation to American secularization. In response the pope described his vision of Catholic higher education. He asserted that a Catholic university must have the following characteristics:

1. A Christian inspiration not only of individuals but of the university community as such.

2. A continuing reflection in the light of the Catholic faith upon the growing treasury of human knowledge, to which it seeks to contribute by its own research.

3. Fidelity to the Christian message as it comes to us through the church.

4. An institutional commitment to the service of the people of God and of the human family in their pilgrimage to the transcendent goal that gives meaning to life.[10]

During the last decade of the twentieth century and into the twenty-first, *Ex Corde Ecclesiae* has been a source of much debate, sometimes acrimonious, among American Catholic episcopal and academic leaders. In many ways the encyclical stirred up the old passions of the controversies at the turn of the previous century. Was the pope's challenge the beginning of a new "Americanism" controversy? Would the Catholic struggle for a respected and secure place in the American academic community be diminished by the requirement once again that theologians take an oath? Has the

American Catholic Church's earlier distrust toward American culture come full circle?

Reviewing the history of Catholic higher education in the twentieth century, Notre Dame historian Philip Gleason describes how the frequent antagonism of American Catholic thought toward American secularist values has changed toward greater acceptance. According to Gleason, although Catholic educators once challenged modernity and resisted the assimilation of values, they began to accept modernity at an accelerated pace first after World War II and then again after the Second Vatican Council.[11]

Another Notre Dame historian, John T. McGreevy, has examined academic perceptions of American Catholicism prior to 1960 as American Catholics learned "to think on one's own."[12] He describes the prejudice that many in the American academic community, not to mention American society in general, had toward Catholics. According to McGreevy, Roman Catholicism was viewed by the educator John Dewey to be essentially antidemocratic; it was believed by social psychologists such as Theodor Adorno to have fostered authoritarian personalities as witnessed in Nazi Germany; it was perceived by the anthropologist Margaret Mead to isolate Catholic youth from mainstream America; and it was judged by personality theorist David C. McClelland to restrain motivations for achievement and initiative through the structures of compliance of its educational system. As McGreevy and more recently Mark Massa highlight, it was no accident that Paul Blanshard's *American Freedom and Catholic Power* was a mid-century bestseller, with a readership that included many in the academic community.

The church's triumphant posture and often defensive style readily contributed to the antagonism. The oath against heresies, required of Catholic theologians by Pope Pius X and lasting until the *aggiornamento* of the Second Vatican Council, was an easy target for academic bias toward Catholic scholarship. The controversy surrounding *Ex Corde Ecclesiae*, with its requirement of an oath (*mandatum*) by Catholic university theologians, has led some to wonder if the American Catholic Church will once again become separatist in its relations with American culture.

On the other hand, many in the Catholic academic community are themselves questioning how well Catholic colleges and universities carry out their mission. When these institutions market themselves as "Catholic" what do they mean? Given the often conservative connotations of the word "Catholic" in American culture, some have even shied away from the use of the word.[13] Analyzing how well Catholic universities carry out their stated ideals, theologian Michael Buckley has criticized many Catholic higher educational institutions for producing mission statements that minimize their institution's Catholicity and separate intellectual life from religion.[14] Buckley believes that one of the essential problems that may well lead to the demise of Catholic higher education is the segmentation of knowledge, in which departments and disciplines, seeking to imitate the neutrality and objectivity of the natural sciences, distance themselves from theology and religious studies. Buckley believes that the Catholicity of Catholic higher education should lie at the heart of an institution's identity and that fundamental questions of theology are relevant to every discipline. Theology should not be seen as one discipline among many.

Given that theology and psychology deal with similar issues, although from different perspectives, it would seem that Buckley's analysis applies in a special way to psychology. In this respect, interdepartmental dialogue in Catholic institutions seems to be one of the necessary constituents of maintaining a Catholic institution's identity. Otherwise, distinct disciplines may seem unrelated, or, worse, in conflict. For instance, issues raised about human development may well profit from the wisdom offered by religious traditions. Psychology can go only so far in helping an individual respond to questions of ultimate meaning and purpose. Likewise, the spiritual aspirations and values proposed in Catholic theology's tradition may at times need to be challenged by psychology's practical empiricism. William James's seminal work, *The Varieties of Religious Experience* (1902), represents one instance of this collaboration; there are numerous successors.

Holy Cross College historian David O'Brien presented some of the central issues of the *Ex Corde Ecclesiae* debate in his book, *From the Heart of the American Church,* referring in his title to the English translation of *ex corde ecclesiae* ("From the Heart of the Church").[15] For O'Brien the debate needs to be placed in the context of American Catholic higher education's response to three publics: the church, the academic community, and the American people. Given psychology's secure role in American academia and the widespread influence of "pop psychology" on American values, psychology informs each of O'Brien's publics. As shown earlier in this volume the new psychology emerged by separating itself from its metaphysical and theological roots, and psychology's growth and pervasive influence have occurred through its steady expansion and segmentation. The fifty-one divisions of the American Psychological Association demonstrate the multitude of mutations in professional psychology; yet only two of these divisions (Division 24, Philosophical Psychology, and Division 36, Psychology of Religion) deal explicitly with philosophical and religious concerns, reflecting psychology's general aversion to metaphysical and spiritual issues.

Catholic institutions have established programs that have promoted the relationship between psychology and religion and to some extent their collaboration. To what degree such a relationship involves an "integration" will continue to be the subject of debate. As is evident from the controversy surrounding *Ex Corde Ecclesiae,* many Catholic leaders are wary of accommodating too much to the influence of secular disciplines such as psychology. Still, the very existence of such programs suggests that psychology's relationship with religious belief will continue to be of interest among religious institutions, intellectuals, and professionals of various religious denominations. While accepting and appropriating many of psychology's principles and practices and seeking to nurture a dialogue with psychology, many American religious leaders appear to be well aware of the dangers of accommodation.

Interfaith Dialogue

As we saw in the controversies surrounding Fulton Sheen, there were tensions between the Catholic and Jewish communities with regard to psychoanalysis. Given that many psychoanalysts were Jewish and that Catholic writers such as Allers and Sheen were concerned over the tendency of psychoanalysts to be atheistic, deterministic, materialistic, and pansexual, such controversies were understandable. As responses to Sheen's criticisms showed, however, not all psychoanalysts, Catholic or Jewish, considered psychoanalysis to be opposed to religious belief. A more conciliatory position was exemplified by Leo Bartemeier and became the public position of Pope Pius XII in his decisive address in 1953 before the International Society of Psychotherapists.

Shortly after the pope's blessing upon psychotherapy and psychoanalysis the summer programs at St. John's College began. From their inception the sessions were taught by Christian and Jewish and faculty and attended by Christian and Jewish clergy. Earlier ecumenical efforts in the mental health movement included those of Thomas Verner Moore and William Bier.

The ecumenical efforts of William Bier in particular should not go unnoticed. As we saw in chapter 4, he was at times advised against some ecumenical ventures: the biennial pastoral symposiums that Bier coordinated at Fordham were ecumenical in their participation. Bier was a leader in the transformation of the American Catholic Psychological Association into the more ecumenical Psychologists Interested in Religious Issues.

The *aggiornamento* that distinguished the Second Vatican Council and its Decree on Ecumenism (*Unitatis Redintegratio*) had a major impact on the emergence of ecumenism. American Catholics became more engaged with non-Catholics in common projects. Although the ecumenical spirit contributed to the demise of such Catholic organizations as the American Catholic Psychological Association and the National Guild of Catholic

Psychiatrists, it also led to less suspicion and greater collaboration between Catholic and non-Catholic professionals. Questions of psychology and religion common to all religious denominations are now being addressed in a collaborative way.

The Catholic tradition of *cura animarum,* while acknowledging the valuable features of contemporary movements of spirituality in popular American culture, stands for something significantly different. The American Catholic institutional, intellectual, and professional appropriation of psychology can enhance the ministry of *cura animarum,* but it must not be confused with the popular interest in the soul and caring for the soul. Whereas the latter seeks to make a significant contribution to American culture, the former seeks to build God's kingdom.

From its earliest days in American culture, psychology has challenged religion's status as the primary "keeper of the soul." Beginning with the empirical findings of the new psychology, followed by the uncovering of unconscious drives and instincts by psychoanalysis, psychology has posed a threat to religion's traditional role and authority. Although the threat has for the most part subsided, the challenge remains. In recent years, the findings of psychology concerning behavior, consciousness, and unconsciousness have included spiritual themes. Spirituality in the field of psychology has taken a variety of expressions, from New Age spirituality to the enthusiastic spirituality of Evangelical psychologists. As American Catholicism continues to seek its identity in a democratic nation and in a pluralistic atmosphere of religious belief, it will be hard-pressed at times to make distinctions between the secular and the spiritual realms. Questions about the overlap of religious spirituality and the spirituality inspired by secular psychology will need to be addressed.

Conclusion

This history of American Catholicism and psychology affords a unique opportunity to view the evolving relationship between a religious denomination and a scientific discipline. From its earliest tradition Catholicism committed itself to an integration of faith and reason, and for many years relied upon the Thomistic synthesis as the best means to do so. While the quest of this integration remains at the heart of Catholic thought (see Pope John Paul II's 1998 encyclical *Fides et Ratio*), and the principle that grace builds on nature continues to inform the work of authors such as Meissner and van Kaam, Thomistic rational psychology is no longer viewed as the primary means for carrying out the quest for such integration.

As we have seen American Catholicism no longer is as combative as it once was toward psychology and in fact has found wisdom in many of its insights. Perhaps we can hope for thoughtful approaches that incorporate the rich reflections of theology and the rigorous standards of empirical psychology.[16] Recently efforts to develop a closer relationship between theology and psychology have been promoted by evangelical Christians, for example, in the *Journal of Psychology and Theology*. Since 1975 the journal, based in the Rosemead School of Theology at Biola University, has made integration a consistent theme. The task of relating psychology and theology has been described by Hendrika Vande Kemp as an effort to "reintegrate" the two fields, separated since psychology's alleged emancipation from theology in the late nineteenth century. According to Vande Kemp, just as there were efforts to keep the "soul" in psychology, writers have persistently sought to maintain a close relationship between psychology and theology. For Vande Kemp, endeavors for integrating theology and clinical psychology have emerged as a "discrete speciality."[17]

From the beginning of the century to the present, the relationship between American Catholicism and psychology, especially in its clinical varieties, has gradually evolved from one of alienation to that of appropriation and mutual respect. Clearly, American Catholicism has developed a new understanding of the various psychological fields and clinical psychotherapies. Such an approach, however, may also be considered as bordering on accommodation to the secularizing tendencies of American society. In this respect, American Catholicism's engagement with psychology reflected the strengths and weaknesses of its overall encounter and dialogue with the modern world in twentieth-century America. One can only wonder how Catholicism's engagement with the psychological disciplines will evolve in the twenty-first century.

The increasing presence of American Catholicism as an established force in American academia suggests that it need not be sectarian or suspicious toward psychology's claims on human consciousness. Catholicism will challenge psychology, however, when scientific and psychotherapeutic claims move into ethical areas and religious practices and beliefs.

American Catholicism's pastoral practices will continue to be influenced by the multitude of discoveries and insights provided by psychological research. In turn, the future of psychology will frequently be inspired and informed by the Roman Catholic Church's classical wisdom in conversation with America of the twenty-first century. Since early in this volume the words of a Catholic pontiff found common ground between theology and psychology in the common quest "for the knowledge of the soul," it is only fitting that a more recent pontiff should have the final words. In showing his support for the general psychological enterprise, Pope John Paul II in 1993 in an address before the American Psychiatric Association and the World Psychiatric Association remarked:

By its very nature, your work often brings you to the threshold of the human mystery. It involves a sensitivity to the often tangled workings of the human mind and heart, and an openness to the ultimate concerns which give meaning to people's lives. These are areas of utmost importance to the Church, and they call to mind the urgent need for a constructive dialogue between science and religion for the sake of shedding greater light on the mystery of man in its fullness.[18]

Notes

Introduction

1. Thomas Moore, *Care of the Soul: A Guide for Cultivating Depth and Sacredness in Everyday Life* (New York: Harper & Row, 1992); Jack Canfield and Mark Victor Hansen, comps., *Chicken Soup for the Soul: 101 Stories to Open the Heart and Rekindle the Spirit* (Deerfield Beach, Fla.: Health Communications, 1993).

2. This mandate may be seen in the Gospel of Matthew, where one finds Jesus' final words to his disciples: "Go therefore and make disciples of all nations, baptizing them in the name of the Father and of the Son and of the Holy Spirit" (Matt. 28:19).

3. The *Catechism of the Catholic Church* states that the sacrament is "called the *sacrament of confession,* since the disclosure or confession of sins to a priest is an essential element of this sacrament. In a profound sense it is also a 'confession'—acknowledgment and praise—of the holiness of God and of his mercy toward sinful man" (no. 1424).

4. In speaking of the increasing diversity in the faith and morals of American Catholics, Davidson et al. cite the 1977 findings of Greeley and the 1987 findings of Gallup and Castelli. See James D. Davidson et al., *The Search for Common Ground: What Unites and Divides Catholic Americans* (Huntington, Ind.: Our Sunday Visitor, 1997), 26.

5. Karl A. Menninger, *Whatever Became of Sin?* (New York: Hawthorn Books, 1973).

6. William James, *The Varieties of Religious Experience: A Study in Human Nature—The Gifford Lectures (1901–1902)* (New York: New American Library, 1958).

7. Stanton L. Jones, "A Constructive Relationship for Religion with the Science and Profession of Psychology: Perhaps the Boldest Model Yet," in *Religion and the Clinical Practice of Psychology,* ed. Edward P. Shafranske (Washington, D.C.: American Psychological Press, 1996), 113–47; Chris R. Schlauch, *Faithful Companioning: How Pastoral Counseling Heals* (Minneapolis: Fortress, 1995).

8. Ian G. Barbour, "Ways of Relating Science and Religion," in *Physics, Philosophy, and Theology: A Common Quest for Understanding,* ed. Robert J. Russell, William R. Stoeger, S.J., and George V. Coyne, S.J. (Notre Dame, Ind.: University of Notre Dame Press, 1988), 21–45; Ian Barbour, *Religion in an Age of Science: The Gifford Lectures, 1989–1991,* vol. 1 (San Francisco: Harper, 1990), 4–30; John Haught, *Science and Religion: From Conflict to Conversation* (New York: Paulist, 1995).

9. Donald S. Browning, *The Moral Context of Pastoral Care* (Philadelphia: Westminster, 1976); Donald S. Browning, *Religious Ethics and Pastoral Care* (Philadelphia: Fortress, 1983); Chris Schlauch, "Expanding the Contexts of Pastoral Care," *Journal of Pastoral Care* 44 (1990): 359–71.

10. Moshe Halevi Spero, ed., *Psychotherapy of the Religious Patient* (Springfield, Ill.: Charles C. Thomas, 1985).

11. Anna Marie Rizzuto, *Birth of the Living God: A Psychoanalytic Study* (Chicago: University of Chicago Press, 1979); John McDargh, *Psychoanalytic Object Relations Theory and the Study of Religion* (Lanham, Md.: University Press of America, 1983); William Meissner, *Psychoanalysis and Religious Experience* (New Haven: Yale University Press, 1984).

12. Jones, "A Constructive Relationship," 115.

13. B. Beit-Hallahmi, "Curiosity, Doubt, and Devotion: The Beliefs of Psychologists and the Psychology of Religion," in *Current Perspectives on the Psychology of Religion,* ed. H. Newton Malony (Grand Rapids, Mich.: Eerdmans), 381–91, cited in *Religion and the Clinical Practice of Psychology,* ed. Shafranske, 153.

14. C. Ragan, H. Newton Malony, and B. Beit-Hallahmi, "Psychologists and Religion: Professional Factors Associated with Personal Belief," *Review of Religious Research* 21, no. 2 (1980): 208–17, cited in *Religion and the Clinical Practice of Psychology,* ed. Shafranske, 153.

15. Allan E. Bergin and J. P. Jensen, "Religiosity of Psychotherapists: A National Survey," *Psychotherapy* 27, no. 1 (1990): 3–7, cited in *Religion and the Clinical Practice of Psychology,* ed. Shafranske 153.

16. Edward P. Shafranske and H. Newton Malony, "Clinical Psychologists' Religious and Spiritual Orientations and Their Practice of Psychotherapy," *Psychotherapy* 27, no. 1 (1990): 72–78, cited in *Religion and the Clinical Practice of Psychotherapy,* ed. Shafranske, 153.

17. K. Derr, "Religious Issues in Psychotherapy: Factors Associated with the Selection of Clinical Interventions," Ph.D. diss., University of Southern California, 1991, cited in *Religion and the Clinical Practice of Psychotherapy,* ed. Shafranske, 153.

18. J. L. Lannert, "Spiritual and Religious Attitudes, Beliefs and Practices of Clinical Training Directors and Their Internship Sites," Ph.D. diss., University of Southern California, 1992, cited in *Religion and the Clinical Practice of Psychotherapy,* ed. Shafranske, 153.

19. Edward P. Shafranske, "Religiosity of Clinical and Counseling Psychologists," manuscript, 1995, cited in *Religion and the Clinical Practice of Psychotherapy,* ed. Shafranske, 153.

20. Shafranske, ed., *Religion and the Clinical Practice of Psychology.*

21. P. Scott Richards and Allen E. Bergin, *A Spiritual Strategy for Counseling and Psychotherapy* (Washington, D.C.: American Psychological Association, 1997).

22. See also William R. Miller, ed., *Integrating Spirituality into Treatment: Resources for Practitioners* (Washington, D.C.: American Psychological Press, 1999); Scott Richards and Allen E. Bergin, *Handbook of Psychotherapy and Religious Diversity* (Washington, D.C.: American Psychological Press, 2000).

23. Roger W. Sperry, "Psychology's Mentalist Paradigm and the Religion/Science Tension," *American Psychologist* 43, no. 8 (1988): 607–13.

24. William O'Donohue, "The (Even) Bolder Model," *American Psychologist* 44, no. 12 (1989): 1460–68.

25. Allan E. Bergin, "Values and Religious Issues in Psychotherapy and Mental Health," *American Psychologist* 46 (1991): 394–403.

26. Jones, "A Constructive Relationship," 141.

27. See Donald Browning, *Atonement and Psychotherapy* (Philadelphia: Westminster, 1966); *The Moral Context of Pastoral Care* (Philadelphia: Westminster, 1976); *Religious Ethics and Pastoral Care* (Philadelphia: Fortress, 1983); and *Religious Thought and the Modern Psychologies* (Philadelphia: Fortress, 1987).

28. Donald Browning, "Psychology in the Service of the Church," *Journal of Psychology and Theology* 2, no. 2 (1992): 127–36.

29. Ibid., 135.

30. Thomas C. Oden, *Care of Souls in the Classic Tradition* (Philadelphia: Fortress, 1984), 33.

31. Peter Homans, ed., *The Dialogue between Theology and Psychology* (Chicago: University of Chicago Press, 1968); Peter Homans, *Theology after Freud: An Interpretive Inquiry* (New York: Bobbs-Merrill, 1970).

32. John McDargh, "Theological Uses of Psychology: Retrospective and Prospective," *Horizons* 12, no. 2 (1985): 247–64.

33. James M. Gustafson, "The Relation of Empirical Science to Moral Thought," in *Introduction to Christian Ethics: A Reader,* ed. Ronald P. Hamel and Kenneth R. Himes (New York: Paulist, 1989), 435–37.

34. Mark L. Poorman, *Interactional Morality: A Foundation for Moral Discernment in Catholic Pastoral Ministry* (Washington, D.C.: Georgetown University Press, 1993).

35. John T. McNeill, *A History of the Cure of Souls* (New York: Harper & Row, 1951), 289.

36. E. Brooks Holifield, *A History of Pastoral Care in America: From Salvation to Self-Realization* (Nashville: Abingdon, 1983).

37. Paul E. Johnson, "Fifty Years in Clinical Pastoral Education," *Journal of Pastoral Care* 23, no. 4 (1974): 223–31.

38. Edward E. Thornton, *Professional Education for Ministry: A History of Clinical Pastoral Education* (Nashville: Abingdon, 1970).

39. Charles A. Van Wagner III, *The AAPC: A History of the American Association of Pastoral Counselors (1963–1991)* (Fairfax, Va.: American Association of Pastoral Counselors, 1992).

40. Allison Stokes, *Ministry after Freud* (New York: Pilgrim, 1985).

41. Robert D. Cross, *The Emergence of Liberal Catholicism in America* (Cambridge, Mass.: Harvard University Press, 1958).

42. Thomas F. O'Dea, *American Catholic Dilemma: An Inquiry into the Intellectual Life* (New York: Sheed & Ward, 1958).

43. John T. Ellis, *American Catholics and the Intellectual Life* (Chicago: Heritage Foundation, 1956).

44. William M. Halsey, *The Survival of American Innocence: Catholicism in an Era of Disillusionment, 1920–1940* (Notre Dame, Ind.: University of Notre Dame Press, 1980).

45. Margaret M. Reher, *Catholic Intellectual Life in America: A Historical Study of Persons and Movements* (New York: Macmillan, 1989).

46. Christopher J. Kaufman, *Ministry and Meaning: A Religious History of Catholic Health Care in the United States* (New York: Crossroad, 1995).

47. Philip Gleason, *Contending with Modernity: Catholic Higher Education in the Twentieth Century* (New York: Oxford University Press, 1995), 322.

48. George M. Marsden, *The Soul of the American University: From Protestant Establishment to Established Nonbelief* (New York: Oxford University Press, 1994).

49. Joseph A. Appleyard, S.J., "The Secularization of the Modern American University," *Conversations on Jesuit Higher Education* 10 (Fall 1996): 31–33.

50. Jay Dolan, *The American Catholic Experience* (Garden City, N.Y.: Doubleday, 1985).

51. Gerald P. Fogarty, *American Catholic Biblical Scholarship: A History from the Early Republic to Vatican II* (New York: Harper & Row, 1989).

52. James Hennesey, *American Catholics: A History of the Roman Catholic Community in the United States* (New York: Oxford University Press, 1981).

53. William P. Leahy, *Adapting to America: Catholics, Jesuits and Higher Education in the Twentieth Century* (Washington: Georgetown University Press, 1991).

54. David J. O'Brien, *From the Heart of the American Church: Catholic Higher Education and American Culture* (Maryknoll, N.Y.: Orbis, 1994).

1. From Two Spires to One Banner: Antagonisms and Alliances

1. Nathan G. Hale, Jr., *The Rise and Crisis of Psychoanalysis in the United States: Freud and the Americans 1917–1985* (New York: Oxford University Press, 1995).

2. The popularity of psychoanalysis among American Jewish psychiatrists in the post–World War II period was demonstrated in a study that revealed that 83 percent of Jewish psychiatrists were psychoanalytically oriented. On the other hand, 88 percent of non-Jewish psychiatrists in the period were biologically oriented. See August B. Hollingshead and Fredrick C. Redlich, *Social Class and Mental Illness: A Community Study* (New York: Wiley, 1958), cited in P. Scott Richard and Allen E. Bergin, *Handbook of Psychotherapy and Religious Diversity* (Washington, D.C.: American Psychological Association, 2000), 276–77.

3. Hale, *The Rise and Crisis of Psychoanalysis in the United States,* 191.

4. Ibid.

5. Ibid., 247.

6. This controversy ensued shortly after Thomas Verner Moore resigned from Catholic University and headed to Spain to begin the process that would eventually lead him into the Carthusians. One wonders what would have transpired had Moore been at Catholic University when his former colleague, Msgr. Sheen, was making such strident attacks on psychoanalysis.

7. "Sheen Denounces Psychoanalysis: He Recognizes Confession of Sin as 'Key to Happiness in the Modern World,'" *New York Times,* March 10, 1947, 10.

8. Ibid.

9. Ibid.

10. Dr. Leo Bartemeier cited in Albert Deutsch, "Freudians Refute Msgr. Sheen's Attack on Psychoanalysis," *PM,* June 17, 1947, 24.

11. Dr. Lawrence S. Kubie, in ibid., 24.

12. Msgr. Fulton J. Sheen cited in Albert Deutsch, "Msgr. Sheen Raps Press for 'Garbling' Sermon on Psychoanalysis and Sin," *PM,* June 18, 1947, 24.

13. Dr. A. A. Brill, "Dr. Brill Replies to Msgr. Sheen," *New York Times,* July 6, 1947, 42.

14. Dr. Leo Bartemeier, in Albert Deutsch, "Catholic Psychiatrists Rebut Msgr. Sheen's Attack on 'Godless Science,'" *PM* (July 1947): 24.

15. *New York Times,* April 9, 1952, 21.

16. Pope Pius XII, "Psychotherapy and Religion: An Address to the Fifth International Congress of Psychotherapy and Clinical Psychology," *Catholic Mind* (July 1953): 435.

2. The Turn-of-the-Century Immigrants: Catholicism and the New Psychology

1. According to Misiak and Staudt Sexton only a few other American universities had established psychology laboratories prior to Pace's: Johns Hopkins in 1883 by G. S. Hall, University of Pennsylvania in 1888 by J. McK. Cattell, University of Wisconsin in 1888 by J. Jastrow, Indiana University in 1888 by W. L. Bryan, Clark University in 1889 by G. S. Hall and E. S. Sanford, University of Michigan in 1890 by J. H. Tufts, and Harvard University in 1890 by W. James. See Henryk Misiak and Virginia Staudt Sexton, *History of Psychology: An Overview* (New York: Grune & Stratton, 1966), 56.

2. The psychologist Theodule Armand Ribot seems to have been the first to use the term "new psychology." To a French audience in 1879 Ribot spoke of the achievements of the "new" experimental psychology. See Sigmund Koch, "Wundt's Creature at Age Zero—and as Centenarian: Some Aspects of the Institutionalization of the 'New Psychology," in *A Century of Psychology as Science,* ed. Sigmund Koch and David E. Leary (New York: McGraw-Hill, 1985), 13.

3. Edwin G. Boring, *A History of Experimental Psychology* (New York: Appleton-Century-Crofts, 1950), 333.

4. William James (1842–1910) had already established an experimental "demonstrational" laboratory at Harvard in 1875, but unlike Wundt's laboratory it was not set up for sustained research.

5. *Syllabus of Pope Pius IX* (1864), in *The Papal Encyclicals,* ed. Claudia Carlen, I.H.M. (Wilmington, N.C.: McGrath, 1981).

6. Thomas Bokenkotter, *A Concise History of the Catholic Church* (Garden City, N.Y.: Doubleday Image, 1979), 331.

7. Pope Leo XIII, *Aeterni Patris* (1879), in *The Papal Encyclicals,* ed. Carlen, 17–27.

8. Henryk Misiak and Virgina M. Staudt, *Catholics in Psychology: A Historical Survey* (New York: McGraw-Hill, 1954), 34.

9. Ibid., 34–35.

10. Quoted in ibid., 48.

11. Walter T. K. Nugent, *Crossings: The Great Transatlantic Migrations, 1870–1914* (Bloomington: Indiana University Press, 1992), 151.

12. James Hennesey, S.J., *American Catholics: A History of the Roman Catholic Community in the United States* (New York: Oxford University Press, 1981), 187.

13. Quoted in Thomas T. McAvoy, C.S.C., *A History of the Catholic Church in the United States* (Notre Dame, Ind.: University of Notre Dame Press, 1969), 266.

14. Robert C. Ayers, "The Americanists and Franz Xavier Kraus: An Historical Analysis of an International Liberal Combination, 1897–1898," dissertation, Syracuse University, 1982, 7, cited in C. Joseph Neusse, *The Catholic University of America: A Centennial History* (Washington, D.C.: Catholic University Press, 1990), 74.

15. Eduardo Soderni, "Leo XIII and the U.S. of America," trans. F. Terras, manuscript, Archives of the University of Notre Dame, 19, cited in Nuesse, *The Catholic University of America,* 74.

16. Nuesse, *The Catholic University of America,* 72.

17. McAvoy, *A History of the Catholic Church in the United States,* 321.

18. Charles Maignen, a leading French conservative of the time, using an abridged translation of Walter Elliott's biography of Hecker, considered Hecker's ideas of the indwelling of the Holy Spirit a form of the heresy known as Illuminism. See David O'Brien, *Isaac Hecker: An American Catholic* (New York: Paulist, 1992), 385.

19. William Halsey, *The Survival of American Innocence: Catholicism in an Era of Disillusionment, 1920–1940* (Notre Dame, Ind.: University of Notre Dame Press, 1980), 141.

20. Ibid.

21. Josiah Royce, "Pope Leo's Philosophical Movement and Its Relation to Modern Thought," *Boston Evening Transcript,* July 29, 1903, 14, cited in ibid., 141.

22. Pope Pius X, *Lamentabili Sane,* July 3, 1907. See http://listserv.american.edu/catholic/ church/papal/pius.x/syllabus.txt.

23. Joseph B. Lemius, *Catechism on Modernism: According to the Encyclical "Pascendi Dominici Gregis" of His Holiness Pius X,* trans. John Fitzpatrick (New York, 1908), 117, cited in Margaret Mary Reher, *Catholic Intellectual Life in America: A Historical Study of Persons and Movements* (New York: Macmillan, 1989), 94.

24. Leo Strauss, cited in John T. McGreevy, "Thinking on One's Own: Catholicism in the American Intellectual Imagination, 1928–1960," *Journal of American History* (June 1997): 101.

25. Eudoxe-Irenee Mignot to Domenico Ferrata, October 1914, in Nicolas Fontaine, *Sainte Siège, Action Française et Catholiques Integraux: Histoire avec documents* (Paris: Librairie Universitaire, 1928), 133, cited in John Tracy Ellis, "The Formation of the American Priest: An Historical Perspective," in *The Catholic Priest in the United States: Historical Investigations,* ed. John Tracy Ellis (Collegeville, Minn.: St. John's University, 1971), 71–72.

26. Helen E. Peixotto, "A History of Psychology at Catholic University," *Catholic Education Review* 66 (April 1969): 844–45.

27. J. K. Ryan, "Edward Aloysius Pace," in *New Catholic Encyclopedia,* 10:850–51.

28. Bruce M. Ross, "Development of Psychology at the Catholic University of America," *Journal of the Washington Academy of Sciences* 82, no. 3 (1994): 138.

29. Thomas Hughes, "Psychology, Physiology and Pedagogics," *American Catholic Quarterly Review* 19 (1894): 790.

30. Ibid., 800.

31. Edward A. Pace, "The Growth and Spirit of Modern Psychology," *American Catholic Quarterly Review* 19 (1894): 523.

32. Ibid., 528.

33. Ibid., 544.

34. Ibid.

3. The New Psychology: Footholds in American Catholicism

1. Thomas Verner Moore, letter to Dr. José Ferrer-Hombravella, Burgos, Spain, October 15, 1949, cited in Benedict Neenan, O.S.B., "The Life of Thomas Verner Moore: Psychiatrist, Educator and Monk," Ph.D. diss., Catholic University of America, 1996, 38. See also Benedict Neenan, *Thomas Verner Moore: Psychiatrist, Educator, and Monk* (New York: Paulist, 2000).

2. Thomas Verner Moore, *A Study in Reaction Time and Movement,* monograph supplement to *Psychology Review* 6, no. 1 (New York: Macmillan, 1904).

3. Thomas Verner Moore, "The Process of Abstraction: An Experimental Study," *University of California Publications in Psychology* 1, no. 2 (1910): 73–197.

4. Moore, letter to Dr. José Ferrer-Hombravella, October 15, 1949.

5. Ibid.

6. Ibid. While more than forty psychology laboratories existed by 1900, psychological clinics were a rare enterprise. As noted above, the first mental clinic dedicated exclusively to psychological purposes was established by Lightner Witmer at the University of Pennsylvania in 1896. Witmer was a charter member of the American Psychological Association and like Pace and Moore had studied in Leipzig under Wundt. When he returned from Leipzig Witmer sought to bring a unique American spirit to psychology by naming the new science "practical." He subsequently conceived of psychology as a helping profession that would be independent of both education and medicine. In 1907 Witmer labeled this discipline "clinical psychology" and founded the journal *The Psychological Clinic*. Witmer was also the first to argue that a psychological clinic could be directed by a psychologist rather than a physician.

7. Thomas Verner Moore, "Imagery and Meaning in Memory and Perception," *Psychological Monographs* 27, no. 2 (1919): 67–296.

8. Thomas Verner Moore, *Cognitive Psychology* (Philadelphia: J. B. Lippincott, 1939).

9. T. V. Moore, "The Parataxes: A Study and Analysis of Certain Borderline Mental States," *Psychoanalytic Review* 8 (1921): 252–83.

10. Moore, letter, 1949.

11. Ibid.

12. Thomas Verner Moore to Thomas J. Shahan, Fort Augustus, Scotland, January 25, 1924, rector's papers, department of psychology file, Archives of the Catholic University of America, cited in Neenan, "The Life of Thomas Verner Moore."

13. Ibid.

14. Ibid. In furthering the cause of Catholic education in America, the Catholic University established a college specifically for the education of women religious. This college was known as the "Sisters College."

15. Ibid.

16. Ibid.

17. Ibid.

18. Thomas Verner Moore to Bishop Joseph M. Corrigan, Catholic University, Washington, D.C., July 17, 1936, Archives of the Catholic University of America.

19. Ibid.

20. Neenan, "The Life of Thomas Verner Moore."

21. Thomas Verner Moore, "The Clergy and Mental Hygiene," *American Ecclesiastical Review* 85 (1935): 602.

22. Neenan, "The Life of Thomas Verner Moore," 217. Brennan was a former student of Moore's at Catholic University and received his doctorate there in 1925. Brennan's identity as a Dominican priest led him to embrace a Thomistic approach to philosophical psychology more forcefully than Moore. According to Misiak and Staudt Sexton, Brennan's books, *General Psychology* (1937; rev. ed. New York: Macmillan, 1952), *Thomistic Psychology* (New York: Macmillan, 1944), and *History of Psychology, from the Standpoint of a Thomist* (New York: Macmillan, 1945), are perhaps the best examples of a Catholic scholar's efforts to integrate Thomistic rational psychology with experimental psychology and bring the latter to the attention of a wide range of Catholic students and seminarians (Misiak and Staudt, *Catholics in Psychology*, 246). McDargh points out two other works that sought to integrate Thomistic psychology with experimental psychology: *Psychology: Empirical and Rational* by the British Jesuit Michael Maher (1890; 9th ed. London: Longmans, Green, 1933), which went through nine editions, and *Psychology and Natural Theology* by Owen Aloysius Hill of Fordham University (New York: Macmillan, 1921). See John McDargh, "Theological Uses of Psychology: Retrospective and Prospective," *Horizons* 12, no. 2 (1985): 250. Several decades later, Joseph Donceel, a Belgian Jesuit at Fordham, published *Philosophical Psychology* (London: Sheed & Ward, 1955). For years Donceel's work was widely used in Catholic colleges.

23. Thomas Verner Moore, *The Driving Forces of Human Nature and Their Adjustment: An Introduction to the Psychology and Psychopathology of Emotional Behavior and Volitional Control* (New York: Grune & Stratton, 1950), 45.

24. Thomas Verner Moore, "Letter to Msgr. Fulton J. Sheen," March 2, 1945, Archives of St. Anselm's Abbey, Washington, D.C.

25. Thomas Verner Moore, *Dynamic Psychology: An Introduction to Modern Psychological Theory and Practice* (Philadelphia: J. P. Lippincott, 1924), 260–61.

26. Thomas Verner Moore, "Catholic Psychological Society Lecture on Freud," *The Tablet* 169 (1937): 490–91.

27. Thomas Verner Moore, *Dynamic Psychology: An Introduction to Modern Psychological Theory and Practice* (Philadelphia: J. B. Lippincott, 1924); *Cognitive Psychology* (Philadelphia: J. B. Lippincott, 1939); *The Nature and Treatment of Mental Disorders* (New York: Grune & Stratton, 1944); *Personal Mental Hygiene* (New York: Grune & Stratton, 1944); and *The Driving Forces of Human Nature and Their Adjustment: An Introduction to the Psychology and Psychopathology of Emotional Behavior and Volitional Control* (New York: Grune & Stratton, 1948).

28. Thomas Verner Moore, *The Life of Man with God* (New York: Harcourt, Brace, 1956) and *Heroic Sanctity and Insanity: An Introduction to the Spiritual Life and Mental Hygiene* (New York: Grune & Stratton, 1959).

29. E. Boyd Barrett, S.J., "Some Modern Psychologists," *The Month* 117 (1911): 396–407.

30. E. Boyd Barrett, S.J., "Psychoanalysis and Christian Morality," *The Month* 127 (1921): 96–110.

31. E. Boyd Barrett, S.J., "Pathological Psychology," *Irish Ecclesiastical Review* 21 (January 1923): 13.

32. E. Boyd Barrett, S.J., "Studies in Practical Psychology," *America* (December 13, 1924): 197–99.

33. E. Boyd Barrett, S.J., *The New Psychology: How It Aids and Interests* (New York: P. J. Kenedy, 1925).

34. Barrett left the priesthood and his religious order, the Society of Jesus, for a number of years but subsequently returned to the priesthood. At the time departures from the priesthood were rare. Consequently his book *A Shepherd without Sheep* (Dublin: Clanmore & Reynolds, 1956), an account of his departure and return, became a significant work in Catholic circles.

35. Barrett, *The New Psychology*, 324.

36. Charles Menig, "The Priest's Attitude toward Psycho-analysis," *Ecclesiastical Review* 75, no. 2 (1926): 124.

37. During the same period mainline Protestant thinkers and leaders were considering the pastoral implications of psychological and psychoanalytic thought. For instance, Frances Kolb notes that between 1924 and 1930 more than 120 articles were published in the *Psychological Bulletin* that dealt with issues pertaining to religion and psychoanalysis and the several schools of psychology. See Frances A. Kolb, "The Reaction of American Protestants to Psychoanalysis 1900–1950," dissertation, Washington University, June 1972, 72.

38. "Charles Bruehl, "Pastoralia," *Homiletic and Pastoral Review* (November 1921): 121–32.

39. Charles Bruehl, "Pastoralia," *Homiletic and Pastoral Review* (October 1921): 1–4.

40. During this period Protestant ministers had begun to do exactly that. In the mid-1920s Anton Boisen at the Worcester State Mental Hospital and Richard Cabot at the Episcopal Divinity School in Cambridge promoted the development of clinical training programs that signaled the birth of Clinical Pastoral Education. Furthermore, as Kolb points out, by the 1930s most Protestant theological schools required at least one course in the psychology of religion. See Kolb, "The Reaction of American Protes-

tants to Psychoanalysis 1900–1950," 112. Incorporation of psychology into religious formation was all but nonexistent in Catholic seminaries.

41. Charles Bruehl, "Cura Afflictorum," *Homiletic and Pastoral Review* (June 1922): 955.

42. Charles Bruehl, "The New Psychology Applied to Pastoral Problems," *Homiletic and Pastoral Review* (March 1925): 584.

43. While the *Review* abandoned Bruehl's "Pastoralia" section after 1930, it periodically presented pastoral reflections of a psychological nature. The most notable instance occurred between 1939 and 1942, when a series of articles was published by Henry Schumacher, one of the first Catholic psychiatrists. He received his undergraduate and medical training at St. Louis University and psychiatric training at the Phibbs Clinic of the Johns Hopkins University. Schumacher served on numerous medical boards and at various institutions and was well qualified to write a series of articles for the *Review* dealing with the care of the "mentally deficient." Schumacher's essays covered the general spectrum of mental illness as it was understood at the time. His topics dealt with psychoneuroses, psychopathic states, affective reaction types, schizophrenia, and organic reaction types.

44. Agostino Gemelli (1878–1959) was a Franciscan priest who, like Moore, obtained degrees in medicine and psychology. His experimental research and publications led him to participate in numerous national and international meetings of psychologists and psychiatrists, where he often delivered papers. Gemelli was appointed by Pope Pius XI as the first rector of the Sacred Heart University in Milan and later became president of the Pontifical Academy of Sciences. Through his administrative leadership and numerous publications in psychology and philosophy, Gemelli more than any other Italian opened the doors of Roman Catholicism to psychology.

45. Rudolf Allers, *The Psychology of Character* (London: Sheed & Ward, 1931); *Practical Psychology in Character Development* (New York: Sheed & Ward, 1934); *Sex Psychology in Education* (St. Louis: B. Herder, 1937); *Self Improvement* (London: Burns, Oates, and Washbourne, 1939); and *Character Education in Adolescence* (New York: Wagner, 1940).

46. Allers's relationship with Moore appears to have been strained. As Neenan points out Moore refused to allow Allers to hold a position in the psychology department at Catholic University. See Neenan, "The Life of Thomas Verner Moore," 214.

47. Rudolf Allers, *The New Psychologies* (London: Sheed & Ward, 1932).

48. Rudolf Allers, *The Successful Error: A Critical Study of Freudian Psychoanalysis* (New York: Sheed & Ward, 1940), 199–200.

49. Ibid., 255.

4. From Rational to Clinical Psychology: Three Jesuit Universities

1. Raphael Charles McCarthy, *Training the Adolescent* (New York: Bruce, 1934); *Safeguarding Mental Health* (New York: Bruce, 1937).

2. Eugene Kennedy, Ph.D., interview with C. Kevin Gillespie, S.J., June 4, 2000.

3. Joan Arnold, interview with C. Kevin Gillespie, S.J., November 19, 2000.

4. Magda B. Arnold and John A. Gasson, in collaboration with Charles A. Curran et al., *The Human Person: An Approach to an Integral Theory of Personality* (New York: Ronald Press, 1954); Magda B. Arnold, *Emotion and Personality* (New York: Columbia University Press, 1960); Magda B. Arnold, et al., *Screening Candidates for the Priesthood and Religious Life* (Chicago: Loyola University Press, 1962); Magda B. Arnold, *Story Sequence Analysis: A New Method of Measuring Motivation and Predicting Achievement* (New York: Columbia University Press, 1962).

5. Magda B. Arnold, *Memory and the Brain* (Hillsdale, N.J.: L. Earlbaum Associates, 1984).

6. Eugene Kennedy, Ph.D., interview with C. Kevin Gillespie, S.J., March 9, 2000.

7. Frank J. Kobler, *Casebook in Psychopathology* (Staten Island, N.Y.: Alba House, 1964).

8. Leroy A. Wauck, Ph.D., "The Story of Psychology at Loyola 1929–1979," manuscript, Archives of Loyola University of Chicago, 7.

9. Leonard Gross, *God and Freud* (New York: D. McKay Company, 1959).

10. Leonard Gross, "Psychiatry, Sin and Father Devlin," *Look,* February 3, 1959, 66–73.

11. William J. Devlin, S.J., M.D., quoted in Jack Conroy, "Are Religion and Psychiatry Going to Get Together?" review of *God and Freud, Chicago Sun-Times*, February 1, 1959, Archives of Loyola University of Chicago.

12. Office of the President, Rev. James F. Maguire, S.J., to American Archbishops and Jesuit Provincials, January 19, 1959, Archives of Loyola University of Chicago (Box 31, Folder 6).

13. Paul F. D'Arcy and Eugene C. Kennedy, *Genius of the Apostolate: Personal Growth in the Candidate, the Seminarian, and the Priest* (New York: Sheed & Ward, 1965).

14. Eugene C. Kennedy, *What a Modern Catholic Believes about Sex and Marriage* (Chicago: Thomas More, 1972); *Believing* (Garden City, N.Y.: Doubleday, 1974); *A Sense of Life, a Sense of Sin* (Garden City, N.Y.: Doubleday, 1975); *Sexual Counseling: A Practical Guide for Non-Professional Counselors* (New York: Continuum, 1977); *The Now and Future Church: The Psychology of Being an American Catholic* (Garden City, N.Y.: Doubleday, 1984); and Eugene C. Kennedy and Sara C. Charles, *Authority: The Most Misunderstood Idea in America* (New York: Free Press, 1997).

15. Vincent Herr, S.J., "Religions and Mental Health Memorandum Describing National Institute of Mental Health Project Initiated by the Academy of Religion and Mental Health, 1956–1961," Archives of Loyola University of Chicago, 2.

16. Ibid., 3.

17. Eugene Kennedy and Victor Heckler, *The Catholic Priest in the United States: Psychological Investigations* (Washington, D.C.: United States Catholic Conference Publications), 16.

18. James Joseph Schroeder, "The Catholic Bishop in the United States: A Psychological Profile," *Dissertation Abstract,* 1980: 5584–B.

19. Ibid.

20. Mary Sheehan and Frank J. Kobler, "Toward a Psychological Understanding of

the American Catholic Bishop," *Journal of Clinical Psychology* 32, no. 3 (July 1976): 547.

21. Henryk Misiak and Virginia M. Staudt, *Catholics in Psychology: A Historical Survey* (New York: McGraw-Hill, 1954); Henryk Misiak and Virginia Staudt Sexton, *History of Psychology; An Overview* (New York: Grune & Stratton, 1966); Henryk Misiak and Virginia Staudt Sexton, *Phenomenological, Existential, and Humanistic Psychologies: A Historical Survey* (New York: Grune & Stratton, 1973); Virginia Staudt Sexton and Henryk Misiak, eds., *Psychology around the World* (Monterey, Calif.: Brooks/Cole, 1976).

22. Misiak and Staudt, *Catholics in Psychology,* 262.

23. Virginia Staudt Sexton, "William Christian Bier, S.J., Ph.D. (1911–1980)," *Newsletter: Psychologists Interested in Religious Issues* 5 (Summer 1980): 2.

24. William C. Bier, S.J., "PIRI—Bridge between the ACPA and APA," presidential address to Psychologists Interested in Religious Issues: Division 36 of the American Psychological Association, August 30, 1975, 4.

25. Thomas Verner Moore, "The Rate of Insanity in Priests and Religious," *Ecclesiastical Review* 95 (1936): 485–98.

26. One Jesuit who was tested by Bier upon entering the Society of Jesus in 1948 noted recently that several of his peers had mental breakdowns early in their religious formation, and it was later learned that Bier, on the basis of a psychological battery, had not recommended their entrance (Rev. George Driscoll, S.J., interview with Rev. C. Kevin Gillespie, S.J., Fordham University, February 7, 1996).

27. William C. Bier, S.J., "Psychological Testing of Candidates and the Theology of Vocation," *Review for Religious* (December 1953): 291–304; William C. Bier, S.J., "Practical Requirements of a Program for the Psychological Screening of Candidates," *Review for Religious* (January 1954): 13–26.

28. William C. Bier, S.J., "Sigmund Freud and the Faith," *America* 96, no. 7 (November 17, 1956): 192–96.

29. William Bier, S.J., Papers, Fordham University Library, Bronx, N.Y.

30. Roy Stuart Lee, *Freud and Christianity* (New York: A. A. Wyn, 1949).

31. Rev. Thomas E. Henneberry, S.J., to Rev. William C. Bier, S.J., April 23, 1957, William Bier, S.J., Papers, Fordham University Library, Bronx, N.Y.

32. William C. Bier, S.J., "PIRI—Bridge between the ACPA and APA," 5.

33. William C. Bier, S.J., *ACPA Newsletter* (1955): 6, 7.

5. Sr. Annette Walters, C.S.J.: Psychologist and Prophet

1. Kathleen McLaughlin, "The Role of the Laity in the Thought of John Ireland," Ph.D dissertation, Marquette University, 1991, 135–39.

2. Mary Reuder, Ph.D., interview with C. Kevin Gillespie, S.J. Reuder, a student of Walters, rose to prominence in Division 36 of the American Psychological Association and has written on the Division's history. See Donald A. Dewsbury, ed., *Unifica-*

tion through Division: Histories of the Divisions of the American Psychological Association
(Washington, D.C.: American Psychological Association Press, 1996).

3. *Time* magazine, July 17, 1964, 40.

4. B. F. Skinner to Sr. Annette Walters, College of St. Catherine, St. Paul, Minnesota, July 16, 1964, Archives of Marquette University.

5. B. F. Skinner to Sr. Annette Walters, St. Ambrose College, Davenport, Iowa, July 11, 1969, Archives of Marquette University.

6. Sr. Annette Walters to B. F. Skinner, Harvard University, Cambridge, Massachusetts, December 5, 1970, Archives of Marquette University.

7. B. F. Skinner, in Eugene Kennedy, *Believing* (New York: Doubleday, 1977), 142.

8. Sr. Annette Walters to B. F. Skinner, Harvard University, Cambridge, Massachusetts, February 12, 1974, Archives of Marquette University.

9. B. F. Skinner to Sr. Ritamary Bradley, St. Ambrose College, Davenport, Iowa, March 10, 1978, Archives of Marquette University.

10. Ibid.

11. Annette Walters, C.S.J. "A Genetic Study of Geometric-Optical Illusions." *Genetic Psychology Monographs* 25 (1942): 101–55.

12. Mary Reuder, Conversation with Rev. C. Kevin Gillespie, S.J., July 25, 2001.

13. This phrase was often used by Fr. William Bier, S.J., who for many years served as the executive secretary of the American Catholic Psychological Association. See William C. Bier, S.J., "PIRI—Bridge between the ACPA and APA," presidential address to Psychologists Interested in Religious Issues: Division 36 of the American Psychological Association, August 10, 1975, 4.

14. Sr. Annette Walters to Sr. Kevin O'Hara, College of St. Catherine, Minneapolis, Minnesota, May 7, 1953, Archives of Marquette University.

15. Sr. Annette Walters and Sr. Kevin O'Hara, *Persons and Personality: An Introduction to Psychology* (New York: Appleton-Crofts, 1954), vii.

16. Ibid.

17. Ibid., vii–viii.

18. Henryk Misiak and Virginia M. Staudt, *Catholics in Psychology: A Historical Survey* (New York: McGraw-Hill, 1954).

19. Sr. Annette Walters, ed., *Readings in Psychology* (Westminster, Md.: Newman, 1963).

20. Pope Pius XII as cited in ibid., 1.

21. Sr. Annette Walters to Rev. Michael E. Naughton, St. John's Mental Health Institute, St. John's University, Collegeville, Minn., December 21, 1970, Archives of St. John's University.

22. Eileen Gavin, Ph.D., "In Her Memory: Some Reflections on the Life and Work of Annette Walters, CSJ," *Newsletter of the St. Paul Province,* June–July 1998, 11–12.

23. Eileen Gavin, Ph.D., interview with C. Kevin Gillespie, S.J., College of St. Catherine, St. Paul, Minnesota, February 4, 2000.

24. Ann Patrice Carrigan, S.S.J., "A Prophet in Our Midst: Annette Walters," *New Women/New Church,* November 1979, 6.

25. Sr. Annette M. Walters, C.S.J., "Conditioning Environmental Factors: The Constructive and Destructive Influences in the Religious, Professional, and Related Areas,"

Seventh Annual Institute of Spirituality for Sister Superiors of Religious Houses, August 5–11, 1959, University of Notre Dame, Notre Dame, Indiana, manuscript, Archives of Marquette University.

26. Sr. Ritamary Bradley, interview with C. Kevin Gillespie, S.J., St. Ambrose College, Davenport, Iowa, March 3, 2000.

27. Sr. Antonine, C.S.J., to Mother Mary Luke, S.L., Motherhouse, Sisters of Loretto, Nerinx, Kentucky, July 28, 1965, Archives of the College of St. Catherine, St. Paul, Minnesota.

28. Ann Carey, *Sisters in Crisis: The Tragic Unraveling of Women's Religious Communities* (Huntington, Ind.: Our Sunday Visitor, 1997), 142–44, 252.

29. Sr. Annette Walters and Sr. Ritamary Bradley, "Motivation and Religious Behavior," in *Research on Religious Development,* ed. M. P. Strommen (New York: Hawthorne, 1971), 599–651.

30. Eileen Gavin, Ph.D., interview with C. Kevin Gillespie, S.J., College of St. Catherine, St. Paul, Minnesota, February 4, 2000.

6. Signs of the Times: American Catholicism before the Second Vatican Council

1. James Hennesey, *American Catholics: A History of the Roman Catholic Community in the United States* (New York: Oxford University Press, 1981), 296.

2. Philip Gleason, *Contending with Modernity: Catholic Higher Education in the Twentieth Century* (New York: Oxford University Press, 1995), 209.

3. Ibid., 220

4. George Bull, S.J., "The Function of the Catholic Graduate School," *Thought* 13 (1938): 364–78.

5. Gleason, *Contending with Modernity,* 264.

6. Ibid., 398.

7. Patrick W. Carey, "American Catholic Religious Thought: An Historical Review," *U.S. Catholic Historian* 4 (1985): 137, cited in Margaret Mary Reher, *Catholic Intellectual Life in America: A Historical Study of Persons and Movements* (New York: Macmillan, 1989), 117.

8. A. A. Roback, *History of American Psychology* (New York: Library Publishers, 1952), 353–54.

9. Ibid., 367.

10. One reason for the shift toward secularization was the department's desire to maintain its new status as approved by the American Psychological Association. Another reason, according to John McCall, was the result of a greater influx of non-Catholic graduate students into Catholic University through the GI Bill. McCall was a Jesuit graduate student in clinical psychology at Catholic University during the late 1940s and early 1950s (John McCall, Ph.D., interview with Rev. C. Kevin Gillespie, S.J., Boston College, July 24, 1996).

11. Evidence of this cautious atmosphere was given by Fr. James Gill, who during his philosophical studies at Gonzaga University was required to ask permission to

read such authors as Marx and Freud, whose works were on the church's *Index of Forbidden Books*. He noted with some humor that the works of such authors were under lock and key in the "hell room" (Rev. James Gill, S.J., M.D., interview with C. Kevin Gillespie, S.J., St. John's Seminary, Brighton, Mass., May 28, 1996).

12. Richard Vaughan, S.J., reported that, when he sought admission to graduate study in clinical psychology, he was permitted to apply only to three graduate schools, all of them Catholic: Catholic University, Loyola University of Chicago, and the University of Ottawa (Rev. Richard Vaughan, S.J., phone interview with C. Kevin Gillespie, S.J., February 15, 1996).

13. Quoted from the *New York Herald Tribune*, February 20, 1958, cited by Thomas F. O'Dea, *American Catholic Dilemma: An Inquiry into the Intellectual Life* (New York: Sheed & Ward, 1958), 8.

14. Sr. Annette Walters, C.S.J., "Why Is the American Catholic College Failing to Develop Catholic Intellectualism?" cited in O'Dea, *American Catholic Dilemma*, 10.

15. John Tracy Ellis, *American Catholics and the Intellectual Life* (Chicago: Heritage Foundation, 1956), 47–49.

16. Rev. John Grimes, interview with Rev. C. Kevin Gillespie, S.J., January 10, 1996.

17. Cited in ibid., 34; from *The Pilot* (Boston), October 17, 1947. Subsequently in 1957, John D. Donovan, a Boston College sociologist, found that only 5 percent of the American Catholic bishops had fathers who had graduated from college and another 5 percent had fathers who had attended college. See John D. Donovan, "The American Catholic Hierarchy: A Social Profile," *American Catholic Sociological Review* 19 (1958): 98–112, cited by Hennesey, *American Catholics*, 284.

18. Ellis, *American Catholics*, 42–44.

19. Ibid. In this criticism Ellis no doubt had in mind seminary-like requirements at some Catholic colleges according to which students had to attend daily Mass and lights had be out at a specified hour.

20. Ibid., 56–57.

21. O'Dea, *American Catholic Dilemma*, 155–61.

22. Roland Dalbiez, *Psychoanalytical Method and the Doctrine of Freud*, trans. T. F. Lindsay (New York: Books for Libraries Press, 1941), 325–26.

23. Jacques Maritain, "Freudianism and Psychoanalysis," *Cross Currents of Psychiatry and Catholic Morality*, ed. William Birmingham and Joseph E. Cunneen (New York: Pantheon Books, 1964), 334–56.

24. Agostino Gemelli, *Psychoanalysis Today* (New York: Kenedy, 1955); Joseph Nuttin, *Psychoanalysis and Personality: A Dynamic Theory of Normal Personality*, trans. George Lamb (New York: Sheed & Ward, 1953).

25. Joseph Donceel, S.J., "Second Thoughts on Freud," *Thought* 24 (September 1949): 484.

26. Ibid.

27. André Godin, "Psychotherapy: A New Humanism," *Thought* 28 (Autumn 1952): 421–34.

28. Bruno Bettleheim, *Love Is Not Enough* (Glencoe, Ill.: Free Press, 1950); Carl Rogers, *Client-Centered Therapy* (Boston: Houghton Mifflin, 1950); Karen Horney, *Neurosis and Human Growth* (New York: W. W. Norton, 1950).

29. Charles A. Curran, *Counseling in Catholic Life and Education* (New York: Macmillan, 1952); Carroll A. Wise, *Pastoral Counseling* (New York: Harper, 1951).

30. A number of Jewish converts to Catholicism who had been trained in psychiatry or psychoanalysis played a significant role in the Catholic Church's assimilation of psychological thought. In addition to Odenwald, Stern and Zilboorg were Jewish converts.

31. Archbishop Patrick O'Boyle in James H. VanderVeldt, O.F.M., and Robert P. Odenwald, M.D., *Psychiatry and Catholicism* (New York: McGraw-Hill, 1957), v.

32. Gregory Zilboorg, M.D., *Freud and Religion: A Restatement of an Old Controversy* (Westminster, Md.: Newman, 1958), 6. Later Paul Vitz presented a dramatic account of Freud's atheism and his fascination with religion, especially Catholicism. See Paul C. Vitz, *Freud's Christian Unconscious* (New York: Guilford, 1988).

33. Gregory Zilboorg, *History of Medical Psychology* (New York: Norton, 1941).

34. At the time it was very difficult for a Roman Catholic to obtain a marriage annulment.

35. John Schwiebert, "The Hamm Foundation: The First Twenty-Eight Years," manuscript, 1982, 25.

36. Ibid., 26.

37. While the Catholic clergy's attendance at the St. John's Institute indicates the growing acceptance of psychiatric and psychoanalytic thought, there was a significant dearth of Catholics in the field of psychiatry. For example, the Menninger Clinic, known for its openness to religious belief, reported that in 1958 about one-third of its psychiatric residents were Jewish, half were Protestant, and only one-tenth were Catholic.

38. Schwiebert, "The Hamm Foundation," 35–36.

39. A. Richard Sipe, interview with Rev. C. Kevin Gillespie, S.J., March 13, 1996.

40. David A. Boyd et al., "The St. John's Mental Health Institute," in *Psychiatry, the Clergy and Pastoral Counseling*, ed. Dana L. Farnsworth and Francis J. Braceland (Collegeville, Minn.: St. John's University Press, 1969), 14–15.

41. Dana L. Farnsworth and Francis J. Braceland, eds., *Psychiatry, the Clergy and Pastoral Counseling* (Collegeville, Minn.: St. John's University Press, 1969).

42. According to Michael Mott it was at this workshop that Thomas Merton had private meetings with Gregory Zilboorg. At the time Merton was the novice director at his Trappist monastery in Gethsemani and was experimenting with his novices with certain psychological strategies he had learned from reading Freud and others. Merton was even considering publishing an article entitled "Neurosis in the Monastic Life." Zilboorg confronted Merton about his inexperienced psychologizing and labeled it as "quackery." As a result, Merton restrained his use of "pop psychology." According to Mott the meetings with Zilboorg had a profound impact on Merton's self-understanding of his neurotic and narcissistic tendencies. See Michael Mott, *The Seven Mountains of Thomas Merton* (Boston: Houghton Mifflin, 1984), 290–99.

43. Schwiebert, "The Hamm Foundation."

44. One instance of such collaboration was related by Rev. Charles Healey, S.J., who was a Menninger Fellow in 1969. Healey mentioned that Karl Menninger often would ask him and other Fellows about their views of sin. A short time later, in 1973, Men-

ninger published a book entitled *Whatever Became of Sin?* (Rev. Charles Healey, S.J., interview with Rev. C. Kevin Gillespie, S.J., Cohassett, Mass., June 16, 1996).

45. A. Richard Sipe, interview with Rev. C. Kevin Gillespie, S.J., March 13, 1996.

46. Herman Feifel, ed., "Symposium on Relationships between Religion and Mental Health," *American Psychologist* (1959): 565–79.

7. Paradigm Shifts: Catholicism and Psychology

1. Karl Rahner, *Concern for the Church* (New York: Crossroad, 1981), 78, 80.

2. In describing the significance of the term, Timothy McCarthy contrasts the principle of *aggiornamento* with a principle set forth by Giles de Viterbo (1469–1532) at the Fifth Lateran Council (1512–17). Viterbo's principle held that "men must be changed by religion, not religion by men." This principle influenced the spirit of the pre-Reformation Lateran Council. *Aggiornamento,* the principle that reflected the spirit of the Second Vatican Council, was the direct opposite of Viterbo's principle.

3. "Pastoral Constitution on the Church in the Modern World," in *The Documents of Vatican II,* ed. Walter M. Abbott, S.J. (Piscataway, N.J.: New Century, 1966), 203.

4. Ibid., 238–47.

5. Ibid., 260.

6. Ibid., 269.

7. Ibid., 250.

8. Ibid., 255. In the church's 1917 code of canon law marriage was seen by the code's principal author, Cardinal Pietro Gasparri, in institutional terms. The code emphasized the contractual and legal dimension of marriage and saw its principal purpose as the procreation of children; the martial couple's relationship was a secondary end.

9. *Code of Canon Law* (Washington, D.C.: Canon Law Society of America, 1983), Canon 1055, 387.

10. Jay Dolan, for example, notes that in 1967 the Catholic Church in the United States granted seven hundred annulments. By 1978 that number had risen to twenty-five thousand. See Jay Dolan, *The American Catholic Experience: A History from Colonial Times to the Present* (New York: Doubleday, 1985), 436.

11. Pope John Paul II, "Address to the Roman Rota," *The Pope Speaks* 32, no. 2 (1987): 132.

12. "Decree on the Appropriate Renewal of the Religious Life," in *The Documents of Vatican II,* 478–79.

13. "Decree on Priestly Formation," in ibid., 455.

14. "Decree on the Apostolate of the Laity," in ibid., 500.

15. Sr. Kathleen Gallivan, S.N.D., interview with C. Kevin Gillespie, S.J., Boston College, Chestnut Hill, Mass., February 14, 1996.

16. Rev. John Grimes, phone interview with C. Kevin Gillespie, S.J., January 10, 1996.

17. Robert Cushman, quoted in James Hennesey, *American Catholics: A History of the Roman Catholic Community in the United States* (New York: Oxford University Press, 1981), 311.

18. John Courtney Murray, "Religious Freedom," in *The Documents of Vatican II,* 673.

19. Walter J. Burghardt, S.J., "The Meaning of Vatican II," *Perkins Journal of Theology* (Spring 1967): 30.

20. In 1963, shortly before his death, Pope John XXIII had established the Pontifical Study Commission on Family, Population, and Birth Problems to study the church's position in light of the United Nations' contraceptive policies on population problems. The majority and minority reports of the commission were published in May 1967; the majority recommended a reassessment of the church's teaching so that within certain guidelines contraceptive intervention in marital intercourse would be allowed. Instead of accepting the recommendation of the commission's majority, Pope Paul VI concurred with the minority report and using classical natural-law arguments reiterated the ban, asserting that "each and every marriage act must remain open to the transmission of life."

21. "Report: The American Catholic Psychological Association Meeting," *Bulletin of the National Guild of Catholic Psychiatrists* 16 (June 1969): 45–46.

22. Ibid., 46. One prominent Catholic psychiatrist of the era and a leader in the National Guild of Catholic Psychiatrists, John R. Cavanagh, M.D., was a member of the papal commission and had helped to issue the majority report that was rejected by Pope Paul VI.

23. Cardinal O'Boyle even suspended the faculties of his own confessor, Fr. Horace McKenna, S.J.

24. Andrew M. Greeley, "Going Their Own Way," *New York Times Sunday Magazine,* October 10, 1982, 36, in Dolan, *The American Catholic Experience,* 436.

25. Ibid.

26. Thomas Kuhn, *The Structure of Scientific Revolutions* (Chicago: University of Chicago Press, 1962).

27. Sigmund Koch, class notes, Boston University, Spring Term, 1990.

28. Duane P. Schultz and Sydney Ellen Schultz, *A History of Modern Psychology* (Philadelphia: Harcourt, Brace, Jovanovich, 1992), 506.

29. A study of the catalogues of two prominent Catholic seminaries, St. John's in Brighton, Massachusetts, and St. Mary's in Baltimore, Maryland, indicated that by the early 1970s a wide variety of courses in psychology were permitted by the institution's authorities.

30. Claire Lowrey, Ed.D., interview with C. Kevin Gillespie, S.J., Boston College, February 5, 1996.

31. Carl Jung, *Memories, Dreams, Reflections,* recorded and edited by Aniela Jaffe, trans. Richard and Clara Winston (New York: Vintage Books, 1963), 11.

32. C. G. Jung, "Why I Am Not a Catholic," *The Collected Works of C. G. Jung,* vol. 18, trans. R. F. C. Hull (Princeton, N.J.: Princeton University Press, 1976), 645–47.

33. C. G. Jung, "The 'Exercita Spiritualia' of St. Ignatius Loyola," trans. Barbara Hannah, 2d ed., *Modern Psychology* 4 (1959): 147–264. Notes of lectures given at the Swiss Polytechnic Institute in Zurich (June 1939–40), private circulation; cited in Kathryn M. Fitzgerald, "The Central Role of Imagination in Effecting Spiritual

Transformation in a Context of Ignatian Spiritual Direction," dissertation, Lancaster Theological Seminary, May 1998, 164.

34. Frederic A. Maples, S.J., interview with C. Kevin Gillespie, S.J., St. Paul, Minn., June 1, 2000.

35. *The Collected Works of C. G. Jung,* vol. 14, trans. R. F. C. Hull (Princeton, N.J.: Princeton University Press, 1976), 214.

36. Victor White, *God and the Unconscious* (Chicago: H. Regnery, 1953); *Soul and Psyche: An Enquiry into the Relationship of Psychotherapy and Religion* (New York: Harper, 1960).

37. White, *God and the Unconscious,* xvi. The friendship between Jung and White soured, however, after White took a dim view of Jung's approach to evil.

38. Raymond Hostie, *Religion and the Psychology of Jung,* trans. G. R. Lamb (New York: Sheed & Ward, 1957).

39. Robert A. Repicky, C.S.B., "Jungian Typology and Christian Spirituality," *Review for Religious* 40 (1981): 422–35; John O'Regan, O.M.I., "Staging, Typing, and Spiritual Direction," *Review for Religious* 42 (1983): 614–19; Carolyn Osiek, R.S.C.J., "The Spiritual Direction of 'Thinking' Types," *Review for Religious* 44 (1985): 209–19.

40. The Jesuit psychologist Richard P. Vaughan related his experience of doing psychological batteries for Jesuit candidates during the 1950s. Frequently his recommendations were largely ignored by his religious superiors. He noted wryly that this aversion toward the results of psychological tests changed when he was made provincial! (Rev. Richard P. Vaughan, S.J., phone interview with C. Kevin Gillespie, S.J., February 15, 1996).

41. Ana-Maria Rizzuto, *The Birth of the Living God: A Psychoanalytic Study* (Chicago: University of Chicago Press, 1979).

42. William W. Meissner, S.J., *Psychoanalysis and Religious Experience* (New Haven: Yale University Press, 1984).

43. Michael J. Garanzini, S.J., *The Attachment Cycle: An Object Relations Approach to the Healing Ministries* (New York: Paulist, 1988).

44. Michael St. Clair, *Human Relationships and the Experience of God: Object Relations and Religion* (New York: Paulist, 1994).

45. Catherine Mowry LaCugna, *God for Us: The Trinity and Christian Life* (New York: HarperCollins, 1991), 255–66, 308.

46. Probably the best example of such an appropriation of psychology by a Catholic moralist is the work of John Ford, S.J., especially his monograph *Depth Psychology, Morality and Alcoholism* (Weston, Mass.: Weston College Press, 1951).

47. Richard M. Gula, S.S., *What Are They Saying about Moral Norms?* (New York: Paulist, 1982), 1.

48. The encyclical *Humani Generis* ("On Certain Opinions Which Menace the Foundations of the Catholic Faith") was issued by Pope Pius XII on August 12, 1950. Through the encyclical the pope wished to curtail some views of progressive theologians that he saw as tending toward the heretical. The Dominicans Marie-Dominique Chenu and Yves Congar and the Jesuits Pierre Teilhard de Chardin and Henri de Lubac were among those whose writings were viewed as the *nouvelle théologie* and were restricted by the encyclical.

49. At Louvain the neo-Thomistic spirit fostered by Pope Leo XIII and enacted by Mercier led the church into its new era. Leo Josef Suenens, who later distinguished himself as a major figure at the Council, had served as its rector. Louvain, however, with its progressive influence was a long way from America, where Catholics were cautious and conservative and still feeling the effects of the Americanism and Modernism controversies.

50. Avery Dulles, *Models of the Church* (New York: Image, 1974).

51. Richard McCormick, S.J., *Corrective Vision: Explorations in Moral Theology* (New York: Sheed & Ward, 1994), 4.

52. A major voice for reporting the events of the Council as well as its effects was the *National Catholic Reporter.* Founded in 1964 as an independent Catholic weekly *NCR* communicated much of the controversy surrounding *Humanae Vitae.*

53. McCormick, *Corrective Vision,* 5.

54. *Documents of Vatican II,* 269.

55. McCormick, *Corrective Vision,* 47.

56. Ibid., 6.

57. Karl Rahner, S.J., *Foundations of Christian Faith* (New York: Seabury, 1978), 98–99, cited in Richard A. McCormick, S.J., *The Critical Calling: Reflections on Moral Dilemmas since Vatican II* (Washington, D.C.: Georgetown University Press, 1989), 172–73.

58. Ibid.

59. Joseph Fuchs, S.J., "Basic Freedom and Morality," in *Introduction to Christian Ethics: A Reader,* ed. Ronald P. Hamel and Kenneth R. Himes (New York: Paulist, 1989), 187.

60. Bernard Häring, *Free and Faithful in Christ,* vol. 1: *General Moral Theology* (New York: Seabury, 1978), 6.

61. Ibid., 170.

62. Ibid., 173.

63. Ibid., 175–77.

64. Ibid., 177.

65. Richard McCormick, S.J., *Notes on Moral Theology: 1965–1980* (Washington, D.C.: American University Press, 1981), 171.

66. James M. Gustafson, "The Relationship of Empirical Science to Moral Thought," in *Introduction to Christian Ethics: A Reader,* ed. Ronald P. Hamel and Kenneth R. Himes (New York: Paulist, 1989), 435–37.

67. Carol Gilligan, *In a Different Voice: Psychological Theory and Women's Development* (Cambridge, Mass.: Harvard University Press, 1982).

68. Poorman cites the following works: Norma Hann, "Moral Development and Action from a Social Constructionist Perspective," manuscript, 1987; Norma Hann, Eliane Aerts, and Bruce A. B. Cooper, *On Moral Grounds: The Search for Practical Morality* (New York: New York University Press, 1985); and Norma Hann, "An Interactional Morality of Everyday Life," in *Social Science as Moral Inquiry,* ed. Norma Hann, Robert Bellah, Paul Rabinow, and William M. Sullivan (New York: Columbia University Press, 1983). See Mark L. Poorman, C.S.C., *Interactional Morality: A Foundation for Moral*

Discernment in Catholic Pastoral Ministry (Washington, D.C., Georgetown University Press, 1993).

69. Gula, *What Are They Saying About Moral Norms?*, 23.

70. Ibid.

8. Grace Still Builds on Nature:
Bridge Builders between Psychology and Catholicism

1. Leo Bartemeier in Francis J. Braceland and Peter A. Martin, "In Memoriam: Leo H. Bartemeier, M.D., 1895–1982," *American Journal of Psychiatry* 140, no. 5 (May 1983): 630.

2. Ibid.

3. Howard P. Rome, "Francis J. Braceland, M.D., 1900–1985," *American Journal of Psychiatry* 142, no. 10 (October 1985): 1209.

4. John C. Nemiah, M.D., and Evelyn S. Myers, M.A., "Editorial: Francis J. Braceland, M.D., Editor," *American Journal of Psychiatry* 142, no. 10 (October 1985): 1179.

5. Francis J. Braceland, "Psychiatric Aspects of Chronic Alcoholism," *Ecclesiastical Review* 105 (December 1941): 444–51.

6. Paul C. O'Connor, S.J., "Some Dangers in Alcoholics Anonymous," *Ecclesiastical Review* 106, no. 4 (April 1942): 285–88; F. J. Braceland, "Reply by Dr. Braceland," *Ecclesiastic Review* 106, no. 4 (April 1942): 288.

7. Francis J. Braceland, ed., *Faith, Reason and Modern Psychiatry: Sources for a Synthesis* (New York: P. J. Kenedy, 1955), 27.

8. Francis J. Braceland and Michael Stock, O.P., *Modern Psychiatry: A Handbook for Believers* (Garden City, N.Y.: Doubleday, 1963), 54.

9. Dana L. Farnsworth and Francis J. Braceland, eds. *Psychiatry, the Clergy, and Pastoral Counseling: The St. John's Story* (Collegeville, Minn.: Institute for Mental Health, St. John's University Press, 1969), 8.

10. Charles E. Curran, "John R. Cavanagh as Bridge Builder," *Bulletin of the National Guild of Catholic Psychiatrists* 27 (1981): 3.

11. John R. Cavanagh and James B. McGoldrick, *Fundamental Psychiatry* (Milwaukee: Bruce, 1953); John R. Cavanagh, *Fundamental Marriage Counseling: A Catholic Viewpoint* (Milwaukee: Bruce, 1958); *Fundamental Pastoral Counseling* (Milwaukee: Bruce, 1962); *The Popes, the Pill, and the People* (Milwaukee: Bruce, 1965); *Counseling the Invert* (Milwaukee: Bruce, 1965); and *Counseling the Homosexual* (Huntington, Ind.: Our Sunday Visitor, 1977).

12. Curran, "John R. Cavanagh as Bridge Builder," 35.

13. Eugene Cardinal Tisserant, preface, in Charles A. Curran, *Counseling in Catholic Life and Education* (New York: Macmillan, 1952), xi.

14. Cited in Paschal B. Baute, O.S.B., "A Report on Pastoral Counselor Training," *Chicago Studies* 4, no. 2 (Summer 1965): 185.

15. Charles A. Curran, "Vatican II: A New Christian Self-Concept," *Journal of Religion and Health* 5, no. 2 (April 1966): 100.

16. Charles A. Curran, *Religious Values in Counseling and Psychotherapy* (New York: Sheed & Ward, 1969), 10.

17. Ibid., 8–9.

18. Ibid., 24.

19. Charles A. Curran, *The Word Becomes Flesh: A Psychodynamic Approach to Homiletics and Catechetics, Theory and Practice* (East Dubuque, Ill.: Counseling-Learning Publications, 1973), 41.

20. Ibid., 21.

21. Many of the details of van Kaam's life presented here were acquired in a personal interview: Rev. Adrian van Kaam, C.S.Sp., Ph.D., interview with Rev. C. Kevin Gillespie, S.J., March 3, 1999.

22. Marinus Scholtes, *Become Jesus: The Diary of a Soul Touched by God,* trans. Joop Bekkers, edited with an introduction by Adrian van Kaam and Susan Muto (Pittsburgh: Duquesne University Press, 1998).

23. Adrian van Kaam, C.S.Sp., Ph.D., *The Science of Formative Spirituality: Transcendence Therapy,* vol. 7 (New York: Crossroad Publishing, 1995), xv.

24. Ibid., xix.

25. In 1982, Van Kaam received the William C. Bier award from Division 36 of the American Psychological Association for promoting dialogue between professional psychology and religion.

26. Van Kaam also served as a consulting editor of the *Journal of Individual Psychology* and the *Journal of Humanistic Psychology.* He also helped to establish and served as editor for *Humanitas* (which later became *Studies in Formative Spirituality*), *Envoy,* and *Epiphany International.*

27. Adrian van Kaam, "The Impact of Existential Phenomenology on the Psychological Literature of Western Europe," *Review of Existential Psychology and Psychiatry* 1, no. 3 (1961): 63–92.

28. Adrian van Kaam, *The Art of Existential Counseling* (Denville, N.J: Dimension Books, 1966).

29. Adrian van Kaam, *Existential Foundations of Psychology* (New York: Doubleday, 1966).

30. Adrian van Kaam, *Religion and Personality* (Englewood Cliffs, N.J.: Prentice-Hall, 1964); *Personality Fulfillment in the Spiritual Life* (Wilkes-Barre, Pa.: Dimension Books, 1966); *The Vowed Life* (Denville, N.J.: Dimension Books, 1968); and *Personality Fulfillment in Religious Life* (Denville, N.J.: Dimension Books, 1969).

31. Adrian van Kaam, *On Being Involved: The Rhythm of Involvement and Detachment in Daily Life* (Denville, N.J.: Dimension Books, 1970); *On Being Yourself: Reflections on Spirituality and Originality* (Denville, N.J.: Dimension Books, 1972); and *Envy and Originality* (Garden City, N.Y.: Doubleday, 1972).

32. Adrian van Kaam, Bert van Croonenburg, and Susan Annette Muto, *The Emergent Self* (Wilkes-Barre, Pa.: Dimension Books, 1968); *The Participant Self* (Denville, N.J.: Dimension Books, 1969).

33. Adrian van Kaam, *In Search of Spiritual Identity* (Denville, N.J.: Dimension Books, 1975); *The Dynamics of Spiritual Self-Direction* (Denville, N.J.: Dimension Books, 1976).

34. Susan Annette Muto and Adrian Van Kaam, *Tell Me Who I Am: Questions and Answers on Christian Spirituality* (Denville, N.J.: Dimension Books, 1977); *Am I Living a Spiritual Life? Questions and Answers on Formative Spirituality* (Denville, N.J.: Dimension Books, 1978); *Practicing the Prayer of Presence* (Denville, N.J.: Dimension Books, 1980).

35. Adrian van Kaam, *The Woman at the Well* (Denville, N.J.: Dimension Books, 1976); *Looking for Jesus: Meditations on the Last Discourse of St. John* (Denville, N.J.: Dimension Books, 1978).

36. Adrian van Kaam, *The Science of Formative Spirituality*, vol. 1: *Fundamental Formation* (New York: Crossroad, 1983), 299.

37. Adrian van Kaam, foreword to Han de Wit, *Contemplative Psychology*, trans. Marie Louis Baird (Pittsburgh: Duquesne University Press, 1991), x.

38. William W. Meissner, S.J., *Annotated Bibliography in Religion and Psychology* (New York: Academy of Religion and Mental Health, 1961).

39. William W. Meissner, S.J., "Prologomena to a Psychology of Grace," *Journal of Religion and Mental Health* 3 (April 1964): 209–40.

40. Ibid., 210.

41. William W. Meissner, S.J., "Problem and Problematic," in *Foundations for a Psychology of Grace*, ed. William W. Meissner, S.J. (Glen Rock, N.J.: Paulist, 1964), 4.

42. William W. Meissner, S.J., *Life and Faith: Psychological Perspectives on Religious Experience* (Washington, D.C.: Georgetown University Press, 1987), 58.

43. William W. Meissner, S.J., *Psychoanalysis and Religious Experience* (New Haven: Yale University Press, 1984).

44. Anna Marie Rizzuto, *Birth of the Living God* (Chicago: University of Chicago Press, 1979).

45. William W. Meissner, S.J., *Ignatius of Loyola: The Psychology of a Saint* (New Haven: Yale University Press, 1992), 391.

46. William W. Meissner, S.J., *Thy Kingdom Come: Psychoanalytic Perspectives on the Messiah and the Millennium* (Kansas City, Mo.: Sheed & Ward, 1995).

47. William W. Meissner, S.J., *To The Greater Glory: A Psychological Study of Ignatian Spirituality* (Milwaukee: Marquette University Press, 1999).

48. Ibid., xii.

49. William W. Meissner, S.J., *The Cultic Origins of Christianity: The Dynamics of Religious Development* (Collegeville, Minn.: Liturgical Press, 2000).

9. Monk and Psychologist: Thomas Merton and Henri Nouwen

1. Thomas Merton, *The Seven Storey Mountain* (Garden City, N.Y.: Doubleday, 1948), 155–56.

2. Ibid., 156.

3. Thomas Merton, "The Neurotic Personality in the Monastic Life," *The Merton Annual* 4 (1991): 5–19.

4. Thomas Merton, *Restricted Journals,* July 28, 1959, cited in Michael Mott, *The Seven Mountains of Thomas Merton* (Boston: Houghton Mifflin, 1984), 290.

5. Ibid., 290–99.

6. Ibid., 294.

7. Ibid., 295.

8. Ibid., 297.

9. Ibid.

10. Merton, "The Neurotic Personality in the Monastic Life," 5.

11. Ibid.

12. Ibid., 6.

13. Ibid., 7.

14. Ibid., 12.

15. Ibid., 15.

16. Ibid., 17.

17. Henri J. M. Nouwen, *Out of Solitude: Three Meditations on the Christian Life* (Notre Dame, Ind.: Ave Maria, 1974); *The Return of the Prodigal Son: A Meditation on Fathers, Brothers, and Sons* (New York: Doubleday, 1992). One estimate reported that as of 1998 Nouwen's books in North America alone totaled more than 1.5 million copies.

18. Henri Nouwen, cited in Sue Mosteller, C.S.J., "Funeral Elegy for Henri Nouwen," *Seeds of Hope: A Henri Nouwen Reader* (New York: Doubleday, 1997), 14.

19. Anton Boisen, *The Exploration of the Inner World: A Study of Mental Disorder and Religious Experience* (Philadelphia: University of Pennsylvania Press, 1936, 1971).

20. Henri Nouwen, "Boisen and the Case Method," *Chicago Theological Seminary Register* 67, no. 1 (Winter 1977): 12–32.

21. Henri Nouwen, *Intimacy: Pastoral Psychological Essays* (Notre Dame, Ind.: Fides, 1969).

22. Henri Nouwen, *Creative Ministry: Beyond Professionalism in Teaching, Preaching, Counseling, Organizing and Celebrating* (Garden City, N.Y.: Doubleday, 1971).

23. Ibid., 59.

24. Henri Nouwen, *Reaching Out: The Three Movements of the Spiritual Life* (Garden City, N.Y.: Doubleday, 1975), 47.

25. Ibid., 65.

26. Todd Brennan, "An Interview with Henri Nouwen," *The Critic* 36, no. 4 (Summer 1978): 47–48.

27. Ibid.

28. Ibid.

29. Henri Nouwen, *Genesee Diary: Report from a Trappist Monastery* (Garden City, N.Y.: Doubleday), 182.

30. Henri Nouwen, *Gracias! A Latin American Journal* (San Francisco: Harper & Row, 1983), xiii.

31. Ibid., 16–17.

32. Henri Nouwen, *The Inner Voice of Love: A Journey through Anguish to Freedom* (New York: Doubleday, 1996), 47.

10. Psychology and Spirituality: The New World

1. Hildreth Meiere was one of the greatest artists of mosaic of her time. She had works in such places as the Smithsonian. For an in-depth study of the Jesuits in Wernersville see Kathy Miller Scogna, *A House of Bread: The Jesuits Celebrate 70 Years in Wernersville, Pennsylvania,* author's printing, 2000.

2. The American Jesuit Assistancy refers to the total number of regions or provinces of Jesuit apostolic works in the United States. At present there are ten provinces: California, Chicago, Detroit, Maryland, Missouri, New England, New Orleans, New York, Oregon, and Wisconsin. Since Maryland was the first of the American provinces it has been designated in some Jesuit circles as the "mother province."

3. The Spiritual Exercises of St. Ignatius may be described as experiments in faith and the imagination. The manual of the Exercises is a guide of 366 annotations or suggestions for the one presenting the Exercises. It is designed to help offer retreatants a way of enhancing their understanding of God in Christ and of deepening their choices. Ignatius divided the Exercises into four "weeks," or phases. In the First Week the exercitant is asked to pray over themes related to a sense of being loved into creation by a providential Creator; the Second Week's themes suggest a deeper sense of knowing, following, and loving Jesus Christ; the Third Week's annotations center around the Passion of Jesus; the Fourth Week revolves around the Resurrection of Christ, which leads to a contemplation on the love of God. The four "weeks" were never meant to be actual seven-day periods.

4. No scholar investigated the history of the Spiritual Exercises more thoroughly then Fr. Ignacio Iparraguirre, S.J. He meticulously traced the origins of the Spiritual Exercises and thereby rediscovered the significance of the directed retreat. See his *Historia de la práctica de los Ejercicios de San Ignacio,* vol. 1: *Práctica de los Ejercicios en vida se du autor* (1552–56) (Rome: Bilbao, 1946), and vol. 2: *Desde la muerte de San Ignacio hasta la promulgación del Directorio oficial* (1556–99) (Rome: Bilbao, 1954). Meanwhile, Fr. Jean Laplace, S.J., was instrumental in the emergence of the directed retreat in France and elsewhere in Europe.

5. Before Schemel's work at Wernersville, John English, a tertian under Kennedy, introduced the directed retreat at the retreat center in Guelph, Ontario. In two masterful works, *Choosing Life* (New York: Paulist, 1978), and *Spiritual Freedom* (Chicago: Loyola University Press, 1995), English describes the psychological patterns observable in Ignatian spirituality and gives insight into his own personal journey. For many years English and Schemel collaborated in developing new ways of applying principles of psychological discernment and insight derived from the Exercises. Their most notable collaboration was ISECP (Ignatian Spiritual Exercises for the Corporate Person), an advisory group that combined group and management psychology with the wisdom of the Spiritual Exercises. ISECP developed new forms of psychological and spiritual integration and applied them to the corporate world.

6. Judith R. Roemer, interview with C. Kevin Gillespie, S.J., October 3, 2000.

7. George J. Schemel, S.J., and Judith A. Roemer, *Beyond Individuation to Discipleship: A Directory for Those Who Give the Spiritual Exercises of St. Ignatius* (Scranton, Pa.: Institute for Contemporary Spirituality, 2000).

8. George A. Aschenbrenner, S.J., "Consciousness Examen," *Review for Religious* 31 (1972): 14–21. Aschenbrenner explains that the practice of the "examen" needs to be understood in terms of the overall practice of discernment of spirits. Rather than a daily discipline of self-perfection, it is meant to be an exercise of confrontation and renewal and a means of learning how God is present in the daily moments of "true-spirited spontaneity."

9. William A. Barry and William J. Connolly, *The Practice of Spiritual Direction* (New York: Seabury, 1982), 8.

10. Ibid., 46.

11. Elizabeth R. Zetzel and W. W. Meissner, *Basic Concepts of Psychoanalytic Psychiatry* (New York: Basic Books, 1973).

12. William A. Barry, S.J., "How Freudian Theory and Practice and Religion Finally Kissed and Made Up in One Man's Practice," unpublished manuscript of lecture given at the University of Michigan, February 24, 1999. Also see William A. Barry, S.J., "Past, Present and Future: A Jubilarian's Reflections on Jesuit Spirituality," *Studies in the Spirituality of Jesuits* (September 2000): 23.

13. William J. Connolly and Madeline Birmingham, *Witnessing to the Fire* (Kansas City, Mo.: Sheed & Ward, 1993).

14. Joyce Rupp, *Fresh Bread . . . and Other Gifts of Spiritual Nourishment* (Notre Dame, Ind.: Ave Maria, 1985); *Dear Heart Come Home* (New York: Crossroad, 1996); *Praying Our Goodbyes* (Notre Dame, Ind.: Ave Maria, 1988); *Your Sorrow Is My Sorrow: Hope and Strength in Times of Suffering* (New York: Crossroad, 1999); *May I Have This Dance?* (Notre Dame, Ind.: Ave Maria, 1992); *Little Pieces of Light: Darkness and Personal Growth* (Mahwah, N.J.: Paulist, 1995); *The Cup of Our Life* (Notre Dame, Ind.: Ave Maria, 1997); *The Star in My Heart* (Philadelphia: Innisfree, 1990); *Prayers to Sophia* (Philadelphia: Innisfree, 2000).

15. Robert J. Wicks, Richard D. Parsons, Donald Capps, eds., *Clinical Handbook of Pastoral Counseling*, vols. 1 and 2 (New York: Paulist, 1993); Robert J. Wicks, *A Handbook of Spirituality for Ministers*, vol. 1 (New York: Paulist, 1995) and vol. 2 (New York: Paulist, 2000).

16. Robert J. Wicks, *Availability: The Problem and the Gift* (New York: Paulist, 1986); *Living Simply in an Anxious World* (New York: Paulist, 1988); *Seeking Perspective: Weaving Spirituality in Search of Clarity* (New York: Paulist, 1991); *Touching the Holy: Ordinariness, Self-Esteem and Friendship* (Notre Dame, Ind.: Ave Maria, 1992); *Seeds of Sensitivity: Deepening Your Spiritual Life* (Notre Dame, Ind.: Ave Maria, 1995); *After Fifty: Spiritually Embracing Your Own Wisdom Years* (New York: Paulist, 1997); *Living a Gentle, Passionate Life* (New York: Paulist, 1998); *Sharing Wisdom: The Practical Art of Giving and Receiving Mentoring* (New York: Crossroad, 2000).

17. Evelyn Eaton Whitehead and James D. Whitehead, *Christian Life Patterns: The Psychological Challenges and Religious Invitations of Adult Life* (Garden City, N.Y.: Doubleday, 1979).

18. Elizabeth Liebert, *Changing Life Patterns: Adult Development in Spiritual Direction* (New York: Paulist, 1992).

19. Joann Wolski Conn, *Spirituality and Personal Maturity* (New York: Paulist, 1989).

20. Benedict J. Groeschel, *Spiritual Passages: The Psychology of Spiritual Development "for Those Who Seek"* (New York: Crossroad, 1983); *Stumbling Blocks or Stepping Stones: Spiritual Answers to Psychological Questions* (New York: Paulist, 1987).

21. Groeschel, *Spiritual Passages*, 96.

22. Don Richard Riso, *Understanding the Enneagram: The Practical Guide to Personality Types* (Boston: Houghton Mifflin, 1990), 13.

23. Maria Beesing, Robert J. Nogosek, and Patrick H. O'Leary, *The Enneagram: A Journey of Self-Discovery* (Denville, N.J.: Dimension Books, 1984); Don Richard Riso, *Understanding the Enneagram: The Practical Guide to Personality Types* (Boston: Houghton Mifflin, 1990); James Empereur, S.J., *The Enneagram and Spiritual Direction: Nine Paths to Spiritual Guidance* (New York: Continuum, 1997); Richard Rohr, O.S.F., and Andreas Ebert, *Discovering the Enneagram: An Ancient Tool for a New Spiritual Journey* (New York: Crossroad, 1990); Richard Rohr, O.S.F., *Enneagram II: Advancing Spiritual Discernment* (New York: Crossroad, 1998); Suzanne Zuercher, O.P., *Enneagram Spirituality: From Compulsion to Contemplation* (Notre Dame, Ind.: Ave Maria, 1992); Suzanne Zuercher, *Enneagram Companions: Growing in Relationship and Spiritual Direction* (Notre Dame, Ind.: Ave Maria, 1993).

24. Zuercher, *Enneagram Companions*, 179.

25. In his study of college students Edwards found that there was perceptual overlap between the Enneagram's personality type descriptions and thus did not find support for some of Riso's assertions about the Enneagram. See Anthony C. Edwards, "Clipping the Wings of the Enneagram: A Study in People's Perceptions of a Ninefold Personality Typology," *Social Behavior and Personality* 19, no. 1 (1991): 11–20.

26. Philip Rieff, *The Triumph of the Therapeutic: Uses of Faith after Freud* (New York: Harper & Row, 1966).

27. Christopher Lasch, *The Culture of Narcissism: American Life in an Age of Diminishing Expectations* (New York: Norton, 1978); Paul C. Vitz, *Psychology as Religion: The Cult of Self-Worship* (Grand Rapids: Eerdmans, 1977).

28. Mitch Pacwa, *Catholics and the New Age: How Good People Are Being Drawn into Jungian Psychology, the Enneagram, and the Age of Aquarius* (Ann Arbor, Mich.: Servant Publications, 1992).

Epilogue: Current and Future Issues: Controversy and Collaboration

1. Robert Wuthnow, *After Heaven: Spirituality in America since the 1950s* (Berkeley: University of California Press, 1998).

2. Ibid., 145.

3. Thomas Moore, *Care of the Soul: A Guide for Cultivating Depth and Sacredness in Everyday Life* (New York: Harper & Row, 1992), 5.

4. Wuthnow, *After Heaven*, 157.

5. Erik Mansager, "Individual Psychology and the Study of Spirituality," *Journal of Individual Psychology* 56, no. 3 (Fall): 2000.

6. Ibid., 375.

7. John Haught, *Science and Religion: From Conflict to Conversation* (New York: Paulist, 1995), 13.

8. Rev. James Gill, S.J., M.D., deserves recognition as a leader in promoting psychological awareness among clergy and religious throughout the world. For more than four decades Gill has spoken on psychological issues pertaining to religious life. For twenty years he has served as the editor of *Human Development*, probably the most popular periodical dealing with the psychology of religious life.

9. Both Guest House and the Hazelden Foundation were established under the influence of Archbishop John Gregory Murray of St. Paul. It was the persuasive energies of Austin Ripley that led Murray to recognize the need for a psychological treatment center for alcoholic priests. According to Ripley, Murray was the only Catholic ordinary who believed alcoholism was a disease rather than a moral failing. Murray's backing enabled Riley to purchase of a thirty-five room mansion on two hundred acres at Lake Orion, Michigan. Among those from the medical establishment who supported Ripley in his position that alcoholism should be considered a disease was the psychiatrist Francis Braceland. In 1956 Guest House opened its doors. Presently two Guest Houses exists, one for women religious (Lake Orion) and another for priests (Rochester, Minnesota).

At the same time, Murray supported another treatment center for laity. Originally an exclusively Catholic enterprise, Hazelden soon became nondenominational and today is one of the most effective treatment centers for addiction in the world. Hazelden opened its doors at Center City in 1949 and has since established treatment centers in New York, Chicago, and West Palm Beach, Florida.

10. Pope John Paul II, *Ex Corde Ecclesiae*, in *American Catholic Higher Education: Essential Documents, 1967–1990* (Notre Dame, Ind.: University of Notre Dame Press, 1992), 417.

11. Philip Gleason, *Contending with Modernity: Catholic Higher Education in the Twentieth Century* (New York: Oxford University Press, 1995), 318–22.

12. John T. McGreevy "Thinking on One's Own: Catholicism in the American Intellectual Imagination, 1928–1960," *Journal of American History* (June 1997): 97–131.

13. At Jesuit institutions some prefer the use of the word "Jesuit" (with its scholarly and progressive connotations) to the word "Catholic" (which for some suggests conservative and reactionary). Jesuit university administrators would assert that you cannot have the former without the latter.

14. Michael J. Buckley, S.J., "The Catholic University and the Promise Inherent in Its Identity," in *Catholic Universities in Church and Society: A Dialogue on "Ex Corde Ecclesiae,"* ed. John P. Langan, S.J. (Washington, D.C.: Georgetown University Press, 1993).

15. David J. O'Brien, *From the Heart of the American Church: Catholic Higher Education and American Culture* (Maryknoll, N.Y.: Orbis, 1994).

16. Useful resources for such integrative thought may be found in the recent books published by the American Psychological Association mentioned earlier. In addition, psychoanalyst Joanne Greer of Loyola College has delineated ways in which integration can occur in research: (1) in the study of psychological issues in religious populations

such as clergy; (2) in the observation of religious people from the perspective of their internal religious experiences; (3) in the examination of religious behavior that correlates with specific theological positions; and (4) in testing the validity of theological constructs by applying statistical methods to demonstrate their viability. See Joanne Greer, "Inventing Psychotheology: New Directions in Doctoral Research," *Pastoral Counseling Currents,* newsletter of the Department of Pastoral Counseling, Loyola College in Maryland, 1999, 9–10.

17. Hendrika Vande Kemp, "Historical Perspective: Religion and Clinical Psychology in America," in *Religion and the Clinical Practice of Psychology,* ed. Edward P. Shafranske (Washington, D.C.: American Psychological Association, 1996), 77.

18. Pope John Paul II, "Moral Responsibility of Psychiatrists," *The Pope Speaks* (May–June 1993): 179.

Index

laboratories
  first psychological, in the U.S., 21
  history of European psychological, 21–22
  James's, 177n.4
  Pace and, 32
  universities with early psychology, 177n.1
LaCugna, Catherine Mowry, 106
Ladd, George T., 34
Lamentabili Sane, 30
Lannert, J. L., 3
Laplace, Jean, 150, 197n.4
Lasch, Christopher, 158
Law of Christ, The (Häring), 109
Leahy, William, 7
Lee, Roy Smart, 67
Leonard, A., 90
Leo XIII, Pope
  contradictory attitudes toward science of,
    163
  criticisms of progressiveness of U.S. church,
    28–29
  Ellis on, 31
  Mercier and, 25, 26
  modern science and, 23–24
  Moore's thought and, 38
  Royce on, 30
  Thomism and, 24, 84
liberalism, 23, 28–31
liberation theology, 99, 146
Liebert, Elizabeth, 155, 156
Liebman, Joshua, 17
Life and Faith (Meissner), 131
Lindworsky, Johann, 76
Lippman, Hyman, 91
Loevinger, Jane, 156
Loisy, Alfred, 29
Lonergan, Bernard, 153, 154
Longinqua Oceani, 28
Looking for Jesus (van Kaam), 128
Look magazine, 58, 59
Louvain. *See* University of Louvain
Love Is Not Enough (Bettleheim), 88
Loyola University of Chicago, 56–62, 165
Luijpen, Wilhelmus, 123

MacMurray, John, 106
Maguire, James, 58–59
Mahler, Margaret, 131–32
Maignen, Charles, 178n.18
Mailloux, Noel, 76, 90, 91
Malony, H. Newton, 3
Mann, Thomas, 116
Mansager, Erik, 161–62
Marcel, Gabriel, 139
Maritain, Jacques, 88
marriage, 97, 189n.8
Marsden, George, 7
Maruca, Dominic, 150–51
Marx, Karl, 96, 187n.11

Maryknoll, 146
Maslow, Abraham, 76, 79, 103, 110, 125, 126
Massa, Mark, 166
materialism, 46, 49, 51, 52
May, Rollo, 6, 60, 76, 126, 161
McCall, John, 186n.10
McCarthy, Raphael, 55
McClelland, David C., 166
McCormick, Richard, 108, 109
McDargh, John, 5, 106
McGoldrick, James, 120
McGreevy, John T., 166
McHugh, Antonia, 69–70
McNeill, John, 5
Mead, Margaret, 166
medical psychology, 41
Meiere, Hildreth, 149, 197n.1
Meissner, William, 105–6, 130–34, 154, 160
Memory and the Brain (Arnold), 57
men religious, 105, 139–40, 152
Menig, Charles, 47
Menninger, Karl
  Bartemeier and, 115
  Nouwen and, 142
  overview of work of, 93–94
  on sin, 2, 108, 188–89n.44
Menninger, Roy, 115
Menninger Clinic
  Bartemeier and, 115
  grants to, 15
  Nouwen and, 141, 142
  overview of, 93–94
  religious affiliation of residents at, 188n.37
Mercier, Desiré
  Bruehl and, 48
  the experimental approach to psychology
    and, 14
  extent of impact of, 160
  Hughes on, 34
  Louvain and, 192n.49
  the new psychology and, 24–26
  Pace and, 32, 36
  Thomism and, 24
Mercy Center, 155
Merton, Thomas
  Eastern thought and, 105
  on neurosis in the monastic life, 139–40
  psychology studied by, 136–37
  Rupp and, 155
  St. John's Summer Institute and, 93
  Zilboorg and, 137–39, 188n.42
Messmer, Sebastian, 33–34
Meyer, Adolf, 15, 39, 43, 114
Michel, Virgil, 91
Michotte, A., 45
Mignot, Euodoxe-Irenee, 31
Miles, Francis, 152
Milhaven, Giles, 111